Three Years in the

ARMY OF THE CUMBERLAND

Three Years in the

ARMY OF THE CUMBERLAND

THE LETTERS AND DIARY OF
Major James A. Connolly

EDITED BY PAUL M. ANGLE

INDIANA UNIVERSITY PRESS

BLOOMINGTON & INDIANAPOLIS

The copyright page is continued on p. 400.

973.781

Introduction

In the late summer of 1862 James Austin Connolly, a young lawyer of Charleston, Illinois, found himself, somewhat to his surprise, a major in a newly organized regiment, the 123rd Illinois Infantry. From the date of his enlistment until the fall of 1864 he wrote voluminous letters to Mary Dunn, of Mount Gilead, Ohio, at first his fiancée, later his wife. From the beginning of the Savannah campaign Connolly saw that letter-writing would be difficult if not impossible, and began to keep a diary which he intended to transmute into letters when he had leisure. If the letters were ever written they have not been preserved, but the diary more than makes up for their absence.

Taken together, Connolly's letters and diary constitute an unsurpassed record of campaigning in the West. The writer had a flair for narrative, an eye for people and places, and a smooth and facile style. His running account of the three years that he spent in the Army of the Cumberland adds little to the story of the major engagements in which he participated, for that story has long since been documented in full detail, but it affords a realistic picture of day-to-day soldiering—of rough, spare living in the field, of boredom and fun in camp, of seemingly aimless scouts, of the high excitement of battle.

Connolly was born in Newark, New Jersey, on March 8,

1840. When he was ten years old his parents moved to a farm in Morrow County, Ohio. There the boy attended common school, and after that, one of the small rural academies that then flourished. Deciding on the law, he studied in the office of Andrew K. Dunn of Mount Gilead, the county seat. Within a few months he was admitted to the bar and began practice in partnership with his preceptor.

After a year, Connolly decided that the newer state of Illinois offered greater opportunities than Ohio. For reasons now unknown he chose Charleston, the seat of Coles County in the eastern part of the state. Although he was only twenty years of age he seems to have had no difficulty in establishing himself.

In February, 1862, soon after Grant captured Fort Donelson, Connolly was a member of a committee that went to Cairo and Paducah to see what could be done for Coles County boys wounded in the engagement. A sentence in one of the letters that he wrote to Mary Dunn while on this trip reveals that he had no intention of joining the army, then or ever: "On reaching Cairo and reflecting that I should probably never have an opportunity again of seeing a fresh battle ground, I determined to take all the risk of a military arrest, and watching my chance, slipped by the guard, got on board a government transport lying at the levee, stowed myself away amongst the freight on the lower deck and soon found myself outside the military lines at Cairo, steaming up the river again without passport or ticket." He succeeded in reaching Fort Donelson and remained there several days before returning home.

Yet six months later Connolly was in the army. How that came about he explains in the second of the letters which follow. That he never regretted his decision the whole body of the correspondence makes abundantly clear. That he quickly became a highly competent officer is equally obvious. If he had remained with his regiment, the likelihood is that he would have been promoted long before the end of the war. As it was, he received his

commission as Lieutenant Colonel by brevet after hostilities had
ended. Apparently he valued the promotion lightly, for he was
known as Major Connolly until the end of his life.

Sometime after March 21, 1865, when Connolly wrote the
last of the letters printed here, he received a leave of absence.
He was at Mount Gilead on April 14, when Lincoln was
assassinated. The following day Connolly was ordered to report
to Washington. There he was assigned to the escort which accompanied Lincoln's body to Springfield. Ten weeks later—
July 1, 1865—he was discharged from service.

Connolly returned to his law practice at Charleston. In 1872
he was elected to the General Assembly of Illinois and served
two terms. In 1876 he was appointed United States District
Attorney for the Southern District of Illinois, a position which
called for his removal to Springfield. Cleveland, inaugurated in
1885, promptly removed Connolly from office, but Harrison re-
appointed him four years later. In 1893 he won election to Congress, served two successive terms, then took up the practice
of law in Springfield. He died on December 15, 1914; his body
was buried in Oak Ridge Cemetery, not far from the tomb of
Lincoln.

Connolly's letters and diary were published originally in the
*Transactions of the Illinois State Historical Society for the
Year 1928*. According to a brief biographical foreword by
Frank K. Dunn, the text used had been prepared by Connolly
himself. For some inexplicable reason he had struck out a great
many proper names. As far as possible, these have been supplied
in brackets by the present editor. The extent of other editorial
emendations cannot now be gauged, for the location of the
original letters, if they still exist, is unknown. There is reason
for believing, however, that Connolly made no material changes.
His diaries are in the Illinois State Historical Library, and the
present editor has compared them with the text as printed in
the Illinois State Historical Society *Transactions*. With the

exception of two or three words, obviously misread by someone, the changes were confined to punctuation, capitalization, and abbreviation—changes which most editors today would make for the benefit of the general reader. In the interest of consistency it has seemed better to follow the text of the *Transactions* than to restore the idiosyncrasies of the hastily written original.

As first printed, the letters and diary were segregated. The present editor has intermingled them in chronological order. A few short letters and diary entries of no historical interest have been omitted.

The maps reproduced in this volume are from Fiebeger's *Campaigns of the Civil War.*

The courtesy of the Directors of the Illinois State Historical Society and the Trustees of the Illinois State Historical Library in permitting the republication of this valuable Civil War record is gratefully acknowledged.

PAUL M. ANGLE

CONTENTS

MAPS

Initiation

CONNOLLY's regiment, the 123rd Illinois Infantry, had only a month in camp before it was ordered to Louisville, Kentucky. The young major's first letters describe his adjustment to army life.

[Mattoon], Ill., Aug. 19th, 1862.

Dear [Mary]:

I was elected Major of my regiment at Camp [Terry], yesterday afternoon, by every vote in the regiment. Now if I get my commission, and I have no reason to doubt that I will get it, I suppose I will be in for the war, carrying more sail in the way of rank than I know what to do with just now. I still insist on being in Ohio at the time I have heretofore fixed, and all the necessary arrangements are left with you. Pardon my brevity, I must return to camp at once, and shall certainly expect to get a letter from you tomorrow.

Yours.

[Mattoon], Ill., Sunday evening, Aug. 31, 1862.

Dear [Mary]:

Your very welcome letter of 20th inst., was received last week, and being here alone tonight, with nobody I care a cent

13

about talking to, and nothing to read but the "Revised U. S. Army Regulations" I sat down in my room, and after reading your letter now for the third time, proceed to talk to you through the medium of wretched hotel paper and worse pen. You ask me if I have thought seriously *before* entering the army. Not very seriously, but I *have* thought seriously *since* entering it. I did not write you that I intended to enter the army for this reason: on the 8th of August I had no more idea of doing so than you have tonight; on the morning of the 9th some gentlemen acting as a committee came to me and said: You have done a good deal toward causing the young men of [Coles] County to enlist; another company must be raised in this county and you can raise it, we will all help, be consistent then, and go to work and raise a company. I felt the force of this, and the implied reproach to me, and looking at it entirely as a matter of duty, I dropped my law books on the 9th of August and on the 15th had a company organized and was elected captain; on the next day I brought it to this place to camp, and on the 18th was unanimously elected Major of the regiment to which my company was attached; on the 27th the ladies of [Mattoon], Ill., presented a fine silk regimental flag to my regiment and I had the honor of being selected to receive the flag; on the 28th I was placed in command of the regiment and have been in command of it since, *without any bloodshed or loss of men.* There! that's a full history of my military career so far, and from the dates you will see I had but little time for deliberation or serious thought and you will not wonder that I did not apprise you of my intention.

Our regiment will be mustered into the U. S. service day after tomorrow, and then I will get my commission. Ours is the [123rd] Illinois regiment. Our Colonel has been in service since April 15th, 1861, his commission as captain in the [Seventh] Illinois being dated on that day; when we elected him colonel of our regiment he was Major of his regiment.[1] He was in the battles of Belmont, Fort Henry, Fort Donelson and Shiloh and was promoted to Major for gallantry at Fort Donelson.

I do not know which way we will be ordered from here, but probably south. If we go east I will see you within two weeks from tonight, for we will go via Crestline or Columbus, and I can get a short leave of absence. I should be happy tonight if I could be assured that I would see you in two weeks, but since I can have no such assurance I shall content myself with the assurance that I shall see your picture within the two weeks, and that I shall surely see yourself within a short time, and more, that before the year 1862 closes you will be my wife. I had hoped that before this the day would have been fixed, but the country and the times are too unsettled in condition to fix a day for anything very long ahead, so I shall not insist upon you naming the day until after the position of my regiment shall be more definitely settled. I think beyond all doubt I can be in Ohio in November, but surely by December. November, however, is the time I want to get there. I'm afraid that fruit I was to have put up will suffer somewhat before I get it canned, as well as a good many other domestic plans I had in contemplation, but another year I hope will find the country at peace and then all will be right.

I received a letter from your brother the same day I received yours, but he failed to tell me how to direct to him, so I can't answer him until you send me his full address, the number of his regiment particularly. He advises me strongly against entering the service, but the die is cast. I have no fears or scruples now. "There's a divinity that shapes our ends, etc." I struggled

1. Colonel James W. Monroe. The Seventh Illinois Infantry, in which Monroe had served previously, was the first Illinois regiment raised for Civil War service. It was numbered the seventh in deference to the six volunteer regiments which the state had sent to the Mexican War.

long against leaving my business, but a sense of duty forced me to yield—I couldn't decently stay at home when all other boys and young men were going out. I go now willingly, cheerfully, without any misgivings or apprehension as to the result. My destiny is in the hands of a just God, and while I hope to avoid rashness, I still expect to do my whole duty. Be cheerful; be happy. I feel sure that all will be well with us. I have a great heart full to unburden to you tonight, but pen and ink won't do, so I'll save it until we meet, and may that meeting be the dawning of a happier day for us. Write soon and don't forget that picture for you know I have none.

Yours.

Camp [Terry, Mattoon], Ills.,
September 18, '62, Midnight.

Dear [Mary].

Tomorrow morning at 9 o'clock our regiment starts, in box cars, for Louisville, Ky. I am in charge of the transportation of the regiment and am compelled to remain with it until we reach Louisville. As soon as we are encamped there I expect to leave and go to Ohio. The Colonel says if I will attend to the transportation of the regiment to Louisville I can go to Ohio then, and he will report me present while I go to Ohio and return. I am up for all night watching the loading of camp equipage and baggage. Soldiering in day time and among friends is pleasant enough, but this all night part worries me. Still, I think I shall get along with it very well. We have news of a glorious victory by McClellan.[2] I accept it as a good omen for us, and trust the morning papers may not mar our rejoicing.

Goodby. I think another week will find me with you.

Yours.

2. The Battle of Antietam, September 17. It was a victory only in the sense that it forced Lee to abandon the invasion of Maryland and withdraw to Virginia.

Louisville and Perryville

AT LOUISVILLE, the 123rd Illinois faced the prospect of an attack at almost any minute. Late in August, 1862, Braxton Bragg, commanding the Confederate Army of Tennessee, decided to invade Kentucky from the south. In his initial move he sent General Kirby Smith with 12,000 men into the eastern part of the state by way of Cumberland Gap. On August 29 Smith met and defeated an inferior Federal force under General William Nelson at Richmond, Kentucky. Nelson fell back on Louisville, where he hastily assembled a new body of troops. Smith, instead of pursuing, moved northward, occupied Lexington, and then threw Ohio into panic by advancing on Covington, across the Ohio River from Cincinnati.

Meanwhile Bragg, with the main body of the Army of Tennessee, was marching energetically toward Louisville. By the time that Don Carlos Buell, commanding the Federal Army of the Ohio, discovered what his adversaries were up to, Bragg had a head start in the race for Louisville and could not have been headed off. Instead, however, of continuing to this important objective, he swung off to the right to occupy Frankfort and go through the farce of installing a Confederate state government. Buell slipped into Louisville, planted an adequate garrison there, and then turned east and south to find Bragg and give him battle. The two armies came together on October 8 at Perryville, where Connolly and the 123rd Illinois saw their first action.

After Perryville, Bragg retreated southward. Buell, believing that the Confederate general would offer battle, drew off to the west, grouped his forces around Danville, and awaited reinforcements which he had called for. On October 30 he was relieved and turned over his command to General William S. Rosecrans. While Rosecrans was reorganizing the army Connolly became ill.

Camp in field near Taylorsville, Ky.,
Oct. 3, 1862.

Dear [Mary].

Well, the Louisville battle that was promised was postponed on account of Mr. Bragg having pressing business elsewhere, and here we are, 34 miles from Louisville, having marched that distance in two days, in pursuit of the flying enemy, as we suppose. It may be, however, that he is not flying very rapidly, for this afternoon we distinctly heard the sound of cannon for some two hours or more, apparently not more than ten miles distant; and the rumor is circulating through the camps this evening that a battle is in progress ahead of us, and if so, although our men are expecting a good night's rest, we may be ordered out any minute. One thing is very certain: Mr. Bragg and his rebels must leave Kentucky in a very few days or we *will* have a battle and compel him to leave or surrender. Taylorsville is situated in a basin, surrounded by very high hills and wears the peculiar marks of indolence and slow decay seen in all these southern towns. Our camp tonight is on the top of one of the highest hills, overlooking the town and the Elk River valley. As far as the eye can reach the camp fires of our army can be seen, and the hum of thousands of voices, mingled with the strains of martial music, comes up to our camp and serves to inspire the weary soldier, lying upon the ground, wrapped in his blanket, and without any shelter save perhaps a tree.

All yesterday afternoon and last night it rained hard, but we marched until about 8 o'clock and lay down in our wet clothing and blankets on the ground to sleep. I have a camp cot and tent, but the men were too tired to ask them to pitch tents for anybody, so I lay down on my cot in the open field and slept there, with the rain pouring down in torrents on me until about 2 o'clock in the morning, when I was completely soaked and was compelled to get up. I have experienced no inconvenience from my drenching as yet, except a violent toothache, which is giving me considerable trouble tonight, but a fellow doesn't dare to complain about a little thing like toothache in the army.

I saw Col. John Beatty today and talked with him a few minutes; also Col. Bill Reid, 121st Ohio, and Smith Irwin, his lieutenant colonel. Smith's health is good as usual. Last Sunday, after several hours' diligent search, I found your brother Jerry.[1] He was so busy making out pay rolls for his company that he could scarcely speak to me for two or three hours, but when he did have time we had an extensive talk, and he gave me a rapid history of their long march under Buell in their chase after Bragg to Louisville. He is looking very well after his long march. I also saw the Bird boys from Mt. Gilead, and Tally House, and indeed all the Gilead boys who are in Jerry's company. They all look as though nothing but a bullet could kill them, and notwithstanding their long march I don't think they

1. Lieutenant J. M. Dunn of the Fifteenth Ohio Infantry.

look half as hard as I do after my two days' march on horseback.

I am thoroughly tired, face and hands about as clean as a blacksmith's at his forge, unshaven and unshorn, my trunk at Louisville and no probability of ever seeing it again; no chance of buying anything in this country, and our faces set directly towards Secessia, so you see my chance for clean linen and elegant toilet are decidedly poor. I am sorry I promised to be in Ohio so soon, for it is impossible for me to leave my regiment so long as a prospect for a battle is so squarely before us; that is, I cannot honorably ask for a leave, and although it would be my greatest pleasure to see you, still I must forego it, but I feel quite sure I can be in Ohio in November.

We have received orders tonight (about half an hour ago) to detail double pickets. That indicates a possible attack tonight, but I haven't much fear that all the rebels in Kentucky combined would dare attack the force encamped here tonight. I am tired out and must take to my cot and blankets, there to forget war's alarms and dream of home and peace, if the toothache lets up. You must write me often, for letters from loved ones at home are the best rations a soldier can have. If we have a battle with Bragg, and whip him, and I am in it, and my legs stand fire, I'll write you what I think about it. Address me Major [James A. Connolly, 123rd] Ills. Regt., 10th Brigade,

Jackson's Division, Army of Ohio.

Good night,

P. S. It is now sunrise. Our Colonel is under arrest formally, for some trivial matter, our Lieutenant Colonel cannot be found, having been officer of the pickets last night and we fear he has been taken by the rebels, so that leaves me in command of the regiment this morning. I was notified about 3 o'clock this morning to take command, and I feel like the man who won the elephant. I don't know what to do with it. I have more command than capacity.

Good bye again,

Near Harrodsburg, Ky., Monday, Oct. 13, '62

Dear [Mary].

I have passed through a battle and am safe. The battle was fought between about 18,000 of our forces and I don't know how many rebels.[2] Every General in our Division was killed. General Jackson commanding our Division was killed by a musket ball within a few feet of me. He was on foot and had just advised me to dismount when he fell.[3] Most of the bullets went over our heads and sounded like a swarm of bees running away in the hot summer air overhead. General Terrell, commanding our brigade was killed by a shell within 5 feet of me, and while he was giving me directions for rallying the men.

I was the only one with him; I raised him to a sitting position, and saw that nearly his entire breast was torn away by the shell.

He recognized me and his first words were: "Major do you think it is fatal?" I knew it must be, but to encourage him I answered: "Oh I hope not General." He then said: "My poor wife, my poor wife." He lived until 2 o'clock next morning.[4] Our regiment lost 154 men, 35 of whom fell dead where the regiment first formed line of battle. I was not shocked, surprised

2. The Battle of Perryville was fought at the Kentucky town of that name about sixty miles southeast of Louisville. There the armies of Bragg and Buell came into collision on October 8. Bragg had about 16,000 men, Buell 40,000, but only 22,000 of the Union forces were engaged. Bragg's losses were reported as 510 killed, 2,635 wounded, and 251 missing; Buell's as 845 killed, 2,851 wounded, and 515 missing. Tactically a drawn battle, Perryville was in effect a Union victory since it brought Bragg's Kentucky campaign to an end.

3. James S. Jackson (1823–62), of Hopkinsville, Ky., resigned his seat in Congress in the fall of 1861 to organize the 3rd Kentucky Cavalry (Union), of which he became colonel. He fought at Shiloh, Corinth, Iuka, and Athens, and on July 16, 1862, was commissioned brigadier-general of volunteers. At Perryville he commanded a division of McCook's corps, Army of the Ohio.

4. William Rufus Terrell (1834–62), native of Virginia, graduated from West Point in 1853. He served in the Regular Army until 1855, when he became an assistant in the U. S. Coast Survey. He was commissioned captain in the 5th Artillery (Regular Army) on August 14, 1861, and served with distinction in the Battle of Shiloh. He was promoted to the rank of brigadier-general of volunteers on September 9, 1862.

or startled, but I suppose I was too green to appreciate my
danger. I didn't seem to think of anything else but to keep the
left wing of the regiment up to its work. The Colonel had told
me that was my special duty, and I noticed nothing else for I
was a perfect novice in such things. The Colonel, in his official
report, has given me special praise for my conduct on the field,
but I don't see that I did any more than any body else would
have done. I just couldn't help doing what little I did do; it
seemed to me to be the only thing I could do. I don't care to
fight any more battles, but we are pushing on after the flying
rebels and will fight them again if we can catch them.

The Colonel of the [Fiftieth] Ohio regiment in our Division,
ran away from his regiment and resigned this morning to prevent a court martial and disgrace.[5] Our Colonel was placed in
command of our brigade yesterday. My health is good, but I am
pretty tired of this campaign. I have not had a change of clothing
for two weeks, and for many nights have slept on the bare
ground with no cover but my saddle blanket. I was in Harrodsburg last evening and met a good many who are acquainted
with your uncle Peter. The regiment is ready to march and I
must close. I shall call on your uncle today if we pass his place.

Write as directed before.

Ever yours,

Danville, Ky., Oct. 14, 1862.

Dear [Mary].

We are halting in the streets of Danville for a short time and
I think I can best occupy my time by writing, even though it

5. "Many of the officers, whose names I never knew, did their whole duty.
Some failed, and among them I regret to report Col. J. R. Taylor, of the
Fiftieth Ohio. He, though on the field and in sight of his men, was of no service
to them. The first position that I saw him in was lying on his face, crouching
behind a stump, and twice subsequently I saw him far to the rear of his regiment, while his men were in line of battle, apparently trying to rally some
half a dozen stragglers." Report of Capt. Percival P. Oldenshaw, Asst. Adj.
Gen. and Chief of Staff, 10th Division, 1st Corps, Oct. 15, 1862. *Official Records,* Series I, Vol. XVI, Part 1, pp. 1061–62.

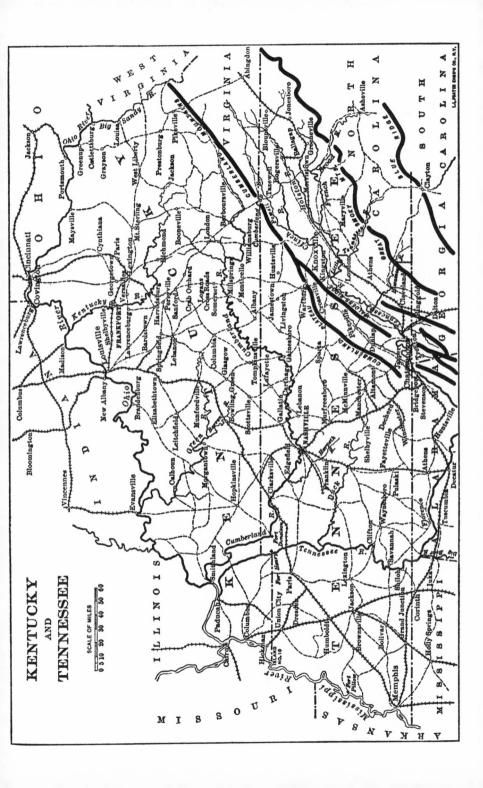

KENTUCKY
AND
TENNESSEE

SCALE OF MILES
0 5 10 20 30 40 50 60

be but a few words. We have marched about 6 miles this morning and it is now about half past nine. During the march I could hear the boom of cannon many miles in our advance, and we suppose that the head of our army has overtaken the rear of the enemy's column. The firing has ceased now and all is quiet again. Danville, although full to overflowing with Union troops, is as quiet as a country village, and the faces of many citizens evince their joy at our coming.

I am not at all disappointed in a soldier's life. From what I saw at Fort Donelson I expected to find a hard one. My greatest doubts and fears are settled, for I have been through one battle and didn't get scared out of my wits nor let my legs run away with me.

One thing is very certain, the bullets and shells flew as thick as I ever want them to in my neighborhood. But a battle seems more dangerous in thinking it over afterwards than it does right in the midst of it. The mind can discover dangers while thinking back over it that were not apparent while the fight was on. Don't mention what I wrote you about the Colonel of the [Fiftieth] Ohio. It is publicly talked of in the army here, and will of course be made public at home, but I don't want its first announcement to come through me. The regiment should not be blamed for what its Colonel did or failed to do. I suppose your brother Jerry is somewhere in the army here, but I can't hear of him. I don't think his regiment was in the Perryville battle, though it might have been. Indeed it is said that not half our army was engaged—that Buell got mad at McCook for bringing on the battle without his orders, and he left him to fight it out without his help. We get such "news" in the army by what we call "grape vine," that is "grape vine telegraph." It is not all reliable.

It is my impression that two weeks more will finish this campaign in Kentucky, and then my thoughts will turn to Ohio more strongly than ever, but I have no hope of getting there until some time in November. Sometimes, as I lie in my blanket looking up at the stars, I almost wish I was at home again, but then I reflect that a few short months and this rough work will all be done, and then, in our snug little home in the prairie state I can forget these days of toil.

Good bye, and at the next good opportunity you shall hear from me again.

Yours

Lebanon, Ky., Oct. 24, 1862.

Dear [Mary] :

I have no assurance that you have ever received a single one of the many letters I have written you since we commenced our tedious, toilsome, terrible march from Louisville after Mr. Bragg.

I have written you 3 or 4 letters since our battle at Perryville, and in each of them promised to give you a full description of the battle the first leisure moment I had. But where are my leisure moments? Every day finds me in the saddle moving along amid clouds of dust raised by a vast moving army; every night finds me, as soon as possible after a halt, wrapped in my blanket under the branches of a tree, and sunrise again finds me in the saddle for another 14 hours of *Buell's famous drill.* The only consolation I have is that marching, while quite as tiresome, is yet much safer than fighting, although so far, one has been as safe for me as the other, but I am perfectly satisfied with my experience in the Perryville battle, and if Buell can arrange his matters so as to fight his next battle without my assistance I shall be under many obligations to him.

It is impossible for me now to give you any more description of the battle than I have already, and I hope you have it. My opinion of the war has undergone a decided change, and I now think it will continue until the rebels are exhausted, and if European powers should interfere in their behalf before that crisis arrives, we will never overcome them, but if they be left to themselves they will still be able to maintain their hostile attitude for another year. To tell the truth the late movements of Buell in Kentucky have sadly disheartened the army of the Ohio, and officers of every grade are flocking to him with resignations. They are worn out with fruitless marches over the dusty pikes and parched uplands of Kentucky, following a leader whose sole aim appears to be "how not to do it."

Oh! for an active earnest leader from the free states! One who sees nothing sacred in negro slavery—one who can say to neutral Kentuckians "Get thee behind me, Satan"—one who will not guard rebel wells and springs to keep our thirsty soldiers from slaking their thirst—one who will hang every rebel guerilla in Kentucky, drive every cowardly sympathiser out of the state and confiscate his property for the use of his soldiers. I am heartily tired of his kind of work, and if I had no hopes of a speedy change of policy I wouldn't hold a commission another day in such service of protecting rebels and their property. If Buell had done what he might well have done at Perryville, he would have captured the bulk of Bragg's army, and even after the battle, had he used ordinary expedition he might have destroyed it. But, as he says, the battle was not according to his programme, and therefore he chose not to gather the fruits of it.[6]

But a truce to martial matters, and yet my head is so full of

6. Kenneth P. Williams' verdict: "Not until four o'clock in the afternoon did Buell learn that a hard battle had been raging and that McCook was being driven back. . . . Because of the direction and intensity of the wind, the heavy musketry firing had not been heard; but Buell's statement that he supposed 'information of anything of serious import' would have been communicated to him is no excuse whatever. He should have been forward. Never before had he deployed the new Army of the Ohio, and he should have wanted to see his men —so many of whom were new—going into position; and he should have wanted them to see him. The afternoon hours of this day were laden with a rare opportunity, and he missed it because he lacked the controlling instinct of a real field soldier." *Lincoln Finds a General*, IV, 133.

them and of limestone dust that I can scarcely think of anything else, and I guess I am sick besides—the Doctor says I am; says I ought to be in bed. But where's the bed? I am to be home—yes, home, in November, but I am proverbial for being behind time, you know; and although I am just as certain now that I will be there at that time as I can be of anything, yet it would just be my luck to be compelled to tag along two or three weeks behind time. Yet the welcome I anticipate will serve in some degree to blunt the keenness of the disappointment if I should be so unfortunate.

I saw your brother Jerry two days since between Perryville and this place. I rode through his regiment as it was resting by the roadside and found him sitting down reading a late paper in a fence corner. I exchanged papers with him and after about a half hour chat left him. He was in good health. I met Colonel Dickey and several other Ohio acquaintances that day. Dickey has resigned and starts home tomorrow. I told him to say "how dy'e" to you for me. Even though you do not receive letters from me regularly you mustn't think I am not writing. I have had but one from you since I left Louisville, but am hoping every day to receive half a dozen in a bunch. This is the only letter I've written that I felt any way certain you would get, and indeed it is somewhat doubtful whether this will get through the great mass of army mail that is here, but I am in hopes it will get through, for there is direct railroad connection between here and Louisville. My regiment went through here yesterday, and being somewhat "under the weather" I remained here to attend to the transportation of our camp equipage and baggage which came here by rail from Louisville. I start with a train of six wagons and guard of ten men tomorrow morning and must reach Woodsonville, two miles south of Munfordsville, by day after tomorrow evening. The distance is 50 miles and I think I can make it, if John Morgan doesn't give us a call.[7] Woodson-

7. John Hunt Morgan, famous Confederate cavalry leader, engaged at this time in harassing the Union troops in Kentucky.

ville is on the railroad between Louisville and Memphis, and it may be we are going to Nashville or Memphis. It is very dry, dusty and turning cold. About six months of this kind of soldiering will satisfy all my military aspirations. Write me often as you can, for I don't suppose I will get more than one out of five of your letters. Direct them to me at Louisville, Ky., "10th Division, 33rd Brigade, Army of the Ohio."

I wish I had time to get my picture taken, just to let you see how hard I do look. I shall do it the first opportunity I have, after a long march in the dust. I think I look tolerably respectable now, for I washed my face this morning, threw away my dirty collar—find I don't need a collar, and swept my coat with a broom that I got from an old negro woman in the hotel kitchen. Good-night.

Yours,

P. S. Next morning. Before mailing this this morning I must tell you that it snowed here last night and the ground is covered with snow now at half past four. Everything seems to be out of joint here in the sunny south. Out of joint myself; high fever all night and splitting headache this morning, but must be off for my 50-mile ride.

Munfordsville, Ky., Nov. 23, 1862.

Dear [Mary].

Can hardly hold a pen, and if the doctor knew I was doing this he would stop me. Three of your letters here but doctor has them and won't let me read them yet. Got here from Lebanon with very high fever, and didn't know much about what I was doing or where I was. Guard took care of me on the way. Much better now. Typhoid fever doctor says. No fever now for several days. Got my clothes on today for the first, and can walk around my room a little. Think I shall go to [Charleston], Illinois, soon as I am able to travel, and put myself under medical treatment, and when well enough hope to get to Ohio, but here it is November now, and all our calculations upset.

My regiment across Green River at Woodsonville yet. Nearly all the men have been sick with measles, and many died. We have not seen a paymaster since we have been in the service, but we got along very well so long as we could borrow from each other, but now we are all broke and are in desperate straits. No difference. I have no use for money now anyhow. I have a few postage stamps but must save them for letters. You see this doesn't look much like my writing. I'm tired and must quit.

Yours,

Munfordsville, Ky., Dec. 7, 1862.

Dear [Mary].

You will notice from my writing that I am not quite as nervous as I was when I last wrote you. In a few days after I wrote you the doctor allowed me to read your letters that had come during my sickness and since then I have received another, and I think they acted as a tonic to revive my strength, for I am daily gaining strength and in a month or two "Richard" will "be himself again." I have lost a trifle in weight, and my "sojer clothes" don't fit quite as snugly as they did. When I came here I weighed about 140 pounds, and now, with my heavy overcoat on, I weigh 83 pounds.

I have not yet received my leave of absence and don't know when I will. It takes a long time for such things to get through the army "Circumlocution Office." My regiment moved from here some days ago, and I learn is now at Gallatin, Tenn. I suppose your brother Jerry is at Nashville. My "nigger" servant that I had has run away since I've been sick, so there's another "thousand dollars" gone. I used to be kind to him, but I won't take any more stock in "niggers." These runaway slaves that come into camp are about the most worthless creatures in the world. "Man proposes but God disposes."

When I so confidently told you I should be home in November, little did I think that I should spend the whole of that month lying on my back in a sick room in southern Kentucky, crazy as a march hare part of the time, and unable to help myself all the time. And we were to be married in November, but Providence prevented it. Why? Undoubtedly for our good, although we may not be able to see it now. That our wedding day *will* come I know, but *when,* I do not know, only I know it shall be as soon as I can get to Ohio. And what a fine condition I'm in to talk of marriage! Fast in the army; it would probably be impossible to get a leave of absence even on account of severe sickness— without a cent of money in my pocket and no paymaster likely to come around for the next 6 months; truly the situation is not one to be envied, but there are brighter days ahead; I can see them and I think of them every day; I am neither going to be killed nor wounded in the war, and at its close, feeling that I have done a man's part, I can retire to my office and a happy little home where you are to be the light.

Address me at [Charleston], Illinois, where I shall be in a week, if I am able to travel there, and I guess I will be.

Yours.

Minor Actions

Soon after writing the foregoing letter Connolly received his leave, returned to Charleston to regain his health, and then proceeded to his old home in Ohio. On February 9, 1863, at the little college town of Gambier, he and Mary Dunn were married. Husband and wife traveled together to Louisville, Kentucky, where Mrs. Connolly remained to visit friends. Connolly went on to Nashville to rejoin his regiment. There, as his letters reveal, he was tempted by an offer of appointment as Inspector, but his conscience bothered him and after a few days' delay he was back in service with the 123rd Illinois.

Rosecrans had spent three months after the murderous Battle of Murfreesboro in strengthening the Army of the Cumberland; he would spend three more. During the first half of 1863 his troops engaged only in minor actions—raiding, probing, trying to keep Bragg off balance, and parrying similar thrusts by the venturesome Confederate cavalry leaders, Forrest and Wheeler. Connolly's letters afford a good picture of this kind of fighting as well as a vivid description of the one engagement of any consequence—the Battle of Milton—in which the 123rd Illinois was engaged.

Six weeks after Milton the 123rd was mounted—an expedient to which Rosecrans resorted in an effort to meet his desperate need for cavalry—and armed with Spencer rifles. For the remainder of their service the men would be grateful for their seven-shooters, which gave them an enormous advantage in fire power over an enemy armed with single-shot muzzle-loaders.

Nashville, Tenn., Saturday Feb. 15, '63.

My dear wife

I reached here yesterday evening, after dark, all well as far as heard from. I soon found General Mitchell, snugly ensconced in the fine residence of a leading rebel of this place, and upon his invitation took up quarters with him.[1] We sat up until after one o'clock this morning discussing Mount Gilead matters and people, and as a consequence we didn't get up until after nine o'clock this morning. Although he wears a brigadier's star, he is still the same old Bob Mitchell, with warm heart and abundant hospitality. I address him as "Bob" and he dignifies me with the name of "Jim", that is in private, not before others, so you see we don't trouble ourselves much with military formality. Some of the men of my regiment got aboard the train yesterday at Gallatin, Tennessee, and I really believe they were glad to see me. They had been left there sick and were just then on their way to rejoin the regiment which is at Murfreesboro, Tenn.

1. Robert Byington Mitchell (1823–82), native of Mansfield, Ohio, veteran of the Mexican War, one-time mayor of Mount Gilead, Ohio (1855), settled at Paris, Kansas, in 1856. In 1861 Mitchell was commissioned colonel of the 2nd Kansas Volunteer Infantry. Promoted to the rank of brigadier-general on April 8, 1862, he commanded the Ninth Division at the Battle of Perryville. For several months after that engagement he was stationed at Nashville.

Last evening the General asked me to remain here to-day and he would go with me to General Rosecrans and have me ordered to duty here as Inspector of this post. I know I am hardly strong enough for field duty yet, and if Rosecrans makes the order I believe I will accept the position for a time, although I have not fully determined yet. While I am writing this I discover that General Mitchell is making out an order relieving his present Inspector and requesting General Rosecrans to appoint me, so I must think and determine quickly. I don't like to be a tail to any General's kite. I'd much prefer to be an independent Major of a good "Sucker" regiment. If my regiment consents to it I'll take it, if not I won't. It is raining hard and has been all day. This is not much of a place after all, and the state house is inferior to the Ohio state house. The streets are very narrow and the hotels dirty; the business buildings smoky and the citizens butternut looking. I was present last evening at an interview between General Mitchell and the Mayor of the City, but the matter talked of is "contraband."

Mitchell's administration is popular here, and the Mayor is anxious that he should remain here. I left Louisville in such a hurry that I forgot to mail those letters, will you please see that they are mailed? Didn't I leave you suddenly though? Well it spared me much of the pain of parting. I hope you are cheerful and happy for I am, and I begin to feel like a soldier again, but you came very near stealing me away from my allegiance and duty, yet I shall remember the fact that my wife always said go and do your duty.

Yours.

Asst. Inspector General's Office.
Feb'y. 19th, 1863.

Dear Wife:

I write you again from Tennessee's capital. The day after I wrote you my last letter, I reached my regiment, about one mile south of Murfreesboro, after wading through much mud for about three miles, carrying my sword and valise, and I declare I never before came so near lying down in a fence corner and giving up, but when I reached camp I found our headquarters tent very large and comfortable, with a plank floor and cots to sleep on, and when night came I turned in early and soon forgot all about wars, weddings and mud. When I reached camp my regiment was out on an expedition and returned next day with 30 horses, 6 prisoners, 15 stand of arms and 30 saddles and bridles captured from John Morgan.

On the evening of my second day in camp I received an order from Genl. Rosecrans directing me to report to Genl. Mitchell, at Nashville, for duty as Asst. Inspector General for the Post of Nashville, and in accordance with that order I reached here last evening and reported for duty to Genl. Mitchell, and am now writing this letter in my office. I, however, requested Genl. Mitchell, this morning, to relieve me and return me to my regiment; the Genl. refuses to do so, and I can't tell yet where I shall drop, but my Colonel and my regiment strongly insist upon my remaining with them, and I feel disposed to respect the wishes of those who gave me the rank I hold, and shall therefore insist upon returning to my regiment. I think I can induce the General to relieve me to-day, and if so I shall return to my regiment at Murfreesboro to-morrow.

My regiment has not been paid yet, and may not be this week but I think it surely will be next week. We were all decently poor when we entered the service last August—have had no pay since, and we now are all equally and abjectly poor, without money enough in the regiment to buy a cigar. This morning General Mitchell, as an inducement to have me stay told me that Mrs. Mitchell would be here after a while and that I should have you come and you could have a pleasant time here together. That, I confess, was the strongest inducement he offered me. It is decidedly too bad that we should be separated so suddenly

after our marriage, and I can't yet feel reconciled to it. But oh!
that splendid future when my days of wandering shall be over!
Then

> "The night shall be filled with music,
>   And the cares that infest the day,
> Shall fold their tents like the Arabs,
>   And as silently steal away." [2]

Be cheerful. Remember the darkest cloud has a bright side,
and we shall find the bright side some of these days. I have
passed over the Stone River battle field [3] but didn't see much
except long lines of rifle pits and hundreds of dead horses.
The surrounding country is a barren waste filled with new made
graves and ruined houses. It has rained nearly all the time I've
been in Tennessee. I met General John M. Palmer of Illinois,[4]
one day as we were plunging through the mud on the Stone
River battle field. He is a large, flaxen haired, ruddy faced,
pleasant looking man.

Your husband.

Nashville, Tenn., Feb'y. 23, 1863.

Dear wife:

Here I am in Nashville yet, but I have received leave from
Genl. Mitchell to go to Murfreesboro to-morrow, and shall
start for there at 6:30 in the morning. While there I shall, if
possible, get Genl. Rosecrans to relieve me from duty at this
Post, and if I fail shall return here day after to-morrow. My
strength is increasing, and I have a very pleasant position here,

2. *Longfellow,* "The Day Is Done."

3. The other name for the Battle of Murfreesboro, fought on December 31,
1862, and January 1–2, 1863.

4. John McAuley Palmer (1817–1900), Illinois lawyer and politician, began
his military career in May, 1861, as colonel of the 14th Illinois Infantry. In
December of that year he was promoted to the rank of brigadier-general. At
Stone River he had fought gallantly as a division commander.

but it is too much parlor soldiering, and knowing that my regiment wants me keeps me in a continual ferment to get away. I made my first official report this evening, in relation to the 23 hospitals in and about this city which I have inspected during the past four days.

In my tour I saw more sick and suffering humanity than I want to see in my whole life again. In one of the hospitals I saw one of your brother Jerry's men, named Chambers, from Morrow County, Ohio.

He called me by name away across the ward and appeared very much relieved to see some one he knew. I have not received any pay yet and feel like grumbling, but I hope to get sight of a paymaster this week. I am more anxious about it on your account than my own, for I can get along anyhow with government rations and government clothing, if necessary, but you can't.

I attended the Washington birthday celebration at the state house to-day, and while there really felt proud that I belonged to the Federal Army. It was such a sight as Tennessee's capital has not witnessed for many a day and will long be remembered by its citizens. Speeches were made by Parson Brownlow, Governor Crawford of Kansas, General Smith of Kentucky, and others, and letters read from Genl. Rosecrans, Genl. Negley, Genl. Mitchell, Daniel S. Dickinson of New York &c &c.[5] Songs were sung by ladies and by soldiers, and the whole concluded by the "Star Spangled Banner" grandly sung by the Nashville

5. Quite a galaxy of notables: William G. Brownlow, Methodist minister, editor, and leader of Union sympathizers in Tennessee; Samuel Johnson Crawford, then an officer in the 2nd Kansas Cavalry; Green Clay Smith of Kentucky, brigadier-general of volunteers; General Rosecrans; Major General James Scott Negley of Pennsylvania; Robert Byington Mitchell; and Daniel S. Dickinson, former United States Senator from New York.

Connolly's reference to "Governor" Crawford is evidence of at least some *post facto* revision. Crawford was not elected Governor of Kansas until November, 1864.

Glee Club, the whole audience joining in the chorus, until the arches rang with the patriotic outburst. If we could whip traitors as easily as we can sing songs and pass resolutions what a glorious thing it would be.

I do wonder how you are getting along. Got the blues any? If I could drop in for an hour or two this evening wouldn't I enjoy it though? If I were commander in chief I would change these headquarters for a day or two.

Your husband.

Nashville, March 2, 1863.

Dear wife:

. . . I am looking every hour for the order relieving me and returning me to my regiment. I have felt depressed under this soldiering on Brussels carpet and in cushioned arm chairs. It seems like a farce to me. Colonel [Monroe] of my regiment tells me my getting married was the worst thing I could do as a soldier; he says it will make me a coward, that I will never go into a fight without thinking of my wife and endeavoring to shelter myself as much as possible on her account. He says it is the case with himself, and that he wishes he had no wife. I don't believe him for he has been in the battles of Belmont, Fort Henry, Fort Donelson, Shiloh and Perryville, and was promoted for gallantry on the field at Fort Donelson, so I think one forgets all about wife, self and everything else but doing his best when he gets in a fight. The officers of this army have to pass a military examination about the 15th of this month and all who are found not up to the mark will be mustered out. I shouldn't wonder if I were found below par for I never could take any interest in studying the confounded military books and I have no taste that way, still I suppose I must brush up a little. So you think of going home to Ohio all alone pretty soon. Be careful of that trunk of mine you are to take home with you. I have no idea now what the contents are except that they are a lot of "frivols" such as I shall never have use for again. If you find anything contraband lay it aside and we'll hold a court of inquiry over it when I get home. . . .

Your husband.

Murfreesboro, Tenn., March 5, '63.

Dear wife:

I received the order relieving me from duty at Nashville two days since, and immediately got on the train and came down here but when I arrived here I found our whole Division, except enough from each regiment to do picket duty, had made the expected advance on Woodbury, and I also found an order placing me in command of so much of our Brigade as remained behind. So you see I run no risk of *ex*-tinguishing myself in the Woodbury fight I wrote you about. It is quite cold here now but dry, and I hope it will remain so until spring fairly opens for I do abominate this Tennessee mud. After I have finished this letter I'll have my horse saddled and start out in search of your brother Jerry. I wrote him from Nashville but I want to see and talk with him. I find a great anxiety here among officers and men to return to their homes, and the men are continually flattering themselves that the war will close about June 1st and they will all get home. Poor fellows! their hopes are doomed to be blasted, the 1st of June will come and still the red tide of war will sweep on more fiercely than ever, still their wives and children will be looking in vain for their return.

We who are in the army are like the "Widow Bedott," we "kaint kalkillate." [6]

Your husband.

P. S. Tell Barbour that I'm paying 15 cents a paper for his "Sunnyside" fine cut chewing tobacco down here. I wish all that profit was going to him.

6. A reference to *The Widow Bedott Papers* (1856), a popular series of humorous sketches in dialect by Frances Miriam Whitcher.

Murfreesboro, Tenn., Mch. 17, '63.

Dear wife:

After many days of waiting, watching and disappointment, I've concluded I'm not going to get a letter from you very soon, so the best thing I can think of to do to-night is to write to you.

As soon as we got up this morning, which was about 7 o'clock, the Colonel proposed that he, myself and our Surgeon go on a fishing excursion to Stone River, whose banks were so desperately contested a few weeks ago. The balmy atmosphere and bright skies of the spring morning induced us to lay aside the sword and shoulder the fishing tackle. We fished all day, most of the time where the battle raged in hottest fury, and returned to camp a little after dark thoroughly tired, but with a very fair string of fish, so I think I might venture to invite you to eat breakfast with our "mess" in the morning. You must be ready for breakfast before 9 o'clock though, for by that time we expect to be far out on the march; at least we have orders to hold ourselves in readiness to march and we expect to receive marching orders early in the morning. We are ordered to prepare 2 days rations in haversacks and two days rations on mules, so the trip will be a short one and we'll be back again in 3 or 4 days. I have not been on any of these expeditions but shall go to-morrow. I think the crack of a rebel gun is all the tonic I need now to make me fit for any kind of soldiering as I was before I was taken sick. We are having beautiful weather now; spring has come; the fields (if this country without fences can be said to have any fields) are looking fresh and green, the trees are budding, some peach trees have already a few blossoms; the few citizens left have commenced making gardens, and the soldiers look more cheerful and happy now that they can once more see the bright sun shining and the grass growing. Poor fellows; the sun will shine as brightly and the grass grow as green over hundreds of their graves by another spring. It is well we don't know what's ahead of us.

I have been practicing law since I came here. One of our young lieutenants deserted when our regiment came through Nashville, and he was arrested at his home in Illinois and brought back here in irons. He was tried on a charge of "desertion in the face of an enemy," before a general court martial at Murfreesboro, and he sent for me to defend him. I went, but I knew he was guilty and I wanted to see him punished, yet at the same time I was very sorry for him. He had been married shortly before entering the service and he left his wife but very little money, expecting to receive pay from the government every two months. In this he was disappointed like all the rest of us. His wife kept writing to him that she was out of money and could scarcely procure the necessaries of life, and finally she wrote him that she had become a mother. The poor fellow could stand it no longer, he didn't know how to get a leave of absence, and he determined to go home and make some provision for his wife and infant child, risking all consequences. This is his story and there was nothing in evidence to contradict it. I don't know yet what the finding and sentence of the court is but I presume they found him guilty, and probably sentenced him to be shot, but I am sure President Lincoln will never let him be shot. It's a hard case, but he had no business to have a wife—*and baby* to think about.

Our Colonel has been home since I was and our Lieut.-Colonel [7] has applied for leave and will probably get it. Probably I may get home by next fall. By the way, did that new suit I had made to wear at my wedding ever come? I understand it was sent from [Charleston,] Illinois in time, but as you know it did not arrive in time and I have never heard whether it finally got through or not, but suppose it has and that you will put it "where moth and rust doth not corrupt and thieves do not break through and steal" for I may need it when I become an American citizen again. It occurs to me that I left a pair of

7. Jonathan Biggs.

boots at the house, and I may need them also when I get back to the United States. How your cares are multiplying! I declare my goods and chattels are scattered hither and yon, from central Illinois to central Ohio and thence to central Dixie—a bad state of affairs for the "head of a family." But it's getting late and I must be up and off early in the morning so I must say good night.

Your husband.

Murfreesboro, Tenn., March 28, '63.

Dear wife:

As our Lieut. Col. is going back home in a couple of hours I will write you a hasty letter and send it by him to mail at some northern office. I received your letter of the 12th on the 20th and the time and place of its reception brought me great pleasure.

It was near sunset, the air was still loaded with the sulphurous smoke of battle, the rattle of musketry and booming of cannon were still ringing in my ears; the dead and wounded lay scattered around me; the browned leaves were marked here and there with little pools of blood where some poor fellow offered up his last sacrifice; our wearied men lay upon the ground in line of battle narrowly watching the dense cedars in our front where the enemy had hid themselves the last time we drove them back. I sat on an old log, my faithful mare near me, still quivering with the excitement of the battle, and as I sat there musing on the fortunes of the day that had lost us one of our bravest captains and two of our best lieutenants, I could see in the distance, the long lines of the enemy commence to move slowly away from us; just then a courier dashed up from our camp at Murfreesboro, his horse covered with foam, bearing with him the mail for our regiment, and also the news that our precarious situation had been heard of at our camp 14 miles distant, and that heavy reinforcements were then on the road to succor us.

But when that mail was distributed I found your letter, and

forgot all about war's alarms; occasionally, however, I would look up from the page to glance at the retreating enemy. What better time or place could there have been for me to receive that letter.

It thrills one to feel that his side has won a victory. I never felt it so completely before, for at Perryville I didn't feel quite sure that we were not whipped, but this time I had no doubt about what happened, and it was the redoubtable Morgan we whipped and sent flying from the field, with a bullet mark of ours on his arm.

He expected to make another Hartsville affair of it but was mistaken in his men. The last letter I wrote you was the evening before we started on our expedition. We started next morning and marched about 15 miles when we bivouacked for the night; early the next morning we started forward again, expecting to meet the enemy, our regiment being in the advance. About noon our mounted scouts brought in word that the enemy's pickets were a short distance in advance. I was immediately ordered forward with 3 companies of our regiment deployed as skirmishers to engage the enemy's pickets and drive them in. We went ahead about a quarter of a mile and my men poured a volley into a squad of cavalry which unhorsed one whom we captured, the rest flying in confusion. Moving on some distance farther we came in sight of a heavy force of the enemy drawn up in line of battle, and we halted; our brigade commander came up and concluding the enemy were too strong for us, the whole column about-faced, bringing us in the rear, and marched back. We bivouacked that night on a wooded hill near Auburn, Tenn., expecting to be attacked during the night, but we were not molested, although the enemy's scouts were all around us all night and kept most of us awake.

In the morning we resumed our march toward Murfreesboro, moving very cautiously, our regiment still in the rear, and we could see the scouts of the enemy following us all morning.

About 9 o'clock in the morning we passed through the village of
Milton, Tenn., and halted on this side to rest. In a few minutes
the enemy appeared in small force in the village. A shell was
thrown at them which caused them to leave suddenly, but in a
few minutes they reappeared in greater force. I was then ordered
to take 3 companies of our regiment back to the village and
open up a skirmish with the enemy, which I did. I concealed my
men behind houses and fences in the village and kept up a
skirmish fire about 20 minutes, in which two of my men were
wounded, but the enemy's cavalry being about to surround us
I brought my men back to the regiment. By this time the enemy
had disclosed his full force and was filing around on our right
and left, in plain view, for the purpose of surrounding our
entire brigade. Our brigade kept falling back in line of battle,
my 3 companies being in the rear covering the retreat. In this
way we fell back about a mile, the enemy keeping up a fire on us
and making several ineffectual atempts to charge us with cavalry
to break our lines. Finally we reached a rocky hill on which our
little brigade of about 1100 fighting men determined to make a
stand and await the attack of the 4000 or 5000 rebels under
John Morgan.

We had but few minutes to wait until on they came rushing
suddenly upon the 101st Ind., which was on our left, and causing some confusion, but the 101st boys fell in with ours and
soon drove the enemy back into the cedars; another charge
came upon our front and we drove them back; again they
charged on the left, but by that time the 101st Ind. was re-
formed and they punished the enemy terribly.

The fighting continued from 10 o'clock in the morning until
4 in the afternoon. The pommel of my saddle and one of my
holsters were carried away by bullets. I then dismounted and in
a few minutes they shot away the collar of my overcoat, leaving
it in rags and knocking me down, but it didn't hurt a bit. The
next day we returned to camp bringing our dead and wounded

with us. We had 6 men killed on the field and about 30 severely wounded, two of our killed being officers. The enemy's loss in killed, wounded and prisoners was about 400. The battle of Milton will not figure among the big battles of the war, but we flatter ourselves that it will be worthy of mention as a handsome victory.[8] They deliberately made the attack with force enough to completely surround us, we had no protection, and they expected to gobble us up as they did the Hartsville brigade but Morgan failed for the first time.

Jerry has probably resigned to-day.[9] I think it the wisest thing he could do for he is not able to stand service in the field. I am getting stronger every day.

Write me a good long letter very soon.

Your husband.

Murfreesboro, April 1, 1863.

Dear wife:

Have just read your letter written at Johnsville and am glad to know you are enjoying yourself. So am I. Saw Jerry this

---

8. Of the Battle of Milton, which Connolly describes here, the *Report of the Adjutant General of the State of Illinois (Revised)*, has a succinct account:

"March 20, the Brigade, consisting of the One Hundred and Twenty-third Illinois, Eightieth Illinois, One Hundred and Fifth Ohio, One Hundred and First Indiana, with two pieces of Captain Harris' Battery—about 1,500 men in all—was attacked and surrounded by Morgan's Cavalry, about 5,000 strong, with six pieces of artillery, near Milton, Tenn., about twelve miles out from Murfreesboro. This was shortly after Morgan had captured a Brigade of infantry at Hartsville, Tenn. In the engagement at Milton, Morgan was wounded, his force driven from the field, leaving their dead and wounded and two pieces of artillery. . . .

"Major Connolly had the pommel of his saddle torn away by a bullet, and dismounting, was in a few minutes seriously injured by a bullet which carried away the collar of his overcoat and blouse. Dr. H. C. Allen, the Regimental Surgeon, had his blouse riddled with bullets while attending to the wounded. Morgan never fought a successful battle after this." VI, 416–17.

As Connolly's letter makes clear, the report of his injury was grossly exaggerated.

9. Lieutenant Dunn resigned his commission on April 1, 1863.

morning. He expects his resignation papers in a few days and he may possibly be home before you get this. We start on another expedition in about two hours, in the direction of Lebanon. We hope to surprise a rebel camp and "gobble" a bunch of prisoners. I had close enough calls in the Milton fight and shall try to take more care of my overcoat and saddle this trip. I command the regiment this trip myself, our Colonel being in command of the brigade and our Lieut. Col. being home on leave. We take 6 days rations, and 60 rounds of ammunition, so we don't propose to be captured without knowing the reason why. I haven't time to write more as it is near marching time, and I must go and hunt up a sutler to get some "fine cut" to last me through the trip.

Your husband.

Murfreesboro, Tenn., April 17, '63.

Dear wife:

Enclosed I send you ———— dollars. Should have sent it by Jerry but he left too soon. Our regiment is under marching orders, but I am not going with it this time. I have not been very well for some days past, nothing but a bilious attack though, to which I am subject occasionally. I am feeling better now but shall not go out into the field until I feel entirely well. Sam Snider called on me a few days since and he was looking very well.

Everything about headquarters is in a bustle of preparation for the march and I shall postpone writing you a letter until this evening when all will be quiet. Don't think now that I'm sick because I say I have not been well, for I am not sick—have been on duty, in command of the regiment all the time, out on an expedition and since return until yesterday. I shall write as often as I can but when I don't feel well I hate to write for fear I may write a blue letter.

Your husband.

Murfreesboro, Tenn., April 20, 1863.

Dear wife:

I am alone in my tent to-night, I have a good solid floor in it, an excellent fire place in one end, graced by a pair of andirons, a cheerful fire is glowing on the hearth for though the days are warm the nights are a little cool; my good *feather bed,* with *feather* pillow is waiting for me; the excellent brass band of the 19th regulars, who are encamped near us, fills the soft night air with splendid music, and while I am content as it is yet if you were here with me I should be happy. You remember when I was at home I was almost entirely out of the notion of soldier-ing much longer, and I really expected that by this time I should be out of the service. But I was not well then, I was petulant, ill humored, weak from my long illness, I know I was. Military rules and orders were interfering with my freedom of action and that engendered in me a rebellious spirit toward everything military, but as time has passed and my general health improved that spirit has passed away and I begin to feel somewhat the spirit of a soldier. I am a better soldier than I was before we were married, not that I am any more rash, or want to fight any more, but somehow I enter into the spirit of things here more, my experience has given me more confidence in myself, but I am in no hurry to get into any more battles, for I think we have done our full share so far. We have been under fire 15 times, we are cut down in 8 months service from 962 men to about 460, 200 of that loss being in battle and skirmish, so that all things considered I don't care to fight any more, at least until regiments in service longer than we have tried their mettle once or twice. Still I know the fighting can't be divided out that way. Fighting goes like fortunes. Some get more than their equal share while many get less.

The other day when I sent you that little money package, I wrote you a short note, the first for many days; I had been un-fit to do anything for ten days but grumble, although I was

compelled by circumstances to be on duty. I saw your brother
Jerry the day before he left his boarding place to go to his regiment. I was quite unwell then, had just got in from a hard trip
of 9 days, and intended to write you next day and send it by
him, but on returning to camp found an order from Division
headquarters appointing me officer in charge of the Division
picket for next day; I wouldn't send up an excuse of sickness but
worried it through, and when I got off that duty and my report
forwarded, I went back to camp, took to bed and called for
calomel and jalap as the only consolation. The order for marching which the regiment had received the day I sent you that
package was countermanded but issued again last evening, and
at 9 o'clock this morning our whole Division started with 6
days rations in the direction of Woodbury, east of here, from
there they will probably go to McMinnville and may possibly
encounter the combined force of Morgan, Wheeler, Wharton
and Forrest,[10] supposed to be about 20 regiments of cavalry
and mounted infantry with 6 or 8 pieces of artillery.

Our force is not more than 9 regiments of infantry, 4 pieces
of artillery and 2 regiments of cavalry, but they won't dare to
fight us if they can help it by running away. Since the Milton
fight our men have no more fear of Morgan and his crew than
they would for that many boys with guns. It is "grape vine"
that Grant's and Burnsides' armies will unite with us within
the next month, and then Bragg must find new camps for we
will have business at Tullahoma and Chattanooga.

In your last letter you say I said something about "bullet
holes." I certainly did. I wrote you a long letter describing our
Milton fight and telling you how and when I got my "bullet
holes," one tearing away part of my saddle holster and shattering the pommel of my saddle, the other tearing away the collar of my overcoat and knocking me down slightly, all of which
caused me no pain and very little uneasiness, but many of the

10. Four Confederate cavalry commanders: John Hunt Morgan, Joseph
Wheeler, J. A. Wharton, and Nathan Bedford Forrest.

men and officers saw me fall and the word passed along the line: "the Major is shot," but when the fighting was over and they all saw I was unhurt we had a jolly time hand shaking for a few minutes. I knew it was a mistake all the time but they didn't. I was some distance in front of the regiment when my saddle was hit, and happened to be the only officer on horseback visible to the enemy. They were in a cedar thicket and I couldn't see them but they could see me. On looking around I saw that all the other field officers were dismounted so I got out of there in a hurry, dismounted and had my horse led back by an orderly; a few minutes later while standing behind our line of men lying down, some "Johnnie" in the cedars who was a tolerably good shot sent a bullet through my overcoat collar and down I went. I expect he thought he shot me but he was badly mistaken. I was conscious all the time, knew I had fallen, but knew I was not wounded, although I was shocked as if by a galvanic battery; in three minutes I was all right again; it seems much worse in writing than the actual experience. Oh yes my clothing in the trunk; you can send it to father's if you choose, but I want it kept for myself as I hope to wear it again some day. . . .

Your husband.

Murfreesboro, Tenn., April 27, 1863

Dear wife:

It is Monday morning again and I'll begin the week by writing to you. I wrote you last Monday, and having occasion to send an express package to [Charleston], Illinois, I enclosed the letter in it, with instructions to mail it there. I thought you would be more certain to get it than if I mailed it here. I suppose you haven't received it yet. After I had started it I received a letter from you in which you said you had received the letter I sent by our Lieut Col. So he mailed it at [Charleston], Ills. I told him to mail it at Louisville and he told me he had mailed it at Indianapolis.

He must have carried it in his pocket ten days. Well I'm glad

it was not in some rebel's pocket. Having received that letter
you will be posted about the bullet holes, for in it I gave you
the full story of the affair. Don't let them worry you any more
than they did me. I feel much better than when I wrote you
last. Have had a good long rest in camp, and wish now I was
out with the regiment. Have had nothing to do for the last eight
days but eat, sleep and ride around.

Our Division has not returned yet. I saw a dispatch from
them this morning at headquarters. They occupied McMinnville
on the 21st, driving out the rebels who fled precipitately without firing a shot. We captured and destroyed two railroad trains
that were used in running from McMinnville to Tullahoma.
Mrs Gen John Morgan was among those captured. We burned
a large cotton and woolen goods factory established there by the
rebel government for the manufacture of army goods. It throws
between four and five hundred women out of employment, that
being their only means of subsistence, their men folks being in
the rebel army. Our forces also burned all the store houses in
the place, and a large amount of army stores consisting of bacon,
flour, sugar and rice; they also destroyed a large portion of the
railroad track between McMinnville and Manchester, 15 miles
from Tullahoma.

Our mounted force pursued the rebels two days in a northwesterly direction toward the Cumberland river and captured
about 300 of them who were sent in as prisoners last evening
but the main body scattered out among the mountains and our
men had to give up the pursuit, their horses being exhausted
and many killed from hunger and fatigue, having been 48 hours
without anything to eat. Our men report that in the region of
McMinnville the country is as destitute of forage and provisions
as a desert. The Division is at Lebanon to-day, I think, and I
shall not be surprised to hear that they burned the place before
leaving. It is a nice town of about 2500 inhabitants, good buildings, and much wealth, but a rendezvous for the rebels who so

frequently destroy our railroad between here and Nashville. About 80 regiments and 25 batteries of this army started out in different directions at the same time our Division started, stretching out like fingers to feel the enemy and get as near Tullahoma as possible. Some of these fine mornings I think we shall find ourselves there and no enemy to resist us, although the bulk of Bragg's army is understood to be there now.

When the regiment returns we are to have a sword presentation. The officers of the regiment have purchased a fine sword and belt for the Colonel and I am to make the formal presentation. The Colonel thinks of resigning before the hot weather of summer commences. He has been in the service and has been in most of the severe battles of the West and he says he thinks he has done his part. I shall be sorry if he does for we can never get a better Colonel or one I will like better. Have you got the blues yet? Be cheerful. Look upon the passing days as so many steps I am taking towards you, and when the number of days have passed that Fate has appointed I will reach you. By the middle of August my first year of service will have been completed. A year in the army looked like an age when I started out but to look at it now it seems very short. When you write tell me all the little items that don't seem to be worth while telling, send me the trifles, the gossip, the rumors that have nothing in them, all such "small change" is very interesting to a fellow in camp.

Your husband.

Murfreesboro, Tenn., April 30, 1863.
Dear wife:

This being the last day of April I had better close out the month by writing you, for the regiment is out yet and I have more time now than I shall have after they get in, which they will probably do to-day about noon. I heard from them this morning; they camped about six miles from here last night and are to move in to-day. We had stirring times here yesterday. I was officer of the day and had just come in from the picket line where everything was quiet, when I received a note from Corps headquarters stating that the enemy were advancing in force on the Manchester pike, and ordering commandants of regiments to hold their commands in readiness for immediate action.

Everything was astir in a few moments. Mounted officers dashing in haste through the camps, over the fields and along the highways; mounted orderlies at full gallop, bearing the long yellow envelope in their belts, batteries hitched up and drivers mounted; regiments in line on their parade grounds; officers inspecting arms and seeing the standard "forty rounds" distributed; long lines of cavalry galloping to the front on the various pikes and the brass bands making the air vocal with their stirring music; tender thoughts were perhaps sent northward to the peaceful North where loved ones are; "if I fall send my body home" was quietly spoken by many to their comrades, but on the surface all was life and gaiety, and the merry laugh and cheerful song rang out from many on whom the setting sun would shine cold in death.

The preparations for battle, to the civilian, seem terrible, but the tried soldier regards them as the farmer does his preparation for harvest, though it must be terrible to the coward whose soul shrinks from the dangers his fancy conjures; the ring of his comrade's musket startles him, the cheerful words of his comrades in line condemn him and he hears his requiem in every bugle note that rings out the call to arms. Well my first motion was to get off my uniform coat and red sash I was wearing over my shoulder and around my waist as officer of the day, having no notion of going into a fight with so much brass and scarlet mounting, because somebody might spoil my wedding coat and fine sash by their careless shooting. Donning an old blouse that proved bullet proof at Perryville, Milton and elsewhere, I proceeded to muster my men, who were somewhat like

Falstaff's, lame, halt and blind, and when I had everything well to bear arms found I had a few over 100 willing men that I could depend on. Seeing that arms and ammunition were all right, I placed them under command of the only one of our captains in camp, and started again for my picket line where I warned the picket officers that the enemy were advancing and would probably be on them before the next morning, and that the safety of the army depended on their vigilance, and that they would be expected to hold their line until reinforcements could reach them.

In the meantime Rosecrans had ordered all the vast pile of government stores to be placed within the fortifications, and had sent a brigade of cavalry, a division of infantry and two batteries out to meet the advancing enemy on the Manchester pike. They met the advance about 4 miles beyond our picket line, drove them back to the main body, then gave the main body a few shells whereupon they returned to Manchester and our scare was over. It was not much after all. All this we learned next morning, but I lost 4 hours of good sleep that night sitting up waiting for the long roll that didn't "roll." Toward morning I lay down and the first "long roll" I heard, which was late in the morning, was the darkey at my tent flap calling out "Major, breakfuss," and so the battle ended like Falstaff's, and even those who "seek the bubble reputation at the cannon's mouth" were entirely satisfied. I hear some one out doors say "they're coming," and I must stop to see what it means, for I expect the regiment is coming.

May 1st. The regiment was coming sure enough, so I had to lay aside this letter to hear the news; we sat up late last night talking over the trip and laughing over the many funny things that always happen on such expeditions. This is the first day I ever saw such as poets sing of for "May day." Everything is bright, cheerful, beautiful and totally unlike the "May day" of our Northern clime. I wish you were here to enjoy it with

me. I imagine you will be here with me some day when we will
travel over these same hills and along these same streams that
I now travel over and along, watching every hill-top for an
enemy's vidette and every cedar thicket for ambushed guerillas.
As we approach Milton I'll show you where our little force
fought and whipped John Morgan; when we reach the village
I'll show you the houses that sheltered my men as we were
bringing on the fight; then we'll turn northward a few miles and
I'll show you "Pierce's Hill" covered with huge rocks where
we, only 250 strong, fought Johnson's cavalry 600 strong,
routed them, captured 25 of their horses, 30 of their guns and
about one third of their blankets, and then made a forced march
to get inside our picket line, wading Stone River breast deep to
the men the water bitter cold, and getting out of their reach
just as the enemy, 1000 strong, appeared on the opposite bank;
then we will turn northeast again and soon come to "Prosperity
Church," nestled down in a beautiful valley where we routed 5
companies of cavalry with 3 companies of our regiment half a
mile in advance of our main body, and then had to "skedadle"
back to the column ourselves, as the enemy returned reinforced.[11]

We'll then move ahead on that road until we come near
Liberty and will see where we captured a company of Morgan's
men right in the middle of the road; then we'll go on northwest
until we reach the handsome town of Lebanon and see where we
got a big scare, being called out in line of battle and standing
so for half an hour before we discovered the enemy were as
badly scared as we were. I think you will enjoy that trip quite
as well as I am enjoying it now, but there are some things to

11. The reference is to an action in which the 123rd Illinois was engaged not
long before the Battle of Milton. According to the *Report of the Adjutant
General of the State of Illinois (Revised)* : "Early in March the Regiment was
attacked beyond Stone River, while halted on Breed's Hill, with arms stacked
and ranks broken, by a large cavalry force, but forming under fire, and repelling the attack, it waded Stone River, carrying off its wounded, and withdrew to Murfreesboro." VI, 416.

be done yet before that trip can be undertaken, the most important of which is the whipping of this "stiff necked and rebellious people." Our regiment got back from their eleven days trip without having fired a gun. One of our men died, however, of apoplexy, and was buried away out in the country. He was one of the best soldiers in the regiment, but his death only caused a temporary ripple like dropping a pebble in a lake.

The regiment is turning over its tents to-day—the cotton houses in which, when "at home," the men have lived since last November, and receiving in lieu of them the shelter tent, or as the men call them, "dog tents." Jerry can describe them to you as he is "an old soldier." We are more fortunate at headquarters though, and besides our allowance of 3 wall tents will manage to "press" about 3 additional ones so I think we can make ourselves comfortable. There is some probability of this Division breaking camp here and moving to Lebanon. I shall not be surprised or displeased if that be true. Lebanon is a somewhat important point, very healthy, excellent water, plenty of eggs, butter, milk &c in the adjacent country, plenty of fine dwellings that would make excellent quarters for officers, and plenty of handsome, impudent female rebels who, if we occupied the place would be likely to shut their mouths or open them only to beg favors. The trouble about moving to Lebanon will be that we won't have a daily mail. Mail is quite as important to soldiers as rations. This paper in large sheets upon which I am writing was captured at Lebanon on one of our trips there. Some Yankee trader smuggled it through the lines I suppose.

We have cedar trees about ten feet high set out in all the streets through our camp and a double row of them about 12 feet high set out the whole length of our headquarter street, which makes a fine shady avenue for these warm days. I have my table out under one of these cedars while writing this letter, and in the next tree to me, right in front of my tent, a couple of red birds have their nest and greet me with fine music every morning about daylight. I was expecting a letter from you to-day but the mail is in and distributed and as none has been handed me I conclude there is nothing for me, so I'll just continue expecting, and stop writing for this time.

Your husband.

Murfreesboro, May 6, 1863.

Dear wife

No letter from you to-day. . . . Expectation has been strained for many days, and the only relief is the cheering news coming from all around the lines of the Union armies. It causes me to forget my petty disappointments and join in the general good feeling that pervades the "Army of the Cumberland." We may be whipped but nothing could make this army believe it possible now. Finally the question is settled and our regiment is to be mounted. Soon as I finish this letter I shall start in command of 3 companies of the regiments, mounted, to join a detachment of [Wilder's] brigade of mounted infantry, at Lavergne, on the railroad between here and Nashville, first, to drive away or capture the enemy now threatening the railroad, and secondly to scour all the country north to the Cumberland river and capture horses enough to mount our regiment. Yesterday and to-day we have been having the cold drizzling rain of May in Tennessee. I don't know whether I shall like the mounting of our regiment, but it will save the men from a lot of marching on foot, and we will still do our fighting on foot, using the horses only for rapidity of movement. We don't intend to become cavalry. As things look now there will be no special need for this army more than the present summer.

You may see in the papers an account of a raid on the railroad near Meridian, Miss. The force making that raid is 1900 men, mounted. One regiment of it, the 80th Illinois, belonged to this brigade and left here about 6 weeks ago to join the expedition. It is a desperate undertaking. They have no tents, wagons or baggage, but are pushing on southward night and day destroying property as they go. They expect to cut all the main lines of railroad between New Orleans, Mobile and Richmond, in the rear of Bragg's army and then surrender if they find they can't get to Banks' army or get back here. We all expect they will return via Richmond as prisoners of war, but if they do the work they are expected to do we can well afford to have them surrender. My men are about ready, they are pleased at the prospect of being mounted. I must close.

Your husband.

Murfreesboro, May 18, 1863.

Dear wife—

Here it is the middle of May and I am not reported killed, wounded or missing. I am back safe from my first trip in command of a mounted force and am feeling better than I have since I have been in the army. The first "May day" of our wedded life came to me "with healing on its wings." Indeed I felt particularly good that day and wrote you a long letter. I see this war in a different aspect from any in which I saw it before. To some extent I have had a peep behind the rebel curtains, and have been surprised at the very little honesty and very great ignorance to be found behind those curtains.

I have been at their houses and talked with the women while I dandled a dirty faced, half clad infantile rebel on my yankee knee; I have gone dashing through their corn fields, their wheat fields, their cotton fields, meadows and door yards with a hundred good yankee "vandals" sweeping along in my train; have eaten at their tables and slept in their feather beds; have gone to their stables and taken my choice of their horses, to their pastures and taken my choice of their mules, to their granaries and hay stacks and fed my hungry horses, while my men went to their smoke houses, milk houses and hens' nests gathering material for high living in camp, and while engaged in this kind of ranging, as you may readily suppose, I came in close contact with the inhabitants, and was compelled to listen to many an entreaty from grey haired matrons and rosy cheeked maidens to spare their last horse that they might raise a little crop to save them from starving but in most cases the last horse had to go, and with it generally went every "likely nigger boy" on the plantation, who had any aspirations for freedom, leaving the women to do their own work as do the blessed yankee girls far away at my Northern home. Now what do you think of your husband degenerating from a conservative young Democrat to a horse stealer and "nigger thief," and practicing his nefarious occupation almost within gun shot of the sacred "Hermitage" and tomb of Andrew Jackson? Yes, while in the field I am an abolitionist; my government has decided to wipe out slavery, and I am for the government and its policy whether right or wrong, so long as its flag is confronted by the hostile guns of slavery.

Soldiering with a mounted command is so very different from infantry service that I must hastily review my first trip for you. We belong now to "[Wilder's]s brigade" of which you have lately seen frequent mention in the papers. The brigade consists of the [17th] Ind. and [72nd] Ind., the [98th] Ills. and my own regiment, with [Lilly's] Ind. battery of 6 rifled Parrott guns and 4 howitzers. All these regiments but mine have been mounted about 5 months. On the morning of May 6th an order came transferring us from the brigade in which we have always been to this new brigade, and that we would be mounted as soon as horses can be obtained.

On the same morning despatches came from General Steedman at Lavergne, a place on the railroad midway between here and Nashville, saying that he had been driven in the day before by about 6000 cavalry and mounted infantry, advancing from Lebanon, and that the railroad was in imminent danger. [Wilder's]s brigade was ordered to mount in hot haste, taking

3 days rations, and proceed immediately to Lavergne. The brigade commander sent us an order to get the spare horses from the other regiments of the brigade, mount as many of our men as possible and join him. We barely got enough to mount one company, and off they started about 9 o'clock in the morning. We then went to the government "corral" and selected 75 horses, without reference to whether they had ever been ridden or not, sent men after them, brought them to camp, saddled, bridled, and mounted them and by two o'clock I started with them to join the brigade and the rest of my command at Lavergne, which place I reached in good time, after a good deal of fun and fuss with our unbroken horses, and went into bivouac, but then came new troubles for me. It was not like going into camp with infantry, for then a commanding officer can dismount, hand his horse over to his orderly, sit down and rest until he gets his supper, smoke his pipe, then wrap up in his blankets and sleep until the reveille startles the quiet of early morning; but here was I with my men tired but not footsore, my horses hungry and thirsty, nothing to feed them with and the men as indifferent about it as though cavalry horses never eat anything. Something had to be done to feed my 125 hungry horses, so I started to see the brigade commander, found him, and he told me where to find corn, and he also told me to have my command in the saddle by 6 in the morning as he would send me in command of a reconnoitering force to hunt up the enemy. Here was a fine fix.

I knew nothing about reconnoitering, never did such a thing and didn't know how to go about it, and here now I was to take four or five hundred men, with a guide, and strike out among the cedar thickets, rocks, hills and ravines of this abominable Stone River country to find the location, strength &c of an enemy who knew the country well, and were reported to be five or six thousand strong. As I laid down on a brush pile in the woods to sleep that night visions of Libby prison loomed up

up before me, and as I started in the morning I looked at my
blankets strapped to my saddle and wondered whether I could
sleep comfortably under them the next night while one of my
southern brethren stood guard over me; but my duty was to
obey and let results take care of themselves; I dare not plead
ignorance, so I was up betimes, and with my own command
reinforced by 150 men from another regiment I struck out into
a bridle path over the hills and after moving northward about
8 miles came to a ford across Stone River. Halting here I sent
150 men across the River with orders to divide into 5 parties of
30 each and scour the country as far as they could safely go, in
search of rebels, "contraband" horses and mules, and report to
me at the ford at 3 o'clock in the afternoon. Posting pickets
then around my remaining force I sat down to await the result; everything was quiet until noon and I went to a house near
by where I found a fine old lady and her handsome intelligent
daughter—intimated that I could eat some dinner, and soon had
a very good dinner.

While eating word was brought from one of my pickets that
he had seen a party of mounted men some distance from him
and supposed them to be rebels. To drop the dinner, mount and
hasten to the picket post was the work of a moment; just as I
reached the post I saw a man dismount and enter a house on a
hill about half a mile distant; I could see the flashing of his saber
scabbard but couldn't distinguish the color of his uniform, but
concluded it was a rebel, as my men were miles away by that
time and I determined to "bag" him, so sending back for 5
men, I made a circuit through the timber and surrounded the
house, then dismounting, with pistol in hand I walked to the
door of the house and on looking in saw one of Uncle Sam's
boys quietly putting himself outside of a chunk of "pone" and
a bowl of milk. I ascertained that he belonged to another force
that had been sent out from Lavergne to operate some 4 miles
west of me, but the Major of the [98th] Ill. who commanded it

had lost his way and was floundering through the woods trying
to find me. My hope of capturing a live butternut having thus
vanished, I sent the man off to find his command and pilot them
through to me, while I returned to my party, and in about an
hour the Major with about 100 men reached me; being his
senior he asked me for orders and I sent him across the river
with his command to follow up and join my men sent out in the
morning, which he did, and he reached them in good time, just
as a party of 100 rebels had attacked a detached party of 50 of
my men. They drove the rebels, killing one, wounding two and
killing two horses.

My scouting parties were all in safely by half past three o'clk
and we moved to Lavergne, having learned that there was no
considerable force of the enemy nearer than Lebanon, and
having captured a few good horses. The next day we remained
at Lavergne, and after drawing rations for two days more
started, on the morning of the 8th, for Lebanon. My command
was the advance guard and I was ordered to keep from one
half to three quarters of a mile in advance of the main column.
Several amusing incidents occurred on that day.

Once we came to cross roads when an orderly from the commander rode up and told me to halt there as the commander
thought of changing the route, so we halted, and while awaiting
orders I saw several horses and mules about a quarter of a mile
distant. I concluded we must have them, so taking twenty men
and some halters off we started through the fields, chased the
mules and horses, got about a dozen and started back, but on
reaching the cross roads my command was gone I didn't
know where. The route had been changed in my absence
and I was in a fix with my captured stock and little party of
twenty.

While pondering on the situation along came one of our
scouts with a prisoner, a guerilla, whom he had chased over the
hills about two miles and finally captured. The meeting was

agreeable for the scout had lost the brigade and so had I, but the scout knew the country and I knew where the brigade was to encamp that night so by uniting our fund of information and keeping under cover of the woods and avoiding public roads and houses we reached the column in about an hour and I tell you I felt much relieved.

Again: on the same day we had halted and were resting in the woods in a little valley when 28 mounted rebels rode up to the top of the slight elevation on our right, and only about ten rods distant. It was a mutual surprise, but I immediately ordered "fire" and away went the rebs and my men after them. Hats, caps, guns and blankets were scattered in every direction, but not a rebel fired a gun; we captured a finely uniformed lieutenant and two privates. The captured lieutenant proves to be the commander of a company who captured a lieutenant who belonged to this brigade, some time ago, and brutally murdered him and the rebel lieutenant is now in irons in the camp of the regiment to which the murdered lieutenant belonged, and he is in much danger of extreme punishment.

Again: On the afternoon of this same day I was ordered to take my command and scour the country for 2 or 3 miles on either side of the road, gather horses, "contrabands" and forage and get into camp any time that night. I had just got into the middle of stony cedar woodland and about a mile from the road when a man riding behind me said: "Major I see a butternut." "Where?" "Yonder" said he, pointing his finger.

I caught sight of the butternut coat just as it disappeared behind a clump of cedar; I ordered 20 men forward and started after him. Losing sight of him I had the men scatter and scour the woods; keeping straight ahead I caught sight of him again, and using my spurs soon came close enough to order him to "halt," but he kept straight on and so did I. Again I ordered him to "halt" and still he kept on; by this time my men were all out of sight in the woods and I was within a couple of rods of the butternut, so I concluded not to rely upon "moral suasion" any longer and took out a pistol and leveling it ordered him again to "halt" and this brought him to, but to my chagrin I found on examination that he had taken the oath of allegiance and had protection papers from Genl Paine at Gallatin. This again was a water haul but he told me where I could find plenty of good rebel forage and my "vandals" were soon swarming around the barn and premises of a stout rebel, where they got plenty of corn and sheaf oats, and we then turned our horses' heads towards the place indicated for camp that night and on reaching there found the rest of the brigade in and we were soon disposed of for the night.

I ate supper at a table that night, drank my coffee out of china cups and slept in feather bed. Near my camp that night the men discovered some sheep in a pasture and we had plenty of fresh mutton for breakfast. The next morning we were nearly out of rations so a wagon train, with an escort of 100 men, was sent across the Cumberland to Gallatin for rations, one regiment was retained at the camp as a reserve, and the remainder of the brigade was ordered forward to Lebanon via the Nashville and Lebanon pike, while I was ordered to take my command and scour the country between the pike and the Cumberland River, moving eastward so as to reach Lebanon that night or early next day, provided the force sent forward on the pike should occupy the place, but if they were driven back I was to fall back if I could and if that were not practicable I was to move north, cross the Cumberland, by swimming or any way I could, and get to Gallatin, from where I was to telegraph to our Division commander.

Here was an order which would throw me on my own resources for 12 or 15 hours at least, and possibly for two or three days. That suited me very well, but here was a strip of country 10 miles long and 8 miles wide that I was to move over without roads, and of which I knew nothing at all except as I had seen it on the map, without a guide and being compelled to depend upon darkies picked up along the way, for all my information, as to the enemy, distances and direction. We also had but one day's rations, and if the enemy should drive us to the Cumberland the prospect was fair that we would be hungry before we reached the "white settlements," but off we started through woods and fields, not being particular about tramping on the corn or cotton, or about putting up fences, and not being entirely certain but what our route would lead directly to Richmond via Chattanooga.

I soon divided my men into 6 parties, keeping 25 with myself and sending the others out in parties of 20 each, with orders to move in an easterly direction, each party scouring 1 to 2 miles of country north and south, and to gather information, "niggers," horses, mules, rebels &c. and to be sure to live upon the best they could find, and each man to bring to camp a ham, canteen of milk, some eggs and cornbread. I then fixed upon a place of meeting about four miles from Lebanon and two miles north of the pike. I was to move with my party direct toward Lebanon and about 3 miles north of the pike, parallel with it, so sending one party between mine and the pike and the other four parties stretching out north of mine toward the river the "forward" was given and away we went for a raid among the Tennesseans. For our adventures that day you must wait until I get home; I will say however, that our forces drove the enemy from Lebanon, all my parties but my own and another got lost and I found them at Lebanon when I got there. We had an abundance of ham, milk and everything good to eat and our days work footed up 55 good horses.

Our rations and the balance of the brigade reached us that night, we remained there next day, and I found a good Union family with a handsome daughter who played the piano and sang the "Star Spangled Banner," "Hail Columbia," "The Red, White and Blue" &c. &c. for us while the soldiers crowded around the house outside listening and cheering every song. You may be sure the people in that house were not disturbed as long as we were there. The following day we started for Murfreesboro and on reaching Stone River turned our horses into a wheat field to graze while the men went to the river to swim.

Saddling up again after a couple of hours spent this way we came into camp here and I hadn't a single sick man, and felt better myself than I have since I've been in the army. It may be that I shall like this mounted service better than I thought I would. I can't tell yet. There is more life, sport, adventure and good living in it, with less hard fighting but more chances of capture. A report has come in tonight that they are fighting at Readyville at one of our outposts, and if it be true we may be ordered out any moment. Col. [Monroe] has finished a letter to his wife and has just got in bed. He says I must stop writing and come to bed, we sleep together, and he says he is cold. It's quite chilly to-night, and if I don't stop he'll bother me so I can't write, so good night.

Your husband.

Murfreesboro, May 22, 1863.

Dear wife:

It is just daylight, and the regiment is mounted and ready for marching. The order came at midnight last night. We take two days rations. I suppose it's for a dash on McMinnville but I don't know. I hear the bugle at headquarters of the brigade sounding the order to march. Should I next write you from "Libby" don't worry.

My brother Charlie was in the Stoneman cavalry dash in the rear of Lee's army on the Potomac. He writes me that he was within 4 miles of Richmond. Maybe I will go all the way there this time, but there will be some "tall running" done before I consent to it.

This is a beautiful morning.

Your husband.

Murfreesboro, May 24, '63.

Dear wife:

I wrote you a very brief hasty note day before yesterday just before we started on an expedition. I was most agreeably surprised on returning night before last to find a letter from you.

If you knew how agreeable such surprises are to me I certainly think you would write me a letter every day. How pleasant it is to come in dusty, hungry and tired from a long scout along the enemy's lines and find a letter from you lying on my table to welcome me back and make [me] forget the fatiguing march. Let these surprises be frequent and you will place me under so many obligations that I shall always have the pleasure of knowing I am in your debt. I told you in my last that I supposed we were going to McMinnville but I was mistaken. We went out on the Manchester pike until we came to the "War Trace" road and then I knew where we were going, viz., to drive in Breckinridge's pickets and "feel" his lines. We did so successfully, killing four of their pickets, wounding two and capturing four, one being a lieutenant of the 2nd Georgia cavalry. We then withdrew, having accomplished all that was intended.

Thus far all the expeditions of this mounted brigade and of its several detachments have been very successful and the question with me now is, can this success always continue? Every community, army and individual has its due average of ill fortune as well as of good fortune, and if the good fortune all comes at once, of course when the supply is exhausted we must take the ill fortune. Well

> "Here's a sigh for those who love us,
> And a smile for those who hate,
> And whatever sky's above us,
> Here's a heart for every fate." [12]

Our brigade is evidently regarded as a useful appendage to this army, for either the entire brigade or a portion of it is in use almost continually; we are sent North, South, East and West, wherever the enemy needs stirring up; we break through their picket lines, drive them out of their camps and capture their stragglers; when the footmen of our Division go out some portion of our brigade starts the evening before to pick up some pickets in the darkness, learn from them the force and position of the enemy, then go forward and bring on a fight—when pushed too hard fall back and let the footmen finish the job, while we hold ourselves in readiness for the pursuit, if our footmen whip, or cover their retreat if they get whipped. We have to do hard riding and a great deal of it—horses frequently drop by the wayside, exhausted, but we always find horses enough to keep the men mounted. That's the kind of service we are engaged in now, and I suppose its purpose is largely to train us in the use and care of our horses when the main campaign begins, for at the beginning we were all perfectly green at it and the men never thought about feeding or currying their horses, but they are learning that they must care for their horses or they may have to go on foot, if their horses fail while out on a raid.

We are under marching orders again and start out at two o'clock this afternoon (we can't stop for Sundays) and it is now nearly noon, so in about two hours from this time I'll be in the

---

12. Lord Byron, "To Thomas Moore." Rendered correctly:
> "Here's a sigh to those who love me,
> And a smile to those who hate;
> And, whatever sky's above me,
> Here's a heart for every fate."

saddle. We take 5 days rations with us and will probably be out 3 or 4 days, there is no way of telling when we start out when we will get back. I told you in my last not to be surprised if I should write you next from "Libby," and now I repeat it. We are going where the enemy is, viz., Woodbury; there is said to be a cavalry brigade, (Wharton's) and if they stay there they must whip us, for we will go there or have a fight in trying, but their one brigade of that kind of cavalry don't amount to much. Just at daylight this morning, or rather just as I got up, which was somewhat after daylight, an orderly came up with a circular from Gen. Thomas announcing that Grant has taken Haines Bluff, 57 pieces of artillery, and has the first line of entrenchments at Vicksburg, with Pemberton and only 15000 men inside.[13]

You should have heard the cheers from the camp of this regiment when that was read to the men. This whole army is practically under marching orders; all heavy camp equipage is back at Nashville, and if I am not greatly mistaken three weeks from this time, and possibly three days, will find the Army of the Cumberland en route for Chattanooga. Vallandingham gone to Fort Warren! good for Burnside! Had the sentence been to the "Tortugas," as first reported it would have suited us better.[14] I do not dare to think of a leave of absence now; our Lieut. Col. is sick and has been for two weeks, and we may consider our-

13. Haynes Bluff, on the Yazoo River fifteen miles north of Vicksburg, fell to Federal troops on May 19. The siege of Vicksburg began on May 22. Pemberton's strength is grossly underestimated here. On July 4, 1863, he surrendered more than 30,000 men.

14. On May 5, 1863, Clement L. Vallandigham [correct spelling], an outspoken if not treasonable Peace Democrat, was arrested by order of General Ambrose E. Burnside, commanding the Department of the Ohio. On May 16 a military commission found Vallandigham guilty of "declaring disloyal sentiments and opinions with the object and purpose of weakening the power of the government in its efforts to suppress unlawful rebellion," and sentenced him to be imprisoned until the end of the war. Lincoln commuted the sentence to banishment.

selves now "in the face of the enemy," an advance and a battle being liable to take place at any time within 48 hours, so to *ask* for a leave at such a time would be almost as bad as open cowardice.

I'll get home though, all safe, and I hope before a great while. Just as soon as I get back from this expedition I'll try and get some photographs. Expect to see a paymaster soon and shall send you all I receive except what I need to live on and pay debts. As I must start soon I shall close, hoping to find a letter on my return.

Your letters reach me now in 3 or 4 days.

Your husband.

Murfreesboro, May 30, '63.

Dear wife:

I have just laid down "Harper's" for May. It has been raining occasional showers all day, the first rain for a long while; the atmosphere is fresh and pure as on a mountain top, and were it not for a neuralgic twinge in my face I should be in the best possible condition, but I am giving myself very little trouble about that, for your letters are reaching me now so frequently and in so short a time after being written that I would be but a "sorry soldier" to complain about such a trifle as a swollen, aching jaw.

The last time I wrote you, which was last Sunday, I told you we started on an expedition at 2 P. M. that day. Promptly at the appointed time we were in the saddle and off, this regiment in the advance.

We moved eastward, in the direction of Woodbury, about 12 miles that afternoon and encamped in a valley, by a mountain stream. By sunrise in the morning we were off again at a swinging gallop, on the road toward McMinnville, our object being to surprise and capture Col. Breckinridge's regiment of Kentucky cavalry, which was known to be on outpost duty at "Ivy

Bluff," about 5 miles from McMinnville. On coming within about 6 miles of their camp we left the pike, two regiments going on the left of it and two on the right, while a detachment of 50 men was left where we separated, with orders to remain there about three quarters of an hour, then to dash forward on the pike, drive in their pickets and advance far enough to let the enemy see their number, then turn and retreat hastily, hoping thereby to draw the enemy out in pursuit, while we who were making the circuit among the hills and valleys, on the right and left, were to close in on their rear and cultivate a close acquaintance with them. This programme was carried out admirably on our part, but the rebs didn't do their part, for when our 50 men, who had been left on the pike, came dashing up to the rebel pickets, the "Johnnies" fled without firing a gun and our 50 troopers followed them into their camp, from which the Kentuckians had, but a few moments before, fled in utter confusion.

We destroyed all their camp equipage, killed ten horses and four men, captured 2 rebel surgeons and ten privates, and 30 head of cattle which they had collected in the surrounding country. Our 50 followed them to within 3 miles of McMinnville, but there being two rebel brigades there the safest thing we could do was to get away from there, which we did as rapidly as military decency would permit.

My regiment with another had taken the right of the pike, and on reaching within about a mile of the rebel camp a courier brought us the information that the birds had flown and that we should rest our horses an hour or two and then return. While we were resting there I observed a new looking log cabin about a half mile distant, in the woods, and concluded I would go over to it and possibly get a drink of milk, so I started over to it alone and soon the inmates of the cabin heard the clatter of my horse's feet, and a woman, with a child in her arms, came to the door, looked out, then quickly stepped back; in an instant I had

a holster open and my hand on a "Colt," for her movement
looked suspicious, but on reining up before the door I saw I had
nothing to fear even if I was alone, for there, on a little stool, in
the middle of the bare floor, sat a "butternut," with blanched
cheek and quivering lip, about 25 years of age, his wife sitting
near him crying, and the child in her arms crying too, while a
little flaxen headed girl about 4 years old came to the door and
stood looking at me; I looked at the picture a moment and felt
a sadness creeping over me as I looked at that young man, sitting in the midst of his little family, and nothing but desolation
around them. I spoke to him kindly, but it took some time before
I could dispel his fears so that he could talk without his voice
trembling and almost giving way, his wife all the time listening
eagerly, anxious to catch, at the earliest moment, some indica-
tion of my intention toward her husband.

I finally drew from him the fact that he was a deserter from
the rebel army and had been home but two days; that he was
conscripted, put into Forrest's cavalry, and was with Forrest
when he captured Straight's command down in Georgia, of
which you read in the papers not long since. He begged me
not to take him prisoner, as he said he never wanted to go back
to them if he could help it. I left him and riding back reported
the facts to the Colonel commanding; he told me he thought I
should take him, but that I might do as I chose, but that I must
not go back there again alone, so I determined to go back and
get him, which I did. His wife simply said "good bye" to him,
her tears had all been shed, long months of loneliness and grief
in that solitary cabin had exhausted the fountain of her tears;
she now saw another cloud rising up between her and the sunlight of her young life, and she stood there in mute despair.

After we had left the house a short distance I looked back and
she was standing in the door, clasping the infant to her breast,
the little girl by her side clinging to her dress—she was looking
after her husband, but no tears were there, perhaps a silent

prayer was stealing from her heart for his safe return. What if
he told the truth when he said he was not a rebel and never had
and never would fire on a Union soldier? I almost shuddered
when I thought of the great wrong I might be committing; of
the hopelessness and utter destitution I might be unjustly bringing on that little household; of the terrible imprecations that
might be heaped on my head by that wronged wife, on her
bended knees, with her little fatherless ones around her, and I
confess too, I was imaginative enough to think that wife's
imprecations, by one word from me, might be changed to effective prayers for my safety, and thus musing, I convinced myself
that humanity bade me return him to his family. When I told
him I had determined to let him return his eyes filled with tears,
and, "God bless you" said he, as he shook me warmly by the
hand and bade me "good bye."

If he does return to the rebel army I shall feel that I have at
least one friend among them who may possibly, sometime, help
me through a rebel picket line, and direct me in a safe course
to where my own flag flies. We got back to camp without any
other incidents of importance, after an absence of four days,
and on my return, sure enough, I found a letter from you awaiting me, which made a pleasant finale to the trip. I begin to
like this mounted service, there is more dash and adventure in
it. Our Illinois Grant is reaping a harvest of glory among the
Mississippi swamps. Hurrah for Illinois! Her Generals and
soldiers are the best in the world, always excepting old "Rosy"
in whom you "Buckeyes" have a slight interest I believe.

This army has received orders, twice within the past ten days,
to hold itself in readiness to march at a moment's notice, with
5 days rations, which, in plain English, means that Rosecrans
is upon the eve of moving out to attack Bragg. I heard to-day,
from a high source, that it will probably be done within ten
days, unless Grant's operations should change the aspect of

affairs. My cheek is so swollen that I can't have that photograph taken now but will in a few days.

So you have purchased some napkins; that's quite a start towards housekeeping. Of course we'll keep house—if we can't afford a house I'll bring my tent home with me and we'll live like the Arabs, except that we won't have a fine mare at our tent door as they have, for my faithful mare that carried me safely through Perryville and Milton lay down and died very suddenly yesterday.

Your husband.

To Tullahoma

WHILE Rosecrans bolstered up the Army of the Cumberland, Bragg held the Army of Tennessee in and around Shelbyville, some eighty miles northwest of Chattanooga. In June, 1863, Rosecrans decided to advance. He planned to maneuver Bragg out of his positions at Shelbyville and Tullahoma, now strongly fortified, and give battle if a favorable opportunity presented itself.

After several feints early in the month, the Army of the Cumberland moved out of its camps on June 23. In the next nine days it drove Bragg from his prepared positions and forced him to retreat to Chattanooga, his base. There was no pitched battle, but there was fighting all along the way. Of that, the 123rd Illinois bore its share.

Henry M. Cist, historian of the Army of the Cumberland, characterized the campaign as one of the most brilliant strategical successes of the war. "The result," he wrote, ". . . gave to Rosecrans possession of Middle Tennessee, and placed the armies back in the relative positions occupied by them prior to Bragg's advance into Kentucky, a little less than one year previous. . . . During these nine days of active campaigning the Army of the Cumberland, numbering less than sixty thousand effective men, with a loss of 560 killed, wounded, and missing, compelled the army under Bragg, numbering something less than forty-five thousand effective men, to retreat a greater distance and out of far stronger positions than the united armies under Sherman were able to compel the same army with but slight additional strength under Joe Johnston, to fall back, in four months of active field campaigning, with a very much larger relative loss." [1]

Murfreesboro, June 4, 1863.

Dear wife:

At two o'clock this morning we received an order to march at 6 o'clock. It is now nearly 6 o'clock and we are nearly ready for the start. I do not know what this move means, but I rather expect that the whole of our army corps moves out to try Bragg to-day.

We however, are ordered around to the enemy's right flank, so that somebody else must do the hard fighting. It may be some time before you hear from me again. If so don't be uneasy about it for we will probably be where we will have no mails. Hope you are feeling as cheerful as I am this morning. Good bye for a little while.

Your husband.

Murfreesboro, June 9, 1863.

Dear wife:

From the date of this you see I am back again. We returned to camp here day before yesterday, and as usual lately I was welcomed back by a letter from you. Out of the saddle and into

1. *The Army of the Cumberland* (New York, 1882), 169–70.

my tent, after a 30 mile ride in 6 hours, I forgot all about being tired as soon as I saw the little white envelope lying on my table. What precious things letters from home are in the army. How much dearer the loved ones at home become as letter after letter from them steals silently in amongst the wilderness of tents, bearing in its folds the story of "Home, sweet home," and words of hope and encouragement for the bronzed, weather beaten soldier. To add to my pleasure on my return, after reading your letter, I discovered a letter from your sister Tempe awaiting my notice, and she may rest assured that it received my close attention. Then again, when yesterday's mail was distributed, I was greeted by another little white envelope of yours, mailed this time at Massillon. Haven't I been a lucky, happy fellow these last three days? And my health is so good now that that alone causes me to feel like a new man, although I wouldn't be very ornamental in a parlor, being sunburnt until I am about as red as three very red Indians; and now while I think of it let me set at rest your anxiety about my *caput*. My hair has grown out finely, blacker than it was before, and very much inclined to curl; that I can't account for; I have some whiskers too, which for a first crop are quite satisfactory, and a moustache too, of which I can't say much yet, but I am treating it very tenderly. Age may bring it beauty and an ebon hue. I only aspire to capillary respectability, not to hirsute perfection.

Now for some account of our late expedition.[2] You have probably seen the general results in the newspapers. As usual we had some fighting, and as usual it was just my luck to be in it. The first day we rode to Liberty, 30 miles northeast of Murfreesboro, surprising Wharton's brigade of rebel cavalry in camp at that place, capturing considerable of their camp equipage, pistols, a barrel of new horse shoes, half a dozen loads of corn, clothing, blankets, saddles &c. They were encamped on

2. Simply a scouting expedition, important to the troops engaged in it, but of no general consequence.

the bank of a stream, and when we drove in their pickets some
of their men were in the stream seining and had caught a fine
lot of fish; we pushed on at a spanking gait right into their
camp after their flying pickets; the main body had taken the
alarm and had just got out of sight, the fishermen leaving their
fish floundering on the bank, and many of the men left their
suppers, smoking hot and untasted, upon their temporary tables
around through their camp; our men were hungry, and the
broiled fish, fried eggs, broiled chickens, onions, warm biscuit
&c, that the marauding "greybacks" had stolen from Union
citizens, soon disappeared, and our men wandered through their
camp, like *real cavalry,* to muse upon the "skedadling" they had
wrought.

We fell back about a mile and went into camp. About dark a
brigade of cavalry, consisting of the 3rd, 4th and 10th Ohio
cavalry, from Murfreesboro, joined us and encamped with us.
Early next morning our brigade commander,[3] who commanded
the whole force, ordered the brigade of cavalry to push on in
pursuit of the enemy, and ordered our regiment, with two pieces
of artillery, to go with them, scattering the other regiments of
our brigade out in different directions after horses, mules, forage
and scattering parties of rebels. We followed the tracks of the
enemy in an easterly direction about 15 miles to Smithville, the
cavalry in advance and our regiment in the rear. All the way to
Smithville, the smoking picket fires by the roadside, and the
scattered blankets, overcoats, dead horses, saddles, broken stir-
rups, cartridge boxes &c gave evidence that there had been
hurrying rebels about there and that they were not very far off.

Our line of march lay through woods and a rugged, moun-
tainous country. On nearing Smithville the sharp crack of a
gun is heard in the extreme advance; we know what that means;
there is a halt, a moment of silence, guns are prepared for instant action; another gun startles the still woods and we breathe

3. Colonel John Thomas Wilder, 17th Indiana Infantry.

quicker; a half dozen reports in quick succession tell us they are making a stand in some force, we can't tell how much; they may outnumber us two to one but they are only cavalry, and this is no time for flinching; we are 15 miles from any support, in the midst of the enemy's country; we have driven them to the wall and now they turn to give us the fight we have been seeking. I wish they would change their minds and continue to run, but they don't, the firing increases, soon a man of the 3rd Ohio cavalry is borne back to the ambulance, shot through the lungs, the company of cavalry, in the advance as skirmishers, is being steadily borne back by the enemy, the whole of our cavalry begins to look shaky and act as though it preferred the rear; the [123rd] Illinois still in the rear awaiting orders, the men cool and looking with pride on their new pets, the Spencer rifles, with which we were lately armed, each with its 7 loads, and they long for an opportunity to try them.

Soon an aide comes dashing up with an order for our regiment to dismount and move to the front on the double quick; the men greet the order with a shout, and in a twinkling we are on foot, our shining bayonets fixed, "battalion right face," "forward, double quick, march"! and away we go, swinging by the cavalry, right on the jaws of death, perhaps, right on to take the place of the cavalry skirmishers who are falling back, right on to where the rebel bullets are singing the death song amid the dense foliage of the woods. Now the regiment becomes a machine, and now comes the hour of trial for its commander—he must ascertain where the enemy is the best way he can—he must see and think for that whole regiment, must direct every movement, and watch every movement of the enemy—he is responsible for the safety and honor of that regiment, and if he makes a mistake disgrace stares him in the face. He must be cool when all others are excited, must stand when all others are disposed to run.

Soon we have driven them through the town and our single

regiment occupies it; the continuous fire of our Spencers was too much for them, but delighted our men. "Major," says the Colonel, "take four companies, advance on this street and drive 'em if you can; be cautious though." At the head of my four companies I move up the street to the edge of the town, when, whiz comes a bullet from a Mississippi rifle right over my head and I dodge after the bullet has passed, of course, while the boys laugh; in a moment two of my companies are sent into the woods on the right and two on the left, while I move forward, concealed by the brush, just in the edge of the road, Soon a continuous fire opens out along the whole line, and the bullets have a merry dance among the bushes and trees around us. The undergrowth hides most of my line from my view, but I know by the sound of the firing that my boys are driving them; occasionally one comes back with a prisoner; I step out into the road and as I do so I see a rebel step out and draw up his gun on me; I step back, *of course,* and call to one of my men to pick him off; two or three respond to my call, but one moves out too far to get a better view and, just as he raises his gun, a rebel bullet goes through his hand, but two Spencers are aiming at the rebel who fired that shot, two reports are heard, and that "Johnnie" will shoot no more.

So we go for a mile, but the rebs are reinforced in my front and we can barely hold them for a little while but can't drive them, my flanks are in danger, we are entirely out of sight of all our brigade of cavalry and of the balance of our regiment; just as affairs are reaching a crisis one of the cavalry men appears in the rear, I call him up and send him back hastily for some artillery, and with a message that I can drive them no further. Soon the artillery comes dashing up, I point out the position of the rebels—the cannon are wheeled around and in an instant the roar of the guns and bursting of shells, with the rattle of musketry, swell out in a grand chorus of war. The shells are dropping into their ranks, scattering men and horses in every direction—a few moments and their bugle is heard sounding the "Assembly" and the "Retreat," and away they go, leaving the field to us—I advance my men until a long view to the front shows no enemy, then we return, pick up 20 of their guns, great numbers of spurs, blankets, hats, coats, &c, look at the dead horses, and 8 dead men, then move back through the long lines of cavalry that open to let us through, with our ten prisoners, most of my men carrying a rebel gun or some trophy of our little fight, and prouder than ever of their new "Spencers." We rejoin the regiment in the town, mount, and are all soon on our way back to Liberty, having advanced as far as we were ordered—reaching Liberty with our prisoners about dark, and going into camp. That same day another regiment of our brigade, that went out in another direction, captured a rebel wagon train loaded with eggs, butter, bacon, also 105 mules which the rebels had captured near Gallatin two days before, and took 20 prisoners.

The next day all the regiments of our brigade were sent out on scouts in different directions, and we were allowed to rest because of our hard work the day before. Along in the afternoon, while the Colonel and myself were lying down with our boots off and nearly asleep, 13 rebels rode up close to our camp, thinking we were gone, and captured one of our men within a few hundred yards of where the Col. and myself were lying. On discovering our camp they fired into it hurting no one, then turned and ran for dear life; soon we had a party of mounted men in pursuit who chased them 5 miles, captured 6 of them, and mortally wounded one. That was the only incident out of the ordinary that occurred with us that day, except the arrival of a courier from Murfreesboro, ordering us back post haste, as the enemy were supposed to be advancing on Rosecrans.

Next morning we started for here at 6 o'clock, the main body arriving here at 3 P. M., but I came ahead with our brigade commander and a small escort, and got here at noon to find your letter lying on my table. We brought in 69 prisoners, among them being one captain and four lieutenants, 200 mules, a wagon load of bacon, 6 wagons, 30 horses &c &c, and lost one man killed and one captured, our man who was shot through the hand being only slightly wounded. This afternoon I took the regiment out to witness the head shaving and "drumming out" of a deserter and two other malefactors. They were odd looking customers, with one half the head clean shaved, as they marched down the lines at the point of the bayonet.

We have been living some time in constant expectation of a general advance, but are getting out of that notion a little just now. When we started on our last expedition I took my valise along, fully expecting that we would not have any baggage or camp equipage until we reached Chattanooga. I can form no idea when the army will move now. I saw Asa Trimble, John Talmage and Sam Snider some days ago. Their regiment was ordered into the field yesterday. They have been at work on the fortifications here ever since the battle of Stone River. I am ordered to take 3 companies of my regiment and move to Liberty at 8 o'clock to-morrow morning, the balance of the regiment going to Lebanon, north of here, and about 30 miles northwest of Liberty, on a "horse stealing" expedition. I am ordered to take 5 days rations and suppose I shall be out 4 days. No fighting this trip, probably, and that suits me. I am sure I'll find a letter from you on my return. Yes, you'll see me some time between now and Christmas, but I can't give any idea when— next fall at farthest. Be particular about marking the number of my regiment plainly on your letters otherwise they may go astray and I don't want to miss any of them.

Your husband.

Murfreesboro, June 16, 1863.

Dear wife:

I wrote you just as we were going out on our last trip and I have become so accustomed to finding a letter from you on my table on my return, that I wrote you I should expect to find one on my return that time, and sure enough the expected letter was here awaiting me, and I believe it was the most welcome letter I ever received, for I had been out 4 days, with the enemy all around us, firing on our pickets all night, frightened citizens coming to us all day and telling us that Morgan was advancing on us with his whole force of 9 regiments while we had only parts of four regiments, and we finally moved into camp here one day sooner than we intended to because of the strong probability that Morgan was trying to get around us with his whole force, so you see I had very strong reasons for getting into camp safely, and was rejoiced at finding your letter after the 4 days of anxiety and watchfulness I had just passed. The principal object of the expedition was to give us an opportunity to capture enough horses to mount us well, and enable us to throw aside about 100 horses that were worn out, for horses like shoes soon wear out in the army.

In order to effect this, 300 men from each of the other regiments of the brigade, and 100 men of my regiment, under my command, the whole under command of our brigade commander, proceeded to Liberty, northeast of here, and the balance of our regiment, together with the rest of the brigade, under command of the Col. of my regiment, proceeded to Lebanon, in the vicinity of which place the "horse stealing" was to be done. Lebanon is north of here, and our force was to proceed to Liberty for the purpose of driving out any rebel force we might find there, and go into camp there so as to hold the place and prevent any rebel force from advancing through there on Lebanon to disturb the "horse stealing" portion of the brigade. On reaching Liberty we found a rebel regiment there, as usual, and drove them out, wounding and capturing one and killing three. It was dark before we halted in the chase. We then went into camp at Liberty, put out our pickets, and in a few moments I was regaling myself upon the rude supper hastily prepared by my servant, the pickets all the while stirring up the echoes of the night by the cracking of their "Spencers," but it gave us no more concern than to cause us to strengthen our picket guard in the direction of the enemy and then roll up in our blankets with clothes and side arms on and horses ready saddled, prepared for a night attack or a daybreak one next morning.

After I fell asleep it began raining and rained, with slight interruption, all night. I knew nothing of it until about two o'clock in the morning, when I was awakened by heavier picket firing and found my hair dripping wet, but I had a rubber blanket outside my other blankets and another rubber blanket on the ground under me, so that I slept just as dry, except my head, as if I had been at home in a feather bed. Long before daylight we were up, the men silently formed in line, under arms, and there we stood until broad daylight, every moment expecting an attack in force from the enemy, and quite ready for it, every man feeling confident that with his new "Spencer" he was good for at least any two rebs in Dixie. But they didn't come, so we stacked arms and ate breakfast. The day was spent lying in camp sleeping, reading, and buying butter, eggs and buttermilk from the country women who always flock to us to exchange such commodities for coffee and sugar.

At 2 P. M. our brigade commander concluded it would be safer to spend the next night a little nearer Lebanon, where the rest of the brigade was, so we started and marched to Alexandria, a distance of 6 miles north west from Liberty, and went into camp there.

These moves the rebels couldn't understand. It was only two days before that we had been fighting them at Smithville and now here we were again, part of us at Lebanon and part at Liberty. They couldn't divine our object in thus moving around, so they were cautious the second night and they didn't disturb our pickets. The next morning after breakfast an orderly summoned me to brigade commander's headquarters, where I was informed that the whole command would immediately move to Lebanon, by the pike, and that I should take my battalion and go ahead on the pike about 5 miles, then turn to the right through a gate, and go to the junction of the Cherry Valley and Middleton roads, a distance of about 5 miles through the woods, then turn left on the Middleton road and march to Lebanon, reaching there not earlier than one o'clock P. M., unless I met too large a force of the enemy, in which case I was to get to Lebanon any way I could. A negro who had lived in that country was sent with me as a guide, and I was to stop at his master's house and get the negro's wife and bring her along, and also take anything else from him I wanted, as he was a loud rebel.

I didn't much like the idea of going into an unknown section of the country, swarming with rebs, with no guide but a negro, who would probably run away at the first crack of a gun, leaving me to find the way as best I could, but I knew I could compel some citizen, on my route, male or female, I didn't care which, to pilot me through, so we started, reached the designated gate and turned off into the woods on a bridle path, which I soon learned was dignified with the title of "Cherry Valley Road." We followed the devious windings of the path mile after mile, keeping a good lookout, and passing an occasional cabin in the woods; finally on coming to a large farm under cultivation, with a comfortable looking house on it, I thought I saw a man, about half a mile distant, moving through the brush along a fence; using my field glass I saw it was a white man with two negroes following him, the three dodging through the brush to keep from being seen, and making for the wooded hills as fast as they could travel. Seeing a couple of negro women nearby engaged in washing, I rode up and inquired who those men were running off through the brush. The wenches didn't know, and it was only after threatening them severely, that I learned from them that it was their master who was going out to hide his two negroes for fear "you Yankees would get 'em." Having no use for the negroes we moved on and met with no further incident until reaching the house where our guide's wife was. This was a snug looking frame, painted white, with a nice dooryard and flower garden, and a handsome young lady standing on the porch at the front door. Halting and dismounting my men, I sent part of them to the barn close by to get corn to bait their horses, while I dismounted and went up on the porch, the handsome maiden retreating into the house at my approach. I took a chair without invitation and proceeded to make myself comfortable as any "Yankee vandal."

I ordered my men to search the premises and pick up any good horses they might find. By this time a little boy made his appearance on the porch, and I sent him into the house for a pitcher of butter-milk which soon appeared and as quickly disappeared; the black guide was in the "nigger quarters" and had found his wife, which the women of the house had discovered, and the hornet's nest was disturbed.

They had vanished from sight, and heroically abstained from murmuring while we took property of every other description, but when it came to touching their "nigger property" they could no longer endure it, but with streaming eyes and loud lamentations came out in search of the commander; I was pointed out as the person they sought, when the old lady besought me to spare her the only woman for housework she had —that herself and the negro woman had been born on that place, were raised together, were playmates in childhood, and that she loved her and had ever used her well; seeing that I paid no attention to this supplication, to which the negro woman seemed to give no attention, the young lady, having dried her tears and put on a pleasant countenance, came forward and in her blandest tones joined her mother's entreaty that I might leave them "Mollie," but "Mollie" said not a word.

I asked the young lady if she was a rebel, "yes sir I am," "then," said I, "you should have more spirit than to ask favors of a Yankee"; "That is true," she replied, "but I have known some Yankee officers that were gentlemen, and I am not ashamed to ask a favor of a gentleman." I admired the sharpness of her reply, but having no idea of complying with her request, and wishing to amuse myself, I changed the conversation by having recourse to flattery, which I soon discovered pleased her, and in a very much shorter time than it takes to tell it, we were pleasantly engaged in conversation, she admitting that she would just as soon marry a "Yankee" as a rebel, and that the "Yankees," generally, are rather a good looking gentlemanly set of fellows, and *not much more* addicted to stealing than the rebels themselves.

About the time I had progressed so far as to have the mother invite me in to eat some bread and milk, one of my men came up by the front door leading a handsome bay mare; the young lady opened her eyes wide with astonishment, and said she: "Major, they have got my saddle mare, you certainly won't take her?" I told her I thought I should; whereupon she remonstrated, but she found it was no use, so she told me I should let some one ride it who would take good care of it; this I agreed to, and told her that the best looking man I had should ride it, and that she might select him and deliver the mare to him herself. She agreed to this and went out with me amongst the men, looked through them, and amid the good natured laughter of the rest selected a fair haired, bashful little fellow about 17, and delivered the mare to him with an injunction that he should treat it kindly, which he laughingly promised to do—glad to get so fine an animal to ride.

Soon the black woman was ready, and mounting her on a horse, I started her and her husband in advance, he carrying her things on his shoulder, and after bidding adieu to my pretty little rebel and her mother (there were no men folks about) we started on the trail of our dusky guides without meeting or hearing of any rebels and reached Lebanon about 3 P. M. where I found all the rest of the brigade awaiting my coming. We rested there about an hour, during which I called upon a Mrs. Green, a sister of ex-Governor Campbell of Tennessee, who is an excellent Union woman, and ate some pie and drank sweet milk in her parlor, while her little daughter, about 12 or 13 years old, played upon the piano for me. The whole command moved out about 8 miles on the Murfreesboro pike that evening, and went into camp. Next morning we started for Murfreesboro, halting at Stone River long enough to let the men bathe, and reaching our camp here about 3 P. M.

We scout so much in the direction of Liberty, Lebanon, etc., and I mention them so frequently, that I will enclose a rough sketch showing the distances and relative positions of these places so that you may get a better idea of them. Alexandria is, even now, a very pretty little place, having many dwellings exhibiting wealth and refinement in the owners, and a very neat two story college building, now closed, of course. I could see the marks of that college all through that town, in the paved sidewalks, painted fences, neat dooryards, tasteful window curtains, neatly dressed, intelligent looking young ladies and clean faced, handsome children. The rebel, whom we wounded and captured a. Liberty, lived at Alexandria, and we brought him there with us in an ambulance and left him with his widowed mother and one sister; the poor fellow died that night, but how much more fortunate was he than many a poor fellow who has no mother or sister with him to soothe his last hours.

From Alexandria to Cherry Valley, which is a small post village, I think the country is the most beautiful I have ever seen. The road winds through a valley about 5 miles in width, skirted by very high hills. The valley is in a very excellent state of cultivation, and as we moved along, the song and laugh of many an ebony harvester saluted our ears. They were just cutting the golden grain, and the crops seemed to be as heavy as any I have ever seen in my favorite prairie state. The atmosphere was so pure and invigorating that I felt as if I could live a century in that peaceful looking valley. The farm dwellings are neat, built in modern style, and well painted, and as we passed house after house along the roadside I thought, what a pity it is that such a war as this should invade such peaceful scenes. So you have had a dream in which I appeared indifferent and careless about meeting you. An individual was once supposed to be, whose memory is now embalmed in "immortal verse," and whose patronymic was Rory O'More, who wisely said:

"Dreams always go by contraries, my dear."

I think if I should get home to meet you now I should appear rather *indifferently,* for I think it doubtful whether I should know how to act, or how to "behave myself before folks." I know Rory O'More's philosophy is right, for I dreamed, some time since, that the rebels had captured me, but I know the contrary is true, although I felt worried about it while dreaming. The papers we get today certainly contain startling news in relation to the invasion of Pennsylvania, and it makes me feel ashamed of my government, to see it exhibiting such weakness and imbecility where strength and vigor are needed. Pennsylvania invaded indeed! Instead of that Hooker ought to be invading Georgia in pursuit of Lee. If Lee does go into Pennsylvania with his army I hope he may never leave until he has ruined every secession tory north of Mason and Dixon's line. I am utterly sick of the stupendous failures of that petted Potomac army.[4]

Vallandingham nominated for Governor of Ohio! Shame! Shame! upon the professed Union men who permitted such a convention in their midst, desecrating by its unhallowed breath

4. Either the newspapers to which Connolly referred anticipated Lee's invasion of Pennsylvania, which would culminate in his defeat at Gettysburg, or Connolly devoted considerable time to writing this long letter. Lee did not cross the Potomac until June 24–25.

the fair escutcheon of a noble state, and at a time too when thousands of her sons are writing the story of her glory in their blood. I can only adequately express my feelings in big sounding "cuss" words, so I must quit.[5]

When you write me again I wish you would send me a lot of postage stamps for I am nearly out.

Your husband.

Wartrace, Tenn., July 5, 1863

Dear wife:

At length I have a little time to devote to you, but the mail leaves for Murfreesboro so soon that I will not have time to scarcely commence telling you all I want to, and this letter, be it ever so short, must get off in this mail, for you have been waiting and watching too long now. I feel good all over this morning, happy as a lark, and I can't tell why, unless it is because we have seen so much hard service, within the past 12 days, have worked so well and fought so well as to win the applause of our fellow soldiers, and that I am through it all safe. Our brigade has rendered notable service in this great army, so much so, that General Rosecrans, two days since, sent a letter of congratulation to our brigade commander saying that we would be mentioned in "orders" as soon as possible, and requesting that 300 men from the several regiments of the brigade, should be sent to his headquarters to serve as his "body guard." You may think this a trifle, but soldiers are in some respects like children, and are pleased with trifles.

On the morning of June 24th, at 3 o'clock, we left camp 5 miles north of Murfreesboro, and started to the "front," in ad-

5. Ohio Democrats, meeting in state convention at Columbus on June 11, nominated Vallandigham for governor by acclamation. The nominee, residing in Windsor, Ontario, carried on his campaign through friends and by correspondence, but was decisively defeated by John Brough, a War Democrat running on the Republican ticket.

vance of everything. As we passed through the camps in Murfreesboro, the rattle of drums, sounding of bugles, and clatter
of wagons, told us plainly that the whole army was to follow
in our wake, and we knew full well, from the direction we were
taking, that a few hours march would bring the brigade to some
of the strongholds of the enemy, so there was silence in the
column as we moved along through the mud, and every ear was
strained to catch the sound of the first gun of our advance guard
that would tell us of the presence of the enemy.

Soon after daylight a heavy rain commenced falling which
continued without interruption all day and night, and has continued ever since, with only a few hours cessation at a time.
About noon the first gun was fired, and then we pushed ahead
rapidly, for we were nearing the formidable "Hoover's Gap,"
which it was supposed would cost a great many lives to pass
through, and our brigade commander determined to surprise
the enemy if possible, by a rapid march, and make a bold dash
to pass through the "Gap" and hold it with our brigade alone
until the rest of the army could get up. We soon came into the
camp of a regiment of cavalry which was so much surprised by
our sudden appearance that they scattered through the woods
and over the hills in every direction, every fellow for himself,
and all making the best time they could bareback, on foot and
every other way, leaving all their tents, wagons, baggage, commissary stores and indeed everything in our hands, but we didn't
stop for anything, on we pushed, our boys, with their Spencer
rifles, keeping up a continual popping in front. Soon we reached
the celebrated "Gap" on the run.

This "Gap" is formed by a range of hills that run westwardly
from the Cumberland mountains, and the pike runs for about
two miles through between these hills; the valley is barely wide
enough to admit the passage of two wagons side by side, and
the hills upon either side command the valley completely; as we
swept through the valley with our 1,500 horsemen on a gallop

we noticed the lines of entrenchments crowning the hills, but
they were deserted; the enemy was surprised and flying before
us, so we pushed onward until we passed entirely through the
"Gap," when a puff of white smoke from a hill about half a mile
in front of us, then a dull heavy roar, then the shrieking of a
shell told us we could advance no further as we had reached
their infantry and artillery force. But we had done enough, had
advanced 6 miles further than ordered or expected possible, and
had taken a point which it was expected would require a large
part of the army to take; but the serious question with us now
was: "Could we alone hold it in the presence of superior force?"
We were at least 12 miles in advance of our army, and from
prisoners we learned that we were confronted with 4 brigades
of infantry and 4 batteries. The mail is ready. Will continue
story in another letter.

Your husband.

Wartrace, Tenn., July 5, 1863.

Dear wife:

Having hurried off the piece of a letter which I so abruptly
closed a few moments ago, so as to get into the mail, I now
resume my talk with you. As soon as the enemy opened on us
with their artillery we dismounted and formed line of battle on
a hill just at the south entrance to the "Gap," and our battery
of light artillery was opened on them, a courier was dispatched
to the rear to hurry up reinforcements, our horses were sent
back some distance out of the way of bursting shells, our regiment was assigned to support the battery, the other three regiments were properly disposed, and not a moment too soon, for
these preparations were scarcely completed when the enemy
opened on us a terrific fire of shot and shell from five different
points, and their masses of infantry, with flags flying, moved
out of the woods on our right in splendid style; there were three
or four times our number already in sight and still others came

pouring out of the woods beyond. Our regiment lay on the hill side in mud and water, the rain pouring down in torrents, while each shell screamed so close to us as to make it seem that the next would tear us to pieces.

Presently the enemy got near enough to us to make a charge on our battery, and on they came; our men are on their feet in an instant and a terrible fire from the "Spencers" causes the advancing regiment to reel and its colors fall to the ground, but in an instant their colors are up again and on they come, thinking to reach the battery before our guns can be reloaded, but they "reckoned without their host," they didn't know we had the "Spencers," and their charging yell was answered by another terrible volley, and another and another without cessation, until the poor regiment was literally cut to pieces, and but few men of that 20th Tennessee that attempted the charge will ever charge again. During all the rest of the fight at "Hoover's Gap" they never again attempted to take that battery. After the charge they moved four regiments around to our right and attempted to get in our rear, but they were met by two of our regiments posted in the woods, and in five minutes were driven back in the greatest disorder, with a loss of 250 killed and wounded.[6]

6. The official history of the 123rd Illinois offers a spirited account of the Hoover's Gap fight: "These two Regiments [17th Indiana and 123rd Illinois] moved out from Murfreesboro long before daylight on the morning of the 24th, in a drenching rain, and by daylight encountered the rebel videttes. From that moment the two Regiments broke into a gallop and kept up the run. The farther they went the larger the rebel force of cavalry kept growing before them, but the rapid pace gave the enemy no time to form, until about 9 o'clock in the morning, by which time these two Regiments had advanced to and seized Hoover's Gap, a place of great natural strength, but they were confronted here with twenty times their own number of infantry, well supplied with artillery to occupy this Gap, and their own supporting forces were at least ten miles in the rear, floundering along through the mud and rain. But the rapidity and audacity of the movement saved them, for the enemy, supposing the force was a large one, checked their advance in column, deployed their force in two lines, brought up their artillery and opened a terrific artillery fire, at the same time sending out reconnoitering parties on the Federal flanks, but as soon as the Gap

On that part of the field an incident occurred worthy of mention, for it shows the spirit of the men of this brigade. A corporal of the [17th] Ind. was shot through the breast at the first fire; he had always said, as indeed all our men do, that the enemy should never get hold of his "Spencer" to use it; he hadn't strength to break it so he took out his knife, unscrewed a part of the lock plate and threw it away, rendering the gun entirely useless, he then fell back amid the storm of bullets, lay down and died.

We held our ground with continual fighting until 7 o'clock in the evening, when we discovered a battery coming up to our support as fast as the horses could run, and such a cheer as was sent up does one good to hear. In a few minutes our new battery was opened and we all felt better. We were nearly exhausted with the rapid march since before daylight in the morning, the continual rain, the half day's fighting, and nothing to eat since about two o'clock in the morning, yet the prospect of assistance nerved the men to maintain the unequal conflict a little longer. About half past seven in the evening along came a weary, jaded regiment of infantry, trying to double quick, but it was all they could do to march at all; we greeted them with such lusty cheers as seemed to inspire them with new vigor, and they were soon in position; then came two more regiments of infantry, weary and

---

was seized, couriers had been despatched back to Wilder, informing him of the situation, and before the enemy had satisfied himself of the force in his front, the other Regiments of the Brigade arrived, and with it the battery of Captain Lilly (Indiana), his guns having been hauled the last mile by men of the Brigade, Lilly's horses having given out with their long run through the muddy roads.

"These reinforcements checked the enemy still more, but by 2 P. M. they made a determined attack along the whole line and on both flanks, but the seven-shooting Spencer rifles proved effective in repelling it, and before another could be made, the head of the infantry of Rosecrans' army began to arrive, and Hoover's Gap was held without further contest, the enemy withdrawing in the night." *Report of the Adjutant General of Illinois (Revised)*, VI, 417.

footsore, but hurrying the best they could to the dance of death; then just at dark came our Division Commander, with his staff, and riding along our lines gave words of cheer to his brigade that had fought so long and well. In a few minutes up came General Thomas, our corps commander, his grave face beaming with delight as he grasped our brigade commander by the hand and said: "You have saved the lives of a thousand men by your gallant conduct today. I didn't expect to get this Gap for three days."

By this time darkness had put an end to the fighting, but there we lay on that hill side in line of battle all night, and I think I slept as well there, without blankets and soaking wet, as I ever did at home. At 3 o'clock in the morning two other brigades came up and took our places in line, so as to be in readiness to renew the fight in the morning, and we fell back to eat and rest. On the morning of the 25th, at daylight, the fight was renewed by the enemy; a heavy skirmish fire was kept up all day, and heavy cannonading, we having 6 batteries in play at once and the enemy an equal number. On the morning of the 25th, too, the sound of McCook's fighting on the Shelbyville road, some 9 miles to our right, reached us, and it was kept up steadily all day.

On the morning of the 26th, Gen. Rosecrans, who had come out to the "Gap," ordered Thomas' corps to advance and our Division was placed in the advance of the corps, our brigade in the advance of the Division and our regiment in the advance of the brigade. We started about ten o'clock.

The enemy fell back before us without firing a shot and beat a rapid retreat for Tullahoma. We moved on all day and encamped within 4 miles of Manchester on the night of the 26th; on the morning of the 27th our regiment started in the advance and went to Manchester on a gallop, we swept by the deserted fortifications of the town on a full run, and while the citizens were at their breakfast tables we dashed into the public square,

scattered out in small parties, and in five minutes every street
and alley was occupied by Yankees, the town was surrounded,
and a rebel major and about 50 soldiers, left as a rear guard,
were captured and marched to the court house. I was immediately ordered to take 100 men and pursue some rebels who were
said to be escaping by the McMinnville road; in a few minutes
I was off without a guide and pursued the rebels about 4 miles
but my horses were worn out and theirs fresh, so I had to give
up the chase and return.

We went into camp at Manchester in the afternoon, and during the whole day Thomas' corps and most of Crittenden's came
up and went into camp. We were now within 11 miles of Tullahoma, that has so long been the boasted stronghold and hope of
the rebs. On the night of the 27th an order came to march at 6
o'clock on the morning of the 28th, with none but serviceable
horses, capable of enduring a very long and fatiguing march, and
the men to take along nothing to eat but five days' rations of *salt*.
As soon as that order came we knew it meant hard work for our
brigade, so the Col. and myself sat down under a tree and wrote
very brief letters to our respective wives, not knowing when they
would ever hear from us again, and I guess it is doubtful
whether those letters got through.

At five o'clock on the morning of the 28th I was in the saddle
and wasn't out of it again until one o'clock on the morning of
the 29th. The brigades left Manchester at 6 o'clock in the morning, and soon leaving the road, we struck off into the woods
until we struck an unfrequented road winding around the base
of the Cumberland mountains. Here our regiment was detached
from the brigade, and the object of the expedition made known,
for the first time, to the field officers, viz: to cut the railroad between Tullahoma and Chattanooga at as many points as possible.
Our regiment was to strike the railroad at Allisonia, the first
station south of Tullahoma, destroy a bridge there, then follow
the railroad and meet the rest of the brigade at Cowan, just in

the corner of Alabama, where we were all to engage in filling up a tunnel so as to prevent reinforcements coming from Chattanooga to Tullahoma. This we were to do provided we could without being captured.

Our regiment branched off from the brigade, following bridle paths through the woods, and swimming the swollen streams that came tumbling in angry torrents from their mountain sources near by. After traveling about 30 miles we suddenly came in sight of the road leading south from Tullahoma, and to our surprise the road was filled with rebel wagon trains, infantry and batteries of artillery moving southward rapidly. Bragg's army was slipping away and we didn't have the strength to stop it. How little did they think, as they were moving along, 12 miles in the rear of Tullahoma, that a regiment of Illinois Yankees was in the woods, within easy musket range of them, quietly watching their movements and noting their numbers. But oh! how the men chafed, as they saw flag after flag pass us and we did not dare attack them. To attack would have been madness, for there was a whole Division (Withers) with infantry, artillery and cavalry, so we lay quiet for more than an hour while they were passing, then noiselessly countermarched, intending to return to where we left the brigade and follow its trail until we overtook it, but when we reached the point at which we left it it was one o'clock in the morning, and we found that Gen. John Beatty's brigade had come there during the day and was encamped.

We concluded to halt there until four o'clock in the morning, so as to rest our horses a little, and send a despatch to Rosecrans informing him how the enemy were evacuating Tullahoma. Col. [Monroe], of my regiment, wrote out the despatch, and I, being acquainted with Gen. Beatty, sent it to him together with a note requesting him to send a courier from his command with it to Gen. Rosecrans. Beatty did so, and after our three hours' rest, we started on the trail of the brigade, at 4 A. M. on the morning of the 29th, and soon started up the Cumberland mountains in a terrible thunder storm. When we reached the summit of the mountains the elemental war was raging in its greatest fury; the reverberations of the thunder rolled through the valleys below us, and the lightning appeared to be flashing below our feet, all this, combined with the dangerous character of our expedition, was enough to try the nerves, but no one dared to fall out, for that would be certain capture at least. About noon of the 29th we struck the railroad again, after descending the mountain side, and found the track torn up, rails bent and scattered all around; we knew this meant that the rest of the brigade had been more fortunate than we and had accomplished their task before the enemy's column reached there, so we pushed on hopefully, and about 2 P. M. when within about five miles of the Alabama line, we overtook the brigade resting in a deep wooded valley.

There was a river in front, so swollen by the continuous rain as to be impassable, and we were compelled to give up the design of destroying the tunnel, and just as an order was issued for us to prepare to bivouac for the night without fires, our pickets on our south front came rushing in saying that the enemy was advancing on us in force.

A rapid retreat was immediately ordered, and back we all started, striking directly into the mountains, without looking for roads. We traveled in the mountains until midnight, then descended from the mountains, single file, by a narrow bridle path, and bivouacked in the valley until morning, without having any very clear idea of where we were. At daylight on the morning of the 30th we started again on our backward march, reaching Manchester again on the evening of the 30th, but when we reached there most of the army had gone forward to Tullahoma.[7] Rosecrans, immediately on receiving our despatch,

7. "While the corps of Generals McCook and Crittenden were concentrating at Manchester, slowly in fact, but as rapidly as the rain and bad roads

ordered the army forward and the next night it occupied Tullahoma. Not more than two hours before our advance reached
Manchester on our return there, General Stanley,[8] who commands all the *cavalry* of this army, in an interview with Rosecrans, said that our brigade would never get back, that it would
certainly be surrounded and captured, and indeed they were still
discussing the probability of our capture when our brigade commander, covered with mud and soaked with the steady rain of
7 days, dismounted from his jaded horse before the door of
Rosecrans tent and walked in upon the astonished Generals to
make report. Rosecrans reply was: "All right [Wilder], I know
you now. Take your brigade any place you can find forage and
rest yourselves until you are again needed. I want you to furnish
me a body guard of 300 of your men."

We bivouacked the night of the 30th at Manchester and on
the morning of July 1st moved out into a beautiful valley where
food and water were abundant, and turning our horses loose
let them eat all day while we slept. July 1st we had no rain, but

---

would permit, General Thomas, in compliance with instruction from General
Rosecrans, commenced the movements which were designed to bring the
campaign to a decisive issue. Early on the morning of the 28th, he sent
Colonel Wilder with his brigade to break the railroad at some point south
of Decherd, and Colonel John Beatty's brigade to Hillsboro, in support of
the movement. He also threw forward toward Tullahoma, Rousseau's and
Brannan's divisions, with some regiments from Reynolds' and Sheridan's,
on their right and left flanks.

"Colonel Wilder reached Decherd at 8 P. M., burned the depot and water-
tank, and destroyed about three hundred yards of railroad, but retired upon
the approach of the enemy's infantry. The next day he moved to the University, broke up the Tracy City railroad, and then dividing his force advanced toward Anderson and Tantallon. The enemy was found at these places
in such force as to forbid attack, and the brigade was soon after united at
University. On his return, he avoided Forrest at Pelham, and reached Manchester in safety about noon on the 30th." Thomas B. Van Horne, *History of
the Army of the Cumberland* (Cincinnati, 1875), I, 306–07.

8. Major General David Sloane Stanley, West Point, class of 1852.

with the exception of that day, it has rained every day since we
left Murfreesboro, and from the morning of June 24th to the
morning of July 1st we lived in the rain, slept in the mud and
rain and were as wet as fish in the river all that time, but it has
not caused me a moment's sickness, and I feel first rate after it
all. Some officers of the brigade have gone to the hospital, some
have tendered their resignations and we used up 500 horses.
From the time we left Manchester until our return there our
horses had nothing to eat except what leaves and grass they
could nip as we went along, and they got so that they would
eat blankets, saddle skirts and anything else they could get into
their mouths. I have frequently read of such privations but never
believed it to be true, but I know such things to be true now;
yet with all its risk and privations I love this kind of service
and would like to be engaged in it all the time. That trip will
never be fully reported, there was too much rough work in it,
consequently we had no reporters with us, but we are satisfied;
every soldier in this army knows our brigade now, and that is a
distinction more highly prized than a dozen newspaper puffs.

On the 3rd of July we came to this place for rest, and spent
the 4th, yesterday, in sleeping and trying to clean up a little.

If it had not rained yesterday I should have gone over to
Shelbyville, 8 miles from here, to see Colonel Reid of the 121st
Ohio, who, I understand is in command of that place. Shelbyville is a Union place, and the loyal citizens there had an old
fashioned 4th of July celebration yesterday. The Tennessee
troops are deserting Bragg in numbers and coming into our
lines, and unless Bragg is reinforced greatly within the next
four weeks Rosecrans will destroy him, as it looks to us here
now. Everything looks favorable now; all our armies are moving at the same time for the first time since the war began, and
if Dix and Meade will do anything in the east the rebellion will
fade with the autumn leaves. We may, however, be too sanguine

in this army; we don't look for a defeat, we don't count on a retreat; with Rosecrans to lead we think we can go anywhere in
the confederacy.

Many wealthy, influential people in this section of Tennessee
are intensely loyal, and I expect Shelby county, Tennessee, is as
loyal today as many a county in Ohio. I do wonder if men will
be permitted to openly advocate the election of Vallandingham
as Governor, in Ohio?

We shoot such men on sight down here and it would be quite
as just to deal with them the same way up there. Never mind,
many of us will live to get home again, and a day of retribution
will come upon those cowards who have been operating with
our enemies. Please let father and mother know I am well and
all in one piece yet.

Your husband.

Chickamauga—and Stalemate

BRAGG'S withdrawal to Chattanooga made that point the objective of the Army of the Cumberland. Rosecrans prepared carefully. His plans called for a feint against Chattanooga from the west by way of the Sequatchie Valley while he put the main body of his army across the Tennessee River southwest of the town. If successful, this movement would force Bragg to give up Chattanooga and retreat southward, where Rosecrans hoped to fall on his adversary's flank and fight a battle on advantageous terms.

The advance began on August 16, with the 123rd Illinois a part of Wilder's brigade in Crittenden's corps, which made the feint. In its initial stages the campaign was a brilliant success. Crittenden's advance led Bragg to concentrate at Chattanooga, and the main portion of the Army of the Cumberland crossed the Tennessee River with little opposition. But Bragg discovered what Rosecrans was up to soon enough to evacuate his base and move a few miles to the south, where he planned to fall upon the scattered Union corps and defeat them piecemeal. Fighting began on September 18, but did not take on the proportions of

a full-fledged battle—Chickamauga—until the 19th and 20th.
In the engagement neither commander displayed even reason-
able competence. Bragg's attacks were poorly coordinated, and
he failed to follow up the successes of his subordinates; while
Rosecrans never succeeded in concentrating his forces and barely
escaped a disastrous rout.

As it was, Rosecrans managed to draw off his army to
Chattanooga, where it was immediately penned in by the Confederates and threatened with ultimate starvation. On October
19 he was relieved—to Connolly's great disgust—and replaced
by Thomas, with Grant in general command of the Military
Department of the Mississippi. Meanwhile—on September 24—
Connolly had been appointed Inspector of the Third Division
(General Joseph J. Reynolds). For the remainder of the war
he would serve as a staff officer.

Camp on Duck River, Tenn., July 11, 1863.
Dear wife:

Yesterday evening I received your letter written the morning
you left Massillon. I hope my letters find you as certainly as
yours find me in all my wanderings. I prized your letters highly
when I received them in our comfortable camp at Murfreesboro,
but how much more valuable are they now, when they reach me
after their long chase among the hills and valleys, the mud and
rebels of Tennessee. I have just finished a letter to ——— and
was congratulating myself over the prospect of a good long rest
in this camp to which we moved day before yesterday, when lo!
I hadn't quite finished the letter when up came an orderly with
an order for us to march at 7 o'clock tomorrow (Sunday)
morning with 7 days rations. That is the way with us, and I am
becoming a perfect Arab with this nomadic life we are leading.
My next letter may be written from Indiana, Georgia, Alabama

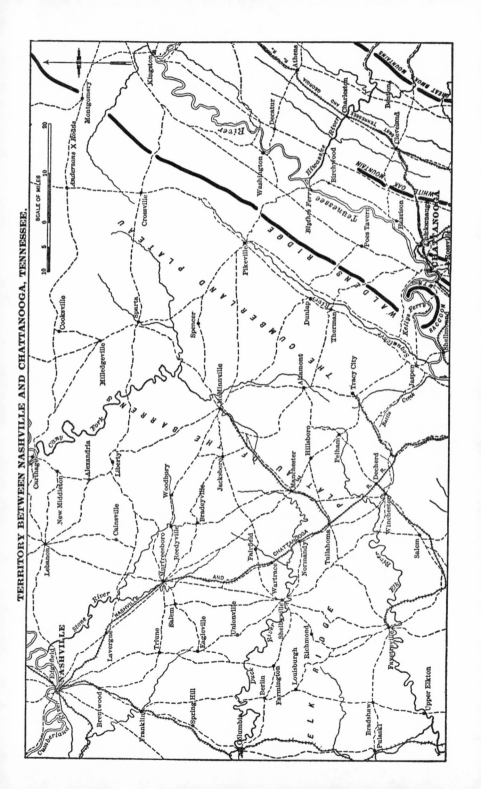

TERRITORY BETWEEN NASHVILLE AND CHATTANOOGA, TENNESSEE.

or possibly from Libby, who knows? I think likely, however, we shall return to this camp. Our headquarters are in the nicest, shady nook you ever saw. There are more blackberries and finer ones here than I ever saw, and I have eaten so many of them that I don't think I shall ever want any more. . . .

I was domestic enough to think how nice it would be to have a good lot of such berries put up for our use, about next winter.

. . . It may be I can get a leave about September, if Rosecrans gets over his fighting humor, but I don't want to be at home when there is a fight on hand, for I should feel ashamed of myself, although I don't really want to fight. I must give you the closing paragraph of Colonel [Monroe's] official report on the battle of "Hoover's Gap." "It would seem invidious to mention individuals, where all did their duty, but I cannot close this report without calling special attention to the conduct of Lieut. Col. [Biggs] and Major [Connolly] who managed their men skillfully and by their coolness under the heaviest fire, imparted steadiness to the whole line." Whew! He didn't know how badly I was scared or he wouldn't have said all that sure.

Buncombe is a great thing in war as well as in politics. The news from Vicksburg, the Potomac and Tennessee is glorious. The rebellion is on the wane and the time is rapidly drawing nearer when we'll "go soldiering" together. . . . I'll stop now for I have much to do before we march, so good bye until after the march, when I'll write you a long letter.

Your husband.

Camp near Rowesville, Tenn., July 21, 1863.

Dear wife:

We returned from our expedition Saturday evening, July 18th and as usual, I was greeted by a letter from you. I shall not tell you how much I wanted to see yourself, if for no other reason than to tell you how much I appreciate your promptness in writing.

The same evening I received a letter from brother Charlie, who had just been released on parole after his capture in that raid around Richmond, also one from sister Maggie, containing mother's photograph, so you see I met with a very gratifying reception on my return to camp. But that is not all that conspires to make me feel happy—it is pleasant to have a good wife at home whose heart and hope is with me and my cause through all these long months of rain, heat, mud and battle; it is pleasant to know that my brother has borne himself manfully in the sternest conflicts of these turbulent times, and is still living unscathed; it is pleasant to know that the stain of treason rests not upon the garments of any with whom I am connected, and it is glorious to know that the old flag of my country floats in triumph, once more, over the Father of Waters, from source to mouth; to know that the bats and owls of treason have been driven from their dens by the gallant boys who fight under that flag; to know that the power of the rebellion is broken and that Providence rifted that dark cloud and let the sunshine through upon the anniversary of our Nation's natal day.

Hail! glorious fourth! at once a Nation's sabbath, the birthday of freedom and the dying day of treason. You at home cannot feel the glow of triumph as we do in the field; those of us who looked to the future with high hopes, staked life, reputation, honor, everything in this contest—taking our lives in our hands we went out for what? for money? no; for power? no; for fame? no; only for an idea, for the idea of Union, Freedom, an intangible something always sought for by mankind, often fought for and never appreciated when possessed; we knew that defeat involved ourselves and all we love in ruin; for months, yes years, we have seen our hopes fading one by one; we have seen our comrades falling one by one; we have listened to their wails coming up from southern prisons and been powerless to aid; we have seen strange flags floating where our own should wave; we have turned our eyes homeward and there, with heavy hearts, seen those who should bind up our wounds and cheer our drooping spirits, turn their hands against us, and shout with fiendish joy as our comrades fell by our sides in the storm of battle—foes in front of us, foes to the right of us, foes to the left of us, foes behind us, true friends only in our own ranks and in the great heavens above us, still we struggled on—one anniversary of our Nation's birth came and with it came sore disaster and disgrace upon our flag; another came and with it disgrace and disaster again; another approached, the loyal heart was sad, the loyal soldier despondent, treason with brazen front encompassed him, his very home was a shelter for treason, his hope was fast settling into despair, when lo! a gleam of sunshine, as bright to him as the beams that first sprang from the omnipotent fiat! another anniversary came, and with it light and hope and joy; he saw his flag now proudly flying over the vaunted stronghold of treason; from camp to camp flew the joyful news upon the wings of lightning; from Mississippi's banks went the freeman's shout, it was echoed by their comrades in Tennessee's valleys and mountains, re-echoed again on Potomac's shores, and was sent on its joyful course to be re-echoed wherever a freeman's heart beats or a blue coated sentinel paces his solitary round.

Our soldiers are happy, their wives are happy, their children are happy, their friends are happy. God speeds the right. When I think of the developments of the last few days it seems to me like a dream, and I almost fear to scan them too closely lest they may disappear and leave me in the old gloom. We of the Cumberland Army have great cause for feeling happy, for we now occupy the strongholds that have caused most of us very serious thoughts for the past 6 months. We really looked forward to the time when we should receive the order to advance on Shelbyville, Hoover's Gap and Tullahoma with a shudder, expecting it would be a field of terrible carnage, but so well did the "wily Rosecrans" (as the "Chattanooga Rebel" newspaper called him) manage his advance that Bragg was whipped almost before he knew we were near him, and the pursuit was so close and rapid that he dared not stop to think of fighting until he had put the Tennessee River between himself and the Yankees.

The excellent news from every point almost makes me think that our respected "Uncle" won't need much of an army by next winter, and the most of us can be honorably relieved from further service. I hope so at least, and shall certainly think so if gold falls to ten or fifteen per cent within a few weeks, for the money market is the best barometer to indicate the condition of public affairs. I wrote you the evening before we started on our last expedition.

We were out just seven days and returned without losing but one man, had considerable skirmishing, captured and paroled 60 rebel soldiers, brought into camp two rebel captains and three lieutenants, and wounded and paroled the rebel Lieut. Col. Gantt of the 9th Battalion of Tennessee cavalry. One of the Lieutenants was A. O. P. Nicholson, Jr., son of the celebrated A. O. P. Nicholson of "Cass-Nicholson" letter notoriety, and former U. S. Senator from Tennessee. Young Nicholson is about my own age and I took quite a fancy to him and we became good friends before we parted. At his earnest request I accompanied him, alone, to his father's house, about two miles in the country from Columbia, to enable him to get some clothing to take with him. I there saw his father and sat talking to him on the veranda for half an hour while the son was in the house getting his clothing. The women never showed themselves. He slept under my blankets with me through the whole expedition until we got back to camp and when he was leaving with the other prisoners I filled a haversack at the sutler's tent with good eatables for him and handed him a little money, for I really felt sorry for him. We also brought in over 800 horses

and mules and nearly 300 negroes; we sent the latter to Tullahoma.

The first day out we arrived at Shelbyville at noon, where I
found Col. W. P. Reid, of Ohio, in command of the Post, and
Col. [Monroe] and myself took dinner with him; toward evening of that day we passed through a village named Farmington,
and on inquiry I found that our village of Farmington, [Coles]
County, Illinois, was named after this one by a man who emi-
grated from here many years ago. At Farmington we found the
Federal flag waving from many houses, children clapping their
hands in greeting and women waving Federal flags and laughing
through their tears of joy. On reaching the square with the head
of our column, about ten well dressed, intelligent looking young
ladies, each with a flag of their own manufacture, met us and
invited us to stay there that night, saying we were the first
federal soldiers they had seen for a year, and we must encamp
there for the night, and they would furnish the officers supper,
lodging and breakfast, and would have a "Union Dance" once
more for our benefit as well as their own, but we couldn't stay.

The next day, on getting within three miles of Lewisburg,
the county seat of Marshall county, I took 50 men and started
ahead on a gallop, with orders to dash in suddenly and surprise
the place. The Spencers were unslung and ready for action,
pistols were drawn and forward we dashed at breakneck speed,
right into the public square before the astonished citizens knew
there was a Yankee within 40 miles of them. When they realized
the astounding fact that we were real live Yankees the women
began to scream, and the merchants shut their doors, but I
ordered the stores opened. We then went to the jail which they
have used during the past two years as a prison for Union
citizens, and in a few minutes the flames were bursting out of
the roof and the jail was in ruins before we left the town. Union
men had no rights which this town respected, and we handled
them accordingly.

The next day, on reaching within five miles of Columbia, the county seat of Maury county, one of the finest counties of the state, I was ordered to take 75 men and go forward rapidly, to surprise that place also; on getting within 3 miles of the town we discovered two rebel officers eating dinner at a farm house, they started to run, and one of them, a lieutenant, got away, but the other, a captain, we captured. I sent him back to the main column, and dashed on to Columbia. On getting in sight of the place I was surprised to find it was evidently a town of about the size of Mount Vernon, Ohio. I knew there were rebel soldiers there and that there were fortifications, but I hoped to surprise them and give them no time to assemble, so with a good pike ahead of us we put spurs and after a run of less than a mile we dashed into the public square by different streets, and the startled soldiers who were sauntering about, and in saloons, stores &c raised the cry—"Yankees!" "Yankees!" and started to run in all directions, some firing as they ran, but my boys, with their Spencers, fired too fast for them and they soon dropped their guns and surrendered. We captured 3 lieutenants and 30 privates here.

While riding along one of the streets a woman called me and told me that Captain Bullock and Lieut. Col. Gantt had left town at the opposite side from which we entered, just as we entered, so taking half a dozen men I started in pursuit of them and ran them 3 miles, getting within half of mile of them, but their horses were fresh and I had run mine 6 miles, so I had to give up the chase for fear of killing my horses, but the second day after this, as I dashed into Centerville, the county seat of Hickman county, with the advance guard, a little after daylight, I had the pleasure of capturing the same two gentlemen who were not expecting us there at all, but Gantt was not secured until one of my men shot him through the arm and leg, as he was running away through a field of standing grain, wounding him so badly that we couldn't take him with us, so I paroled him to report to our military authorities at Nashville as soon as his wounds would permit.

I was then 8 miles from our main body, so I returned to it. We were then 80 miles in a straight line from our camp, and learning that Col. Biffles, with a superior rebel force, had crossed the Tennessee River and was moving toward us, we turned southward, went within about 30 miles of the Alabama line, collecting negroes, prisoners and horses all the time, then turned northeast and moved back to camp. After leaving Columbia and going toward Centerville we passed right by the home of ex-President James K. Polk. It is a large comfortable looking house on a large lawn with buckeye trees all around the front fences. We had a hard trip, but I enjoyed it very much.

I slept in a house every night and took my meals at a regular table. Strange to say, all through the country we traveled they had not heard of the fall of Vicksburg, and even the Lieut. Col. whom I paroled, who was a prominent Tennessee lawyer and educated gentleman, had not heard of it, and could not believe it, when I told him. The officers we brought in with us as prisoners became very much attached to our command, and seemed to be sorry to leave us. They were extremely depressed when they saw the late papers and one of the Captains, after reading the news, said to me: "Major the confederacy is played out, it's humbug, and my fighting is done. Come what may I'll fight no more."

This captain was a rising young lawyer at Columbia when the war broke out but as he said: "It's all gone now." I sympathized with him, for he was not much older than I, and I thought what has become of my start as a lawyer? I can't say what I saw of the people I saw, their feelings, sentiments, farms and homes; I must put that off to another time. . . .

Your husband.

Camp near Decherd, Tenn., August 3, 1863.

Dear wife:

I received your letter of the 15th ult this morning, and while it delighted me to receive it it pained me to read it, for I saw you were disappointed and sad when you wrote it. I have not written you for two weeks I believe. A few days after returning from our last expedition General Reynolds ordered a general Court Martial and appointed me Judge Advocate of the Court; since that time I have been very busy day and night in the preparation and trial of cases, and shall be, I expect, for two weeks more. It leaves not a moment of leisure time, and the time I occupy in penning this hasty letter is just so much time stolen from duties that are pressing me. The weather is getting very hot too, and I assure you it is not pleasant to conduct the proceedings of a court martial with the mercury at ninety in the shade, and be compelled to work incessantly 15 hours out of every 24. The worry is quite as bad as the work, for it is so new to me that I am constantly afraid of blundering, and I want to send up a good record if I have to work every hour. Notwithstanding the hot weather and hard service we have seen lately, my health is excellent—never was better. Our Colonel is home now, very sick, and I expect will not be back for some time. I shall not ask for a leave before he returns. On coming to my quarters yesterday evening I was informed that an officer named Dunn called to see me during the day, that he was light complexioned and wore spectacles.

He left his address but it was mislaid, by the carelessness of some one and I have not been able to find it. I wonder if it can be your brother Henry. He is on duty somewhere in this army, as Topographical Engineer. I know it is unmanly to be repining at one's lot, but I can't help thinking, sometimes, that mine is pretty hard in this war, but then there are thousands whose lot is harder, but I feel that duty demands of me all the sacrifice I am making and I look hopefully to the future to repay me. I wish I could sit down with you tonight and tell you all my hopes and show you the bright future for you and me with which I regale myself occasionally; I know it would inspire you with courage to bear the trials of today. Never give up!

"It is wiser and better,
Always to hope then once to despair."

I know that you are lonely, I know that feelings of gloom and sadness will steal over you, but think, at such times, that I am with you in spirit, that scarcely a waking hour passes over me that I do not send you a tender thought to steal its viewless way through scenes of war and seek admission to the chambers of your heart, to remind you that your husband has not forgotten you. I can begin to see the end of this war, I think, and oh! when "this cruel war is over" how proudly I can go home to my brave wife and feel that our whole duty was done, by me and mine, when our country was in danger.

When I left you at Louisville I expected to see you again in May, for I really believed ill health would compel me to resign, but my health improved, it is now excellent, and it is difficult for me to frame a well grounded application for leave of absence, but as soon as I think the prospect fair I shall apply for one. Six days more and I shall have completed a year of service. Quite a "veteran" am I not? I hardly think another year will be required of me. I've got me a new horse, a magnificent one; we captured him in Hickman county, Tennessee. He is said to be a favorite horse of the rebel General Forrest, that went lame on him out there and was left behind.

He is hard mouthed and stiff necked as any rebel, the scamp ran away with me yesterday and took me clear to the picket line before I could stop him. I bought him of the government and paid $100 for him.

You need never be afraid of me being captured while I ride him, for he is fleet as a deer, and having been trained in the rebel service, he knows how to *retreat.* I'll write as often as I can, but our life is such a nomadic one that our mail comes and goes very irregularly.

Your husband.

Tracy City, on Cumberland mountains, Aug. 18, 1863.

Dear wife:

I have an opportunity of sending you a line by a courier who is going back to army headquarters in the "settlements." We are here in the mountains, shut off from everybody. Just got here, and will bivouac here tonight. Have to write with pencil and use my saddle for writing desk. No wagons or baggage with us. We travel by mountain trails. Our brigade is alone. We are bound for Chattanooga, but don't know where it is or how we'll get there. We shall keep in the obscure trails and hope to surprise the place. Time's up, good bye.

Your husband.

Dunlap, Tenn., Aug. 19, 1863.

Dear wife:

It is now 9 o'clock at night, and as our pack supply train starts back to Tracy City in the morning, I'll send you a hasty note. All day yesterday and today we have been traveling in the mountains but this afternoon we came down the mountain on the east side and are bivouacked tonight in the Sequatchee Valley, 25 miles from Chattanooga, as they tell us here. We had some skirmishing today, and captured 25 rebels, together with a lot of Union men whom they had prisoners, and some of whom they intended to hang here tonight. We happened along in good time for the poor fellows who were to be hung and I tell you they were happy. We have just received an order to march at 6 tomorrow morning, with 6 days rations, but we only have two and a half days rations, so we will have to stretch them out for 6 days. Our Colonel is at home sick, our Lieut. Col. is here sick, and that throws me in command of the regiment. I hope the Lieut. Col. may be well enough to take command in the morning, but am afraid he will not be. This is a beautiful valley, about half a mile wide here, with mountain tops on every side reaching up into the clouds. There is a marked difference between the temperature in the valley and on the mountain tops. Last night at this time I was on the mountain and it was cool enough to make a fire agreeable; tonight, in the valley, the air is sultry. The citizens say they are having a hot summer here, but I can't see that the heat affects me any more here than it did at home. I must be up early so pardon me for not writing more. These mountain marches and short rations make a body very sleepy when night comes. Good night, and think of me as a contented soldier whether feast or famine reigns in my "mess."

Your husband.

Across the river from Chattanooga, Sept. 5, 1863.

Dear wife:

I have deferred writing you for a very long time, you will say. Well I have indeed, but I couldn't help it. I wrote you from Tracy City, on the mountains, about the 16th or 18th of August, then I wrote you another from Dunlap in the Sequatchee Valley, in a couple of days afterwards. The next morning after writing you the last letter we started across the last range of mountains which separated us from the Tennessee River, leaving our baggage behind us. Since that morning we have been marching, fighting, bushwhacking, reconnoitering, living on hard crackers and talking across the river and exchanging papers with the rebel pickets of Chattanooga. Our wagons reached us day before yesterday and this is about the first chance I have had at pen, ink and paper for many a day. I was in command of the regiment for several days while crossing the mountains, and on the morning of the day we reached Chattanooga, or rather the river bank opposite Chattanooga, I was in command of the ad-

vance guard, and the men under my command were the first to
open the fight and fire into the stronghold. Just as we dashed
up to the river bank a ferry boat, which had just unloaded a lot
of mules and a dozen rebel soldiers on our side of the river, was
preparing to return to the Chattanooga side; we began firing
into the boat, and, as we have since learned, killed 6 and
wounded several more, while the boat drifted off down the
river out of our range, and left us sitting there on our horses,
drinking out of the river, and we looking up the main street of
the city. I had started from Poe's tavern, 12 miles up the valley
that morning, in advance of every thing, had moved briskly,
and it was very early when we reached the river. They were
completely thunderstruck at our sudden appearance and audacity,
and so great was their surprise that, if it were not for the river
over which there was no bridge we could have ridden clear
through the city without being molested by its garrison. I sent
a courier back to inform the brigade commander where I was,
and withdrew my men under cover of the timber, but it was
nearly half an hour before they had their guns manned so as to
open their batteries on us. Soon after that the balance of the
brigade and our battery came up on the gallop, our rifled guns
were unlimbered on the hill top opposite the city, and then we
had an artillery duel from that time (about 9 A. M.) until near
dark with a loss of one man and 4 horses on our side but we
don't know the loss in the city. Since then we have been lying
here on the hills opposite the city, watching the soldiers and
citizens, moving about the streets, shelling the railroad depot
every few days, skirmishing along the river bank with soldiers
in the streets of the city, and picking up deserters as they swim
across the river.[1]

1. The official history of the 123rd Illinois contains a graphic account of
this exploit. "August 16, moved eastward from Decherd, over Cumberland
Mountains and Walden's Ridge, reaching the valley on the east side of the
Ridge, at Poe's tavern, about 10 o'clock at night, and there bivouacking until
3 o'clock in the morning, when Major Connolly, of the One Hundred and

We are the *extreme front,* and have remained here at Chattanooga longer than any portion of the Federal army since the war began. I know where the balance of our army is and what doing but it would not be prudent for me to write it here, for this letter may fall into rebel hands, yet I may say that I have the fullest confidence in the success of Rosecrans' present movement. From our present position we can look down into the streets of Chattanooga and even read the sign-boards. We could lay the place in ruins in one day if we chose to do so. Colonel [Monroe] and myself have crossed the river several times in a canoe and spent several hours talking and playing cards with rebel officers under the shadow of Lookout mountain, and they have as often

---

Twenty-third, was ordered to move down the valley with two companies of his regiment, and moving cautiously and without noise, to go as far down the valley as he could. This battalion moved on at a smart pace and noiselessly over the sandy road, until about 6 o'clock in the morning, when, upon making a turn in the road, the battalion suddenly found itself within 100 yards of the Tennessee River, and looking right up the main street of the city, while the high fortified hill, on the Chattanooga side, with its many guns, frowned immediately over the heads of the men of the battalion, but there was a steamboat lying at the bank on the north side of the river, just where the road they were traveling reached the water, which had just unloaded 60 mules and twelve rebel soldiers, who were bringing the mules out to pasture. In an instant the battalion was flying down the road to that steamboat, the mules and soldiers were captured, and the Spencer rifles began firing into the boat, which dropped its gang plank into the river, and backed out from the bank, drifting down with the current, as the helmsman was compelled to desert his wheel. In the excitement of the attack some of the men rode their horses belly-deep into the river, in their eager desire to capture the boat. The enemy in the city were completely surprised; they didn't know there was a Federal soldier within 100 miles of the city, so the little battalion stood there and fired across into the streets at every rebel uniform that showed itself dodging about the streets, for full ten minutes before a single shot was returned from the other side. Couriers were sent back to notify the Brigade Commander, and, in a very short time, the rest of the Brigade, with Captain Lilly's battery, was on the hills opposite Chattanooga, and Lilly, with his rifled guns, soon found himself able to send his shells entirely over the city and to any part of it. The Regiment remained there with its Brigade, picketing the river for miles above and below Chattanooga, until Sept. 9, when Crittenden's Corps entered Chattanooga."

crossed to our side and talked and played with us. We find them intelligent gentlemen and good fellows.

I doubt very much whether you have received any of my letters since I left Decherd, for mail communication has been largely interdicted, and I suppose you are somewhat uneasy about me, but you never need feel so, for I am getting along finely and am having an experience that will be a treasure to me in the future. I am like a vegetable, ripening rapidly under the intense artificial light of this war. I am very anxious to get home, but here we are in the face of the enemy, sleeping at night under the very shadow of the hills whose tops bristle with rebel cannon; in momentary expectation of an attack. Last night the enemy built a pontoon bridge, and this morning it is lying on the bank on the opposite side of the river, only about 650 yards from us, but too low for our guns on the hills to reach it; we expect them to attempt to launch it tonight and cross over a body of troops to this side. If they attempt it we must prevent them if possible, otherwise we shall be compelled to burn our baggage and fall back to a supporting force which is a good way off, so you see, under such circumstances, it would be considered an exhibition of the "white feather" to ask for leave of absence, and I must defer it until matters are more settled.

I would write you more details now but that confounded pontoon bridge is on my mind so much that I can hardly think of anything else, besides I have very slender hope that this will ever reach you and therefore feel very little like spending much time in writing, possibly for the amusement of some Johnnie who may get this. If you should get it though, let me again impress you with the fact that probably for the next three months our mail communication may be very much interrupted and you may hear from me but seldom and you must not, therefore, feel disappointed because you don't hear from me regularly as before.

Commending you to the same Providence that has protected

me in my rough pathway, and hoping that a *restored union*, in a double sense, may soon dawn upon us. . . .

Your husband.

Camp on Chickamauga River South of Chattanooga,
Sept. 16, 1863.

Dear wife:

I wrote you a hurried note yesterday, just before getting into the saddle to go, I knew not where, and am glad I have an opportunity to write you again today. This is a day of rest for us, which is something rare lately. Since we crossed the Tennessee River we have had almost continual fighting, and pretty hard too, up to yesterday. All the cavalry of this army has been on our right flank for some time, and we have been operating on Crittenden's left flank, and we have had our hands full night and day. Everything you see in the papers that has been done by Crittenden in this advance, has been done by our brigade, and Crittenden, being the Corps Commander, has received the credit for it. We went ahead of his corps and cleared the way in his front, so that his infantry has moved along without seeing a single rebel soldier except those we sent back as prisoners.

We bivouacked one night within 6 miles of Dalton, Georgia, after fighting and driving Pegram's division of cavalry all day, and had them swarming around us all night; at daybreak in the morning we started in retreat and I was placed in command of the rear guard of 3 companies—about 120 men—and had to cover the retreat of the brigade, resisting the advance of the enemy for some 6 hours before we got to a safe place. I didn't lose a man, but at one time got about 3 miles in rear of the brigade and we had to run like greyhounds to prevent being surrounded and cut off. That afternoon we ran into another Division of Forrest's cavalry and had a hard fight with them, in which we lost 35 men, but we drove them with a heavy loss, and pursued them until we came within full sight of Buckner's army corps. Here was a fix. It was night, and we had taken the wrong road in the hurry of pursuit without knowing until we came in full sight of Buckner's camp fires, and our little brigade found itself thundering at the very lines of an army corps. Our audacity, however, served us, for the rebels supposed, of course, that none but a large force would venture so far and accordingly prepared for a "big fight." While they were so engaged our brigade commander seized a citizen for a guide and "cut across lots" and by marching until one o'clock in the morning through woods and fields reached Crittenden's lines at Lee & Gordon's mills, but Crittenden, not looking for Federals in that direction, supposed he was attacked and his pickets fired on us and fell back. The mistake was soon discovered and we got inside his lines, and men and horses, tired and hungry, dropped down to sleep together, having not a mouthful to eat since sometime before daybreak the morning before; after about two hours rest we were up and off again still without anything to eat but some hard crackers which we stuffed in our pockets and ate as we rode along.

That is a specimen of the way we live in this brigade. Infantry soldiers who march on foot know nothing about this kind of soldiering. Sometimes they have hard marching and scant fare, but whenever we start out we move and skirmish continually, sleep but little, and eat whenever we can catch a chance as we move along. The dust is about 6 inches thick on all these Georgia roads, the weather is extremely hot, but the nights are a little too cool and there has been no rain for a long time.

My health is excellent; indeed the excessive fatigue and hardship I have endured since we have been mounted have been a mine of wealth to me, for I am hardened and strengthened, and I think the bad effects of a sedentary life are entirely worn away. If you could see me in my rags and dirt as I am now, you would laugh immensely, and if my dear mother could see me she would laugh first and then cry to see me looking so much like a beggar

man; my coat is out at the elbows and all the lining torn out, my
vest is lost, my shirts all gone but two, and they so small they
wont button anywhere, my boots with huge shiny legs but soles
"gone up," and my hat the very picture of misery and dilapida-
tion, but my boots will hold my spurs, and I have a fine horse
and saddle and my regiment a good reputation, and that's sufficient, for I can look the "brass and blue" ornamental fellows
squarely in the face and feel proud of the rags I have won in my
country's service. I would wear better clothes if I could get them,
but I am dressed as well as the rest of our brigade, and we are
so constantly moving that we can't get time to "go to town" to
get anything better. But it doesn't make any difference in the
field, for a fine uniform does not make a soldier. I remember,
when I saw Jerry at Louisville about a year ago, when he had
been trailing after Buell in his famous retreat from Tennessee
to Louisville, following after Bragg, he was some ragged and
dirty, and I was tricked out like a butterfly with everything new
and glittering. I then thought he was a very careless fellow and
that I would never look as he did, but I am now as much worse
as possible, yet feel a thousand times better and happier, for I
have learned something about actual soldiering, and since then
have seen our flag go forward from victory to victory and have
a right to feel that I have contributed in some small degree to
that end.

We captured a large rebel mail at Tyner's on the railroad 9
miles east of Chattanooga, some days since, and I read probably
200 of the letters, and heard as many more read, and such a
gloomy, despondent bunch of manuscript, relating to the Southern Confederacy, I never dreamed of. They all agreed that the
Confederacy was ruined, that they were whipped, that it was no
use fighting any longer, that they intended to desert, &c. &c.
Among them I read letters written by officers of Buckner's staff
acknowledging they were whipped, and one, advising his
brother-in-law in Richmond to convert his property into gold

and make preparation for them both and their families, to fly the country, as they couldn't possibly hold out much longer. Day before yesterday a captain and his company deserted, all together, and came marching in to our lines. The newspapers don't tell one hundredth part of the facts in regard to desertion from the rebel army; there is a perfect stampede among the troops from the states, except Virginia, South Carolina and Florida; they come swarming into our lines daily, we pick them up in the mountains, in the valleys, and by the road sides, and there are many who go to their homes and never come to our lines.

It would seem to be good policy not to force a general engagement at this time so long as such desertion continues, for every desertion makes one less rebel to fight. Something must be done though, soon, for two such hostile armies can't lie so close to each other many days without breeding trouble. As I write I can hear the popping of guns on the picket line, and almost any moment that popping is liable to bring on a general engagement, although Rosecrans told General Reynolds, yesterday, that he didn't expect to get a fight out of Bragg this side of Atlanta. It was hinted to me this morning that I would probably be appointed Division Inspector on General [Reynolds'] staff. I shall not ask for it, but if appointed shall be pleased and if not shall be content. We were away down near Dalton, Georgia when I received yours of September 2nd. It worked its way almost through the rebel picket lines. . . .

Your husband.

Fryer's Island, Tenn. River, Sept. 22, 1863.
Dear wife:

Have been through all the Chicamauga battle the papers have told you about and am safe and in good health. Our brigade commenced it on Friday morning and fought all day until ten o'clock at night trying to keep the rebels from crossing Chicamauga creek, then we fought in line with the infantry all day Saturday and Sunday, and Monday morning this brigade withdrew through Chattanooga to this Island in the Tennessee River opposite the north end of Mission Ridge, and we are an outpost here to prevent the rebs from crossing the river here and getting in the rear of Chattanooga. Our army is falling back to Chattanooga. We are *somewhat* whipped but will get over it. The rebs were too numerous for us, they didn't have enough desertions.[2] I had to run for it Friday morning but a fast horse saved me, lost my hat in the race—that wretched hat I told you about in my last letter—and I went bare headed all Friday, Friday night and Saturday until late in the afternoon, when I picked up a hat on the field which I am wearing now and it is better than the one I lost, but not much at that. These are stirring times with us, soldiering in earnest.

Your husband.

Headquarters [Reynolds'] Division, 14th Corps.
Chattanooga, Oct. 4, 1863.

Dear wife:

Should I not be thankful that I am alive and able to write you this pleasant Sunday morning? Thankful that I am one of the spared amid the ranks of this decimated army? I am indeed thankful.

For 72 hours in succession I was in the midst of the storm of

2. A cursory dismissal of one of the major battles of the war—an engagement which cost the Union army 16,170 men in killed, wounded, and missing, and the Confederate forces a loss of 18,454. At Chickamauga the 123rd Illinois, as a unit in Wilder's Brigade, fought valiantly. Samuel C. Williams, writing of Wilder in the *Dictionary of American Biography,* comments: "In the major battle of Chickamauga, engaging as a distinct unit, it [Wilder's Brigade] acquitted itself brilliantly, and Wilder was recommended by Maj. Gen. George H. Thomas for promotion to the rank of brigadier-general 'for his ingenuity and fertility of resource . . . and for his valor and the many qualities of commander displayed by him in the numerous engagements of his brigade with the enemy before and during the battle of Chickamauga.' "

battle, without food or sleep, dear friends and companions dropping all around me and yet God has spared me. Well, war is a
great thing, and I tell you that amid the terrible fighting of
Saturday and Sunday, whenever I had time to think, I had some
very serious thoughts about how I was going to get out of that
tornado alive. Something made me stick, and here I am and
glad of it but wish I could get home for a little while. Some days
since I was talking with Gen. John Beatty, and we arranged to
apply for leave of absence at the same time and go home together
before the election in Ohio, but in a couple of days I saw I could
not honorably ask for a leave at that time; I called on Beatty
again this morning and found he had arrived at the same conclusion, so we reluctantly concluded to defer our applications
until a more opportune time and then go home together if
possible.

Does it seem strange to you that other officers can get home
as frequently as they do while I can't get home for ten or twelve
months? If many of those officers knew how they are talked
of, and in what estimation they are held on account of their frequent leaves of absence and dodging fights, they would either
never ask for leave or would resign at once and go home to stay
with the non combatants, and I know you would rather have me
stay during the war than go home in the hour of action and so
incur the reproach of my comrades.

Many officers are going home now on account of sickness
but there is no use of me thinking of getting home on that
ground for I don't believe I could get sick if I should try. I
wrote you before the big battle, from some place down in
Georgia, that I had a hint that I would be assigned to duty as
Inspector of our Division. A few days after the battle I received
an order to report at Division headquarters for duty as Division
Inspector, accompanied by a letter from Major General
[Reynolds], the Division Commander, saying he had just sent
me such an order, and that if I would like a position on his staff,

as Inspector, to come prepared to stay. I concluded to accept it and try it a while, although I did not like it at Nashville, but I think it will be different in the field and I will probably like it better. I began duty as Inspector of this Division on September 26th and have been busy since with office work and in learning how.

I can give you some information about your brother Henry. During the battle he was on the staff of General Brannan, as Topographical Engineer. Gen. Brannan's adjutant general told me today that "Lieut. Dunn behaved with great gallantry during the battle of Saturday and Sunday, and on Sunday evening was sent with a message by Gen. Brannan, in carrying which he ran into the enemy's lines and was captured." He is doubtless a prisoner in the hands of the enemy, and unhurt. I am sorry to know he was captured, but am glad it is no worse. They captured my hat on Friday and would have captured me but I ride a horse that the Southern Confederacy can't catch in a fair race, and we had a fair race that time for about two miles.

Gen. Beatty told me he saw Sam Snider lying on the battle field, with a pretty severe wound in his shoulder, but could do nothing for him except to give him a drink of water. Wounded men suffer from thirst as much as from ordinary wounds. One of your letters, I forget its date, was handed me on the battle field, on Saturday afternoon, during a brief lull, and just before our heaviest fighting began, indeed I was reading it as the enemy came charging on us.

Good bye. I surely will get home soon.

Your husband.

Chattanooga, Oct. 9, 1863.

Dear wife:

It is now about 6 o'clock in the morning and I have been up an hour, so you see I am an early riser sometimes when I can't help it. There is a captain here from my regiment who is going home today on sick leave, and I'll send this little letter by him, to be mailed somewhere in the U. S. An order will be issued today breaking up the present organization of the Army of the Cumberland and reorganizing it. Maj. Gen. [Reynolds], on whose staff I now am, is to be Chief of staff in the new organization, and that, of course, will relieve all his staff, so I suppose I will receive an order to rejoin my regiment, but where it is now I don't know. If I receive such order I shall try to get a leave of absence before returning to the regiment. If I should try to get a staff position under the new organization I know I could get it, but I shall not try, for I believe I will be better satisfied serving with my regiment, among my personal friends and home acquaintances. If I should be appointed on another staff it will prevent me from getting home as soon as I otherwise would, but one thing is certain, I'm going home soon. Address me:

Major [J. A. Connolly], [123rd], Ills. Vols.
Inspector [Reynolds'] Div. 14th A. C.
Chattanooga, Tenn.
and I will get it at the regiment if nowhere else.
Your husband.

Chattanooga, Oct. 21, 1863.
Dear wife:
So you have the blues have you? Oh well, cheer up! Remember, *we are suppressing the rebellion,* and you agree with me that it must be done at all hazards; you are doing your part of it, quite as well as I, in bearing with bitter disappointment and almost neglect. We men are not bearing all the burdens of this war, our women are bearing their full share.

I had been doing my part of it, I confess, with dark forebodings for some little time, until the news of the Ohio and other elections came like a rift of sunshine, breaking through the clouded skies, giving promise of brighter and better days. I remember receiving your last letter, but oh, how long since, and what changes have taken place!

I remember I was reading that letter as the fight was thickening around us on Saturday at Chicamauga; the thunder of the artillery and rattle of musketry kept growing closer and closer as I read, and before I had finished it the rebel yells and whistling bullets told us that our time had come, so forward into the leaden hail we charged to meet their coming charge and broke it with the constant fire of our Spencers but I got through it with your unfinished letter crumpled up in the pocket of my blouse, and finished reading it when we had cleared the Johnnies from our front. We got through the three days of fighting without losing many men. We think our Spencers saved us, and our men adore them as the heathen do their idols.

I wrote you before that I had been assigned to duty on the Division staff, as Inspector, after the battle. I remained as Inspector until our Division commander was taken from the Division and made Chief of Staff to Gen. Rosecrans. Gen. Thomas, who commanded the corps, then sent for me, and told me I might either return to my regiment or be assigned to some other Division as Inspector. "Well," he said, "you make a good Inspector, Gen. [Reynolds] tells me, and perhaps you had better remain unless it interferes with your promotion in your regiment," so I chose to continue as Inspector, for I don't care about promotion. I have all the rank now I care for. I was assigned to duty on the staff of Gen. [Baird], as Inspector of his Division, viz. 3rd Div. 14 A. C.,[3] but change appears to be the order

3. In the reorganization of the Army of the Cumberland the divisions of Reynolds and Brannan were consolidated and placed under the command of General Absalom Baird.

Baird, with whom Connolly would serve for the remainder of the war, was a professional soldier. Born at Washington, Pennsylvania, in 1824, Baird attended the United States Military Academy and graduated in the class of 1849. He saw service in the Seminole War, served six years as an instructor at West Point, and was on duty in Texas when the Civil War broke out.

of the day, and I don't know where I may be ten days hence, for night before last a telegram came from the Secretary of War, ordering Gen. Rosecrans to report at Washington and placing Gen. Thomas in command of the Army of the Cumberland, and now the question comes who will command the 14th army corps in place of Gen. Thomas? Rumor says that Gen. [Reynolds], our old Division commander, will.

I have no idea where I will go other than to my regiment, and am not likely to know until the very moment the order is issued, for I shall not ask for any place or position but shall do as the private soldier does, go ahead under the orders I have until I get different ones. I suppose I look odd amongst the rest of these staff officers, with my great big boots and worn clothes, while they are all tricked out in fine uniforms, gold lace, brilliant shoulder straps, fine boots, fine handkerchiefs, &c &c. I laugh about it myself sometimes, and wonder what they do think about that seedy looking Major, but thank fortune I don't care a cent what they do think, if their opinions are based upon the quality of my clothing, for I have no better; my venerable Uncle Samuel is indebted to me considerable and I haven't money enough to pay for a paper of "fine cut" and if a Paymaster don't come pretty soon I'll be as poor as Don Quixote was in his military career, and if Bragg don't get away from here pretty soon, so we can get some forage for our stock, my fine horse will only exist as a sorrowful memory of better days. Did you ever expect to see your husband reduced to such poverty? Well, don't laugh at me just because I'm poor. I could relate actual experiences of my own since reaching Chattanooga in my present pen-

---

From the rank of captain, which he held at the beginning of the war, he rose steadily to that of brigadier-general (April 28, 1862). Baird was transferred to the 14th Corps in August, 1863, at the request of General Thomas. "At this time, which marks the beginning of his distinguished military service, Baird was in the prime of life, active, energetic, ambitious; a just commander, a strict disciplinarian, and an aggressive fighter." C. A. Bach in the *Dictionary of American Biography*.

niless condition that would be amusing enough to cure any case of hypochondria, and my own experience is probably not any harder than that of nine tenths of the officers of this army, except that those who had good clothes when the trouble began have better clothes than the rest of us now. The usual salutation in Chattanooga now is: "How much money have you got," the universal answer being "Pretty well broke."

But it will not do for me to expose the secrets of Chattanooga in this letter, for our mails have to go by wagon road 60 miles over the mountain, before reaching the railroad, the chances are pretty good that some of our mails will fall into rebel hands, and I don't want them to gather any crumbs of comfort out of my letters. If this should fall into rebel hands, let me say by way of parenthesis, to the rebel who reads it: "I have captured and read hundreds of rebel letters, to this *one,* so I'm ahead of you Johnnies on that score." These changes of position that I have been undergoing for some time have prevented me from having any opportunity to get a leave, but I'm living in the greatest hopes of any fellow you ever saw, for I know that when I ask for one I'll get it, and I shall ask for it just as soon as I can decently.

I presume you have seen by the papers that Col. [Monroe] of my regiment was killed in a fight with Wheeler's cavalry, near Farmington, Tennessee.[4] It is sad news indeed to me, for he was a gallant and accomplished officer, and during our entire period of service we have been bosom friends. It grieves me to think that we have passed together through so many severe fights, have talked together so much about death upon the battle field, and that in so few days after being separated from him he should meet his death. He fell like a brave man by a bullet through his heart while charging a rebel battery, but the regiment, inspired by his example, rushed on and took the battery and routed the rebels.

4. On October 7, 1863.

It was in the long chase after Wheeler, who had crossed the river after Chickamauga to cut the railroad which supplied our army with food, and this battery had stopped the cavalry leading the chase, so they stopped, and as usual, sent back for one of the regiments of mounted infantry to clear the way. My regiment was the one selected, they dismounted, and took the battery but lost one of the bravest and best officers in the army. That is the only fight my regiment has ever been in when I have not been with it, and while it creates a vacancy, yet neither the Lieut. Col. nor myself can be promoted because we number less than 500 men and under existing orders, no new field officers can be mustered. The field officers of a majority of our regiments are in the same condition, vacancies occur, but officers cannot be promoted to fill them. This works great injustice in many instances, and there is general dissatisfaction amongst officers in regard to it but the rule is inflexible and we must submit. . . .

Tattoo long since sounded, the hour of midnight is near and I must be up with the lark, to inspect the picket lines before it is light enough to give the rebel pickets a good sight of me, for I have to ride part of the line in full view of them, and I ride fast along there, the pickets on both sides being concealed in their holes.

Your husband.

P. S. Send me some postage stamps by Gen. Beatty.[5]

Chattanooga, Oct. 27, 1863.

Dear wife:

> "The melancholy days have come,
> The saddest of the year, &c."

and, to be in keeping with the face of Nature, my letters should be "sicklied o'er with the pale cast of thought," but I didn't

5. In civil life General John Beatty had been a banker at Cardington, Ohio, a small town only a few miles from Mt. Gilead.

come into the army to think; a soldier has no business to think, unless it may be to devise means for sending over the river Styx the greatest number of his enemies, but since the rebels are going to sticks fast enough anyhow, I have determined to take things easy and not bother myself with thinking, so if this letter should contain no news or anything else but nonsense, just attribute it to the fact that I've quit thinking and gone into plain soldiering in the most comfortable manner possible. Oh yes, I do think sometimes. When the reveille calls me to the light of a new day; when our daily cannonade breaks on my ear at midday, and when the

"Bugles sing truce and the night cloud has lowered,"

then thoughts of home come stealing over me, and I think of many things more pleasant than those surrounding me here, although soldiering is not so very unpleasant to me, but I am satisfied this is not exactly my sphere, and I am satisfied there is something in civil life that I would fit into better, if my duty to my Uncle Samuel would only permit me to devote myself to it. What a pity I'm not a Major General. I could then go home and make a visit every now and then, and no one think anything of it. If I couldn't get home any other way, I could make a blunder, sacrifice two or three thousand men, be relieved of my command, be ordered to report at Cincinnati, Columbus or Washington, go there and draw my pay regularly and spend a season in fashionable society. That would be fine wouldn't it? Yes; but you say there is more or less disgrace attached to such a course. Aye, "there's a rub," and I hope those who take such a course may feel that disgrace most keenly all their lives.

In fixing up my new quarters at Division headquarters here I was given a new wall tent for myself, and it became necessary to get a stove, as the weather is getting cold, especially at night; my clerk said he knew a man in the 14th Ohio, who had one to sell, so I sent the clerk to have him bring it up. The next day a quiet, clean, elderly private presented himself at my tent with a little copper stove, cone shaped and evidently made by himself, with some small copper pipe to fit it. I asked him his price and he replied "ten dollars." I remonstrated with him about his exorbitant price—the old man's eyes filled with tears as he replied: "Major I have a wife and six children at home whom I have not seen for over two years; I have done duty all the time, and never missed a fight where my regiment was engaged; I have done this for $13 a month all the time, and have sent nearly every cent of it to my wife, and it has supported her, but winter is coming on, my children need clothing, and if you give me ten dollars for this stove you'll never miss it out of your salary, and I'll send it home to my wife to buy shoes or something for the children." I took the stove then, and would have done so if he had asked me $25 for it. How many such cases there are in the army! Poor fellows! they are the patriots; *they* form the bulwark that must save our country; *they* are the heroes who charge batteries, win battles and enwreathe our starry flag with glory, but who, alas! fill nameless graves today in every valley and on every hill side from the Ohio to the Gulf. When will our people cease to emblazon the names of Generals, Colonels, Captains, &c., &c., in characters of brightness, while they forget the unadorned privates who did the actual fighting?

Chattanooga is the great point of interest now. The Potomac is "played out" as the boys say. Vicksburg "went up" and is paroled; Charleston is condemned to "Greek fire," and everybody is coming to Chattanooga. Grant is here, Hooker is trying to fight his way here,[6] and I have been out at the front all day listening to the booming of his guns as he thunders away for a passage over Lookout Mountain. Halleck is on his way here and will only be *in the way*. General Smith late Chief Engineer of the

6. Hooker, relieved of the command of the Army of the Potomac on June 28, 1863, was given the 11th and 12th corps when they were sent to the Army of the Cumberland in the fall of the year.

defences of Washington is here,[7] and indeed, Major General and Brigadier General stars are getting to be as plentiful as corporals chevrons. I'm afraid that's one trouble with our army just now—we have too many Brigadier stars and not enough of that other kind of "Stars" that fights and lives on "hard tack" at $13 a month. Notwithstanding the scanty "Bill of Fare" prevailing here now, my mess had turkey and real Irish potatoes (none of the dessicated affairs) for dinner yesterday. The turkey and potatoes were intended for company dinner we intended giving to another staff, but our forage scouts specially sent out by us had to go 55 miles up in the country to get one small turkey and about a peck of potatoes, so, as we didn't have enough to go around we ate it ourselves and needed more to satisfy hunger. Tonight we sent out a wagon across the river, with a guard, and an officer in charge, furnished with money from the different messes about our headquarters, to buy something for us to eat. They will probably have to go 60 or 70 miles up the valley before they can find a chicken or potato. . . .

Another change took place in this army today. General John M. Palmer of Illinois, was assigned to the command of the 14th corps, and that is the corps in which I am now and have been ever since the Army of the Cumberland was organized. We all regret losing General Thomas. . . .

Your husband.

Chattanooga, Nov. 5, 1863.

Dear wife:

It is now ten o'clock at night. I took up a paper tonight and read the remarks of General Rosecrans at Cincinnati; I laid the paper down, mad, indulged myself with a mental denunciation of all Generals, except "our Rosy," took up the paper again and

7. General William F. Smith, who had served with distinction in the Army of the Potomac, was sent to the Army of the Cumberland as Chief Engineer at this time.

read Henry Ward Beecher's address at Manchester, England, and felt much better; am decidedly in favor of Beecher and his political theories; hurrah for Beecher, Gerrit Smith, Wendell Phillips, and every other *earnest man,* who has sense enough to know what is right politically as well as morally, and has courage enough to proclaim it and act it.

I am as confirmed an abolitionist as ever was pelted with stale eggs, but I rarely think of it except when I see the operations of old stay-at-home politicians to drag down and ruin every earnest man who, in these days of action and earnestness, is supplanting them in the affections of the people. Rosecrans relieved! Then comes the starveling crew of home politicians to defame his character, to defame a name that should stand bright on the pages of history, to steal away laurels that such as they can never win. If such men and such reports are to mould public opinion, God help the Republic! I have no patience to think about it, much less to write about it. The scoundrels! How can men be so depraved? General Rosecrans was my *beau ideal* of a leader; I would follow him with the devotion of the crusaders for "Peter the Hermit." This entire army *was* an army of crusaders under his leadership. He was the light and life of this army. When the order for his removal was made public this army said nothing, it was dumb, the blow was too sudden and too severe for speech; we all now pursue our way quietly, as soldiers bound to obey the orders of our superiors; we used to obey because we loved our leader, but let it be announced tomorrow that Rosecrans was to command us again, and every silent tongue in this quiet army would find a voice, whose loud acclaim would almost wake again to the deadly shock our sleeping comrades on Chickamauga's banks.[8] But enough; we'll triumph under

8. "Rosecrans was generally regarded as an able commander and has been called the 'greatest strategist of the war. . . .'" [Henry M. Cist, *The Army of the Cumberland*]. He accomplished an incredible amount of work, and in campaign seemed to be able to do without sleep. He had a hot temper, which

Grant, just as well as Rosecrans, and perhaps it is right that *Generals* should be dealt with unjustly sometimes, as well as privates.

Yet this kind of work sets a "still small voice" talking with me occasionally, something in this wise: "What are *you* here for? You left a comfortable home, and a growing practice, you have roughed it in the field for over a year, you have a wife at home, and you have a long life before you if you would only return to where you would be *safe,* you are scheming neither for place nor pelf here, you can make more money at home, why not, then, go home, live like a Christian, and enjoy the passing days? The Generals, who risk nothing but reputation, will have their names blazoned in history while yours will be hidden away in the army rolls." And what do you think? I sometimes think that "still small voice" whispers to me a great deal of truth, and yet I dare not listen too much to its counsels, for they are selfish, and not in accord of the spirit of the times. Selah! as the Good Book says.

Let's change the "key note." When I commenced this letter a splendid brass band was playing a delightful "Quickstep" near my quarters, and in the midst of my indignation I found myself beating time with my feet, and it brought vividly to my mind the scenes and persons of "the days when we went gypsying, a long time ago," but not so very long ago either, so I laid down my pen, and for a few moments thought, thought of that circle of youth and gaiety, of the music, the merry laugh and light

---

he was not always able to control, and was often hasty and indiscreet in speech. He especially resented interference from above with his plans, and seemed to persist the more obstinately in his own decisions. These characteristics brought him into conflict with his superiors, as in the Tullahoma and Chickamauga campaigns, and ultimately led to his relief. He was, however, well liked in the army and was affectionately called 'Old Rosy' by the soldiers." Oliver L. Spaulding, Jr., in the *Dictionary of American Biography.* Rosecrans, born in 1819, was forty-four years old when he was removed from command of the Army of the Cumberland.

hearts of the ball room, but now how changed! that merry laugh struggles forth now, with but the doleful cadence of a sigh, the light heart is burdened with sorrow, that circle is broken, here and there I see a soldier's grave containing all that's left of some of those early friends, others I see engaged in a fruitless struggle with "the fickle Goddess," but all scattered, dead and dying, some with honor, some without.

"The lights are dead, the music fled,"

Well, what of it? Does it make me feel sad? Not a bit of it. I don't feel half as gloomy after these reflections, as I did last night after sitting up until midnight to read Alexander Dumas' account of the life and death of Louis XV. Every fellow has to "paddle his own canoe," even Louis XV had to, and a sorry voyage he made of it.

In your last letter you seem to think I don't give you enough description of battles, armies, scenery, etc. If you were as tired of battles and armies as I am you wouldn't care to spend much time on them for they are very unpleasant things to be in and one does not like to reproduce memories of unpleasant things. My letters have been barren and uninteresting of late I know, but you must recollect we have been on very short rations—the rebels say we are starving—and how can a starving soldier write an interesting letter? If "Miss Flora McFlimsey" [9] was in such agonies because she had "nothing to wear," imagine my condition with "nothing to wear" and "nothing to eat."

Nodier, a French savant, insisted that the toad lived upon his own skin, which he shed once a year, and which served to sustain him until the next shedding season. I wish I was that kind of a toad just now, I'd thrive in this rainy season, and Bragg might cut our cracker line as much as he pleased, he couldn't affect my rations. I commenced some days since to jot down my own recollections of the advance on Chattanooga,

9. A popular comic poem of the time. It was one of Lincoln's favorites.

the evacuation, the battle of Chickamauga, and the retreat to Chattanooga. I may be too lazy to finish it, for I find my memory crammed with incidents enough to fill a volume, and like "The Discontented Pendulum" give up in despair at the length of the task before me. Still I shall try to muster up perseverance enough to finish it, for bye and bye many of these incidents will have passed out of my mind, and I would like to have the record made up here in the heart of the Confederacy, so as to remind me hereafter, of those days of adventure and jolly soldiering that even now seem as days of romance in my soldier life. Bless me! My sheet is almost full and I have but one postage stamp, and it is impossible to beg, borrow or steal another in Chattanooga, so you must be content with this, for if I run into another sheet the postage will be six cents and Uncle Sam won't trust me for the other three cents. An officer of this staff received a letter to-day from a friend in Libby prison, and he says your brother Henry is there with him and is well. Out of money, out of clothes, out of rations and out of postage stamps, I must quit.

Your husband.

Chattanooga, Nov. 15, 1863.
Dear wife:

I write you briefly tonight, with a heavy heart. I have just received and read yours of the 8th inst. It is the first announcement to me of the death of my dear brave brother Charlie. Oh God! comfort my dear mother in her affliction! Poor boy, another victim. . . .

I cannot write tonight, my mind wanders off to my dear dead brother whose soldier life has been such an active stirring one, always at the front, a leader in daring enterprise, with well won promotion awaiting him. But it is some consolation to know that he went like a soldier, shot in the forehead, while leading his men in the deadly charge, and falling on the enemy's breast works. I am but a weak child tonight. One by one my friends are falling; a sister goes to her grave without my farewell kiss; a brave soldier brother yields up his life while fighting for our flag; my Colonel, my bosom friend and companion on many a weary march and hard fought field, has fought his last battle, and the loss of each of them comes to me tonight with accumulated force, and makes me feel discouraged and disheartened. . . . I really ought not have written you such a letter as this, but I couldn't help it, I shall try and write a more cheerful one to mother tomorrow. I see by your letter that you were with her when it was written. Don't let her see this for it will only make her sad. . . .

Paymaster Rhodes of Delaware, O., is here paying some of the troops of this Division and I will get 4 months pay from him tomorrow. Would rather have something good to eat, money is no good here. Can't even buy clothes with it, although I need them very much. It is rumored today that Gen. Reynolds is to command the 14th corps. That will suit me. . . .

Your husband.

Chattanooga, Nov. 17, 1863.

Dear wife:

I wrote you only a couple of days ago, but I have spent this evening, so far (it is now ten o'clock) in reading the letters of an English officer at the siege of Delhi, India, written home to his wife, and I see by their dates, that he wrote to her daily, unless prevented by military duty, and it made me think that perhaps I didn't write as often as I should, so I just laid down my book, took up my pen, and here I am "hard at it" writing you a letter when I really ought to be asleep, for I must be up and out on the picket line at the front, by daylight in the morning. Your last letter brought me very sad intelligence, and I answered it in a most gloomy and despondent mood, which I should not have done I know, but I couldn't help it, I wrote just as I felt and just as I should have talked if I had been at home. Next day after writing it I stated to Gen. [Baird] on whose staff I now am, the fact of my brother's death, killed in action, and that I would like to have 20 days leave of absence, if I could be spared from my post. He replied: "Certainly Major, I will approve your application and should be glad to see you get it but I fear they will not approve it at Department headquarters, for before your return there will probably be some active work for this army." I told him if there was probability of active work before my return I should not make application, but would stay at my post. . . .

When I settled in Illinois among strangers, and hung out my modest shingle, with fear and trembling, I felt as if I was "starting in life" and with pretty big chances against me, but I "made it go" and was getting "fixed to my notion" when this confounded war turned up and upset everything. That's the time Fortune flanked me; when I quit the service I'll have to start life again, so this time, you see I'm preparing to flank Fortune, and if possible start a little ahead of her in the race. . . .

I am not at liberty to tell you what I know of contemplated army movements, but I can say that I shall not be surprised if, within ten days the blow will be struck that will strike the heart of the rebellion. Movements are in operation at the very moment I am writing these lines, which, if they can be kept from the knowledge of the enemy 48 hours will, in all probability, damage Bragg's army as much as anything that has ever been done. If the plan is not frustrated in some way, you will, of course, read of it in the newspapers before you get this, so that when you do get it you will read it either as a guess that was true or as one that was false at the time it was made, and even though it may be stale when you get it, I give it as a bit of gossip in the best informed army circles today. Tomorrow morning may change it all, the enemy may not then be found in our front, or he may have doubled his force, or he may open his batteries on us from fifty points where he commands this devoted city. Such is army life here—like the views in the kaleidoscope—changing with every turn of the cylinder, yet here we are, tens of thousands of men wrapped in their blankets, sleeping soundly, all save the lonely pickets, under the cannon of the enemy, equally indifferent whether the morning light brings a battle or day of ease, our dreams and visions of home the same whether our reveille be the cannon's roar or the bugle note.

If Gen. Thomas knew how bad I want to get home he would send me a leave of absence tomorrow, I know, for he is a most kindly old gentleman, but I'm not going to acknowledge it to him or anybody else but you. Nothing like keeping up your courage. The world respects even a *show* of courage. Keep yours up. I'll get home sometime for good and when I do

> "The night will be filled with music,
> And the cares that infest the day,
> Shall fold their tents like the Arabs,
> And as silently steal away."

Good Night.
Your husband.

Chattanooga, Nov. 19, 1863.

Dear wife:

Last night, after finishing a letter to you, I determined to keep a diary until I wrote you again, and send you the diary for my next letter. My resolution to do so is very firm but I don't know how it will hold out. My servant, who is a free black, from Cincinnati, and came into the army as servant for Col. Reid of Delaware, Ohio, came into my tent at daylight this morning and built a fire, then aroused me and went out to saddle and bring out my horse for me; I was very sleepy and disliked the idea of getting up to go out in the dense fog, so I lazily rolled over and went to sleep again, but in a few minutes, my African: "Major your horse ready, want him?" "Yes." I drawled out sleepily, and rolled over again, wishing I could sleep a couple of hours longer, but it was no use wishing, I had to get up, hurry into my clothes and mount. The morning was cold and my horse feeling fine even if he was hungry, so I was soon wide awake, galloping through the silent camps to the front. At the picket reserve I met Gen. Starkweather, whose brigade was then on picket and whom I was to relieve with Turchin's brigade.[10] While sitting there on our horses, talking and awaiting the arrival of Turchin's brigade, a picket from one of the outposts further to the front, came and reported to Gen. Starkweather, with a rebel deserter who had just came through our lines; the General ordered him taken to the Provost Marshal and nothing further was thought of it, all despatched in a business like way; it occurs so frequently that our soldiers think nothing of it.

I couldn't help thinking, as I looked at him: "You're a cowardly rascal." I like to see them desert; I wish they would *all* desert and go to their homes, but at that moment I respected his misguided comrades who remained at their posts more than I did him. About half past six o'clock Turchin's brigade came filing out through the fog; I gave some directions to the brigade Inspector and he started with the "reliefs" to the different out-posts; waiting a few moments to see that everything was going right, I started back to my quarters; found my cot made up, tent swept out, light boots blacked, a good fire and a late Cincinnati Commercial on my table; read the paper until breakfast was ready at half past eight; after breakfast took a snooze of about an hour and a half, by which time the "Daily Reports" from Brigade Inspectors were in; made up my own "Daily Report" from them and had it approved by the General, sent it off by an orderly to the Corps Inspector, and my routine work for the

10. Brigadier General John C. Starkweather; Brigadier General John Basil Turchin (Ivan Vasilevitch Turchininoff), Russian-born veteran of the Crimean War who began his Civil War service as colonel of the 19th Illinois Infantry.

day was done. Had nothing to do then but sit in my snug tent and read the papers, sleep, write or do whatever I chose. Captain Johnson of General Negley's staff called a few moments. He is a fine looking officer, about 6 feet tall, slender, and has a moustache and imperial like Shakespeare's in the pictures.

He was a New York salesman at the commencement of the war but with more grit than some other New York salesmen we know of. After a two o'clock dinner I rode out without any particular aim or destination. In town I met Colonel Nodine 25th Illinois, Colonel Hays 10th Kentucky, Lieutenant Bales Carter Quartermaster 125th Ohio, formerly of Fredericktown, Ohio, and later of Mount Vernon, Ohio, also, met Doherty, correspondent of the Louisville Journal; next met a citizen who starts to Louisville tomorrow morning and gave him some money and my "size" to buy me a uniform coat (you see I found a paymaster) then rode back to my quarters and slept until supper was ready; after supper took up a novel—"Ten Thousand a Year"—and read it a couple of hours, until tattoo, laid down the novel, commenced this diary, and now, having finished it for the day, shall take up "Ten Thousand a Year" and read it a while then "turn in." [11]

November 20, 8 o'clock P. M.

I have just come from Gen. [Baird's]s room and he said "Major we must all be out at 4 o'clock to-morrow morning; we will get up at 3 so as to get a cup of coffee; we will fight tomorrow probably." That is refreshing news certainly, to a man who is by no means anxious for a fight, but that is what I agreed to do when I entered the army, and if we fight every day I have no right to complain, so here we go, a fight tomorrow morning and a glorious triumph for us I hope. I was

11. A popular novel of the law (1839) by an English lawyer, Samuel Warren.

up at daylight this morning and on the picket line; two deserters came in while I was there. On returning to camp I met Gen. Carlin just going out. He was Corps officer of the day to-day. I have met him at the picket line before. I think he is a careful, painstaking officer, possessed of what Napoleon called "two o'clock" courage—he's not afraid to get up and stir around in the morning when his subordinates are sleeping.[12] I won't write much to-night except to say that the enemy attacked Burnside in force day before yesterday, and now surround him in Knoxville, so we must fight in the morning, to create a diversion in his favor, and thus save Burnside and East Tennessee. Pontoons are to be thrown across the river about 3 miles above here, tonight, and Sherman's corps, with Davis' Division of the 14th corps, are to cross there at daylight, while Hooker on our right flank beyond Lookout Mountain, attacks to divert the attention of the enemy from Sherman, and, if all goes well, we attack the centre at Missionary Ridge, and all working together, drive them from Lookout Mountain and Missionary Ridge. Let us see now how near my predictions come true.

Saturday, Nov. 21.

Well, my prediction in yesterday's diary didn't come true. Last night, about an hour after Gen. [Baird] told me what I have written above about to-morrows movement, an orderly came to him in haste with a message. He opened it and read: "The movement for to-morrow morning is countermanded." That ended the trouble about getting up early in the morning. Immediately on hearing this I went over to Gen. Davis' [13]

12. Brigadier General William Passmore Carlin, West Point, 1850. A Captain in the Regular Army when the war broke out, Carlin was soon commissioned colonel of the 38th Illinois Infantry. After distinguishing himself at Perryville, he was promoted to Brigadier General of Volunteers. Later, he would be given command of a division in the Army of the Tennessee.

13. Brigadier General Jefferson C. Davis, commanding the Second Division of the 14th Corps.

headquarters, and from there, (in company with my friend Capt. Howard of the 18th U. S., who is Commissary of Musters for Gen. Davis' Division) went to Gen. Reynolds headquarters, but found no one at home, so we went over to Gen. Grant's headquarters where we met Gen. Rawlins, Col. Lagow, Capt. Hudson and Capt. somebody else, all of Grant's staff. There learned that Bragg had notified Gen. Grant, yesterday, to remove the non-combatants from Chattanooga, which we laughed at as a joke. Returning to Gen. Reynolds headquarters we there met Capt. Floyd, Reynolds aide de camp, and took him with us to Capt. Howard's room where we found Col. Smith, of the 16th Illinois. We sat down and talked over the prospect of a fight while Capt. Howard (who is a capital little fellow), busied himself in making an elegant punch, of which of course, we all partook. Capt. Floyd then returned to his quarters, and Col. Smith, Capt. Howard and myself all turned in to Howard's big old fashioned bed together, for it had commenced raining and we didn't want to get wet going home in the rain.

There, that's the conclusion of my Friday's operations. I was up at 6 o'clock this, Saturday, morning, came home here to my own quarters through quite a rain, breakfasted at eight, dined at two, supped at seven, and did nothing all day but sit in my tent and read the papers and my novel "Ten Thousand a Year" which now, at ten o'clock P. M., I have just laid down for the purpose of writing up this diary for to-day, after which I shall take it up again and read until sleepy. I like to read a good novel any time, but it is particularly pleasant to get hold of a good one in camp, with which to while away the long slow hours of a rainy day or lonesome evening, and I am specially interested in this one for the author is, evidently, a lawyer, quotes Blackstone, Chitty, Co, Litt, &c. quite glibly; talks about *nisi prius,* the *absque hoc,* "lessor of the plaintiff," &c. &c. like an old stager, and indeed has so skilfully interwoven into the plot of his story the abstruse principles of the English law relating to

"Conveyances" and "Descents and Distributions" that in reading his pages I can almost imagine myself at home in my comfortable office, reading up for a land case. After all, that same office, humble as it is, and my law books, few though they be, have more charms for me than all this "pomp and circumstance of glorious war," and after we get this rebellion crushed I don't want to take a contract to crush any more; I prefer to settle all disputes hereafter by jury trial. Now for my "Ten Thousand a Year."

Sunday, Nov. 22.

Up rather late this morning, caused by sitting up to finish my "Ten Thousand a Year." Confound the "Ten Thousand a Year." After wading through the large volume I discovered that the last pages were torn out, as I thought, but on turning to the title page, I discovered for the first time, that the story was "complete in two volumes." The other volume can't be obtained in Chattanooga, so now I'm in a bad fix—can't digest the story in this unfinished condition, and can't get the other half for a digester.

When I got up this morning, at eight thirty, breakfast was ready, and three letters were lying on my desk. By the address I saw, as I was dressing that one was from you, one from Mr. ——— and one from Mt. Vernon, Ohio, but I didn't know the handwriting on it. It then became a grave question with me whether I should read my letters before or after breakfast. If I am not in a hurry I like to keep your letters unopened a while, for the purpose of thinking about the contents, speculating as to whether they are gloomy or cheerful, whether they bring good news or bad news, whether they bring tidings of deaths or marriages among my friends and former associates, whether any of my old associates have had better luck or worse luck than I, so in accordance with this practice I determined to breakfast before opening my mail. Having finished breakfast I opened the Mt. Vernon letter first, and great was my surprise to find it was from Miss Martha ———. She writes me such a letter as Joshua R. Giddings might be supposed to write to some young politician of the Democratic persuasion who had long resisted Joshua's arguments, but who had suddenly discovered their truth and beauty, and had opened himself out like a sunflower to bask forever after in the full rays of the sun of Abolitionism.

Martha and I used to have some strong political arguments, and in her letter she reminds me that she has finally beaten me, and that I have come to her way of thinking. You know she was a noisy Abolitionist. But she is mistaken. I am not an Abolitionist, i.e., a *political* abolitionist. I have no affiliation with or sympathy for the *political* abolitionist, for they are a canting hypocritical set of cowards, having courage only to support their peculiar opinions with their tongues; they can't be found in our armies now, but are at home, holding their little tea party conventions, mourning over "man's inhumanity to man" and adopting addresses to the President entreating him to proclaim to the world that the negro is the equal of the white man, and that it is an abolition war. The fanatical fools! Can't they see, without conventions or proclamations, that it is an abolition war? If they were honest they would turn out and help fight the battles, instead of whining around home because the President won't ratify *God's own decree* by signing "A. Lincoln" at the bottom of it. Such abolitionists as Smith, Giddings, Phillips &c. I don't object to now, for they have, to a great extent, dropped their cant, and are, and have been striking sturdy blows for the government.

You see I am a *practical* but not a *political* abolitionist. But this is enough; I am simply "thinking out loud," moved to these thoughts by Miss Martha's letter. In your letter you say: "You know I can make good coffee." You can't imagine what a luxury a cup of that coffee, with "sure enough" cream and white sugar, with a piece of bread and butter would be down here just now. When I get home I shall appreciate plain bread and butter more than I ever did before I was "brass mounted." I see by the despatches of to-day that the Cabinet has actually been considering the recall of the seceded states. That begins to look like business, but what bothers me is that the most serious part of that business will have to be transacted in a very rough way, probably in a day or two, by this very army.

I have been looking at the rebels, with a good glass, all day, filing along Mission Ridge in long columns, moving toward our left; evidently there is something up, and I think both sides are massing for a fight. Howard's Corps [14] came across the river just at dark to-night, and it is here in Chattanooga, for the first time, to-night. While I write I can hear the rumble of artillery crossing the pontoon bridge, and I can also hear the whistles of the locomotives of the rebels, just on the other side of Mission Ridge—say three and a half miles from where I sit. What are those locomotives doing? Are they bringing rebel reinforcements, or are they hurrying Bragg's army away on another retreat? Hardly the latter I think, but I'll know to-morrow morning. We'll have to whip Bragg this week unless he runs away again.

Was glad to get your letter and the postage stamps. You ask me if I have read the speech of Gantt of Arkansas. I have. A party of my regiment, under my command, last July, shot in two places, and captured his brother, Lieut. Col. George Gantt, at Centerville, Hickman Co., Tenn. I got his horse, saddle, bridle and pistols, had him carried to a house in Centerville, which is the county seat, had his wounds dressed, and as he was too badly wounded to take along, paroled him to report to the Federal Commander at Nashville as a prisoner of war as soon as he should be able to travel. He wrote a letter to his wife in

14. Major General Oliver Otis Howard was ordered to Tennessee from the Army of the Potomac in the fall of 1863.

Maury Co., Tenn., which I took and sent to her. I don't know whether he has ever reported or not. He was said to be one of the leading lawyers of Tenn before the war. Must get this off to-morrow. It will take two stamps and that is all I can spare now. Will try to continue the diary, and if I should be captured in the coming fight will have plenty of time in Libby to write, but expect to spend most of the time there devising plans of escape.

Your husband.

Lookout Mountain
and Missionary Ridge

GRANT had no sooner reached Chattanooga (on the evening of October 23) than he ordered into effect plans, already prepared, for relieving the siege. Within five days food and supplies were plentiful.

The next move was to sweep Bragg from his strong positions on Lookout Mountain south of Chattanooga and Missionary Ridge east of the town. The attack, made on November 24 and 25, succeeded beyond all expectations.

Chattanooga, Thursday, Nov. 26, 1863.

Dear wife:

I have just come down off Mission Ridge, up which we fought our way yesterday afternoon. My horse carried me up there without a girth to my saddle, but I can't tell how. We captured quite a good sized army in the way of prisoners and artillery. Right in front of our Division as we climbed the mountain, were massed 42 pieces of artillery, belching away at us, but they couldn't even scare us, as they couldn't depress their guns to reach us, but had to blaze away far over our heads. We captured all these guns. One of the first officers I saw at these guns was old Quartermaster General Meigs,[1] wild with excitement, trying himself, to wheel one of these guns on the rebels, flying down the opposite side of the mountain and furious because he couldn't find a lanyard with which to fire the gun.

Our advance to the base of the Ridge was the grandest sight I ever saw. Our line stretched along the valley for miles, in the open field, in plain view of the rebels on the mountain top, and at a given signal all moved forward as if on parade, through the open valley to the foot of the mountain, then without further orders, slowly, steadily, but broken into irregular groups by the inequalities of the face of the mountain, that long line climbed up the mountain, mostly on hands and knees, amid a terrible storm of shot, shell and bullets; the rebels were driven from their entrenchments on the mountain side, and on our gallant boys went, officers and men mingled together, all rank forgotten, following their old flag away to the mountain top, a struggle for a moment and our flag was planted here and there by scores of color bearers, on the very crest of the Ridge, battery after battery was taken, battle flags and prisoners captured, and the men indeed seemed perfectly frantic—rushing down the opposite side of the mountain after the flying rebels, regardless of officers, orders or anything else.

I slept on the ground on top of the Ridge last night, and when I waked this morning found myself lying within three feet of a dead man who, I thought, was lying there asleep when I laid down there in the dark last night. I have no time

1. One of the great soldiers of the war. Montgomery C. Meigs, graduate of West Point, class of 1836, was appointed Quartermaster General of the Army on May 15, 1861, and served in that capacity until the end. Described as "old" by Connolly, Meigs had, in fact, attained the advanced age of forty-seven in the fall of 1863.

LOOKOUT MOUNTAIN   151

to write more; one brigade of our Division started in pursuit
this morning, the rest of the Division may be off when I get
back to where I left it, so I must hurry.

Thank God I am again unhurt, and in excellent health.
Chattanooga is full of prisoners. They are non combatants
now, and Grant will remove them to a safe place in accordance
with the notice Bragg gave him some days since.

                                            Your husband.

                                    Chattanooga, Dec. 7, 1863.
Dear wife:

I received your letter written Nov. 26, on the 3rd day of
this month, and when your letter was brought to my tent I
was lying on my cot indulging in some vigorous remarks
concerning mules in general, and one mule in particular, which,
about two hours before, had given me a hard kick on the leg
as I was riding past him, cold and hungry, just returning with
my Division from the pursuit of Bragg and his valiant cavaliers
whom we so handsomely "cleaned out" as the soldiers say.
On Monday, Nov. 23rd our Division was ordered to move out
just in front of the fortifications. We did so, and the rebels,
as they looked down on us from Lookout Mountain and Mission
Ridge, no doubt thought we had come out for a review. But
Sheridan's Division followed us out and formed in line with
us. Wonder what the rebels thought then? "Oh, a Yankee
review; we'll have some fun shelling them directly." But out
came Wood's Division, then Cruft's Division, then Johnson's
Division, then Howard's entire Corps of "Potomacs." "What
can those Yankee fools mean," Bragg must have thought, as
he sat at the door of his tent on Mission Ridge and watched the
long lines of blue coats and glistening guns marching around
in the valley below him, almost within gun shot of his pickets,
and yet not a gun fired. All was peace in Chattanooga valley
that day.

The sun shone brightly, the bands played stirring airs; tattered banners that had waved on battle fields from the Potomac to the Mississippi streamed out gaily, as if proud of the battle scars they wore. Generals Grant and Hooker, and Sherman and Thomas and Logan and Reynolds and Sheridan and scores of others, with their staffs, galloped along the lines, and the scene that spread out around me like a vast panorama of war filled my heart with pride that I was a soldier and member of that great army. But what did it all mean? Bragg, from his mountain eyrie, could see what we were doing just as well as Grant who was riding around amongst us. The rebels thought they had us hemmed in so that we dared not move, and so near starved that we could not move. Two o'clock came, and all was yet quiet and peaceful, gay as a holiday review; we could see crowds of rebels watching us from Mission Ridge and Lookout Mountain, but three o'clock came, and a solitary shot away over on our left, among Wood's men, made every fellow think: "Hark!" A few moments and another shot, then a rat-tat-tat-tat made almost every one remark: "Skirmishing going on over there." Wood's line moved forward, a few volleys, still Wood's line moved forward, and Sheridan's started forward, heavy work for a few minutes then all was quiet; two important hills were gained; cheer after cheer rang out in the valley and echoed and reverberated through the gorges of Lookout and Mission Ridge; still it was only 5 o'clock Monday afternoon. The bands commenced playing and the valley was again peaceful, but we all knew there was "something up," and Bragg must have thought so too. We lay there all night, sleeping on our arms.

Tuesday morning, Nov. 24th, broke bright and beautiful; the sun rose clear; but for whom was it a "sun of Austerlitz"? Grant or Bragg? We talked of Austerlitz and Waterloo at headquarters that morning. During the night the moon was almost totally eclipsed. We talked of that also. It was con-

sidered a bad omen among the ancients, on the eve of battle;
we concluded also that it was ominous of defeat, but not for
us; we concluded that it meant Bragg because he was perched
on the mountain top, nearest the moon. Daylight revealed the
hills which Wood and Sheridan had won the day before, bristling
with cannon of sufficient calibre to reach Bragg's eyrie on
Mission Ridge. About 9 o'clock in the morning some 30 heavy
guns opened on Mission Ridge. It appeared then that we were
to advance right down the valley and attack the rebel centre,
but, hark! Away off on our right—3 miles away, on the opposite
side of Lookout—we hear firing. What can that mean? Suddenly the cannon, with which we have been pounding away
at Mission Ridge, are silent, and all eyes are turned westward
toward Lookout Mountain. The sounds of battle increase there
but it is on the other side of the mountain from us and we
can see nothing, but the word passes around: "Hooker is
storming Lookout!" My heart grows faint. Poor Hooker, with
his Potomac boys are to be the forlorn hope! What? Storm that
mountain peak 2400 feet high, so steep that a squirrel could
scarcely climb it, and bristling all over with rebels, bayonets
and cannon? Poor boys! far from your quiet New England
homes, you have come a long way only to meet defeat on that
mountain peak, and find your graves on its rugged sides!
Lookout Mountain will only hereafter be known as a monument
to a whole Corps of gallant New Englanders who died there
for their country! But hold! Some one exclaims: "The firing
comes nearer, our boys are getting up!" All eyes are turned
toward the Mountain, and the stillness of death reigns among
us in the valley, as we listen to the sounds of battle on the
other side of the Mountain while all was quiet as a Puritan
sabbath on our side of it. How hope and despair alternated in
our breasts! How we prayed for their success and longed to
assist them, can only be known by those of us who, in that
valley, stood watching that afternoon and listening to the

swelling diapason of their battle. But the firing actually did grow nearer, manifestly our men were driving them; Oh! now if they only can continue it, but we fear they cannot! I have a long telescope with which I can distinctly see everything on our side of the mountain. I scan the mountain with it closely and continuously, but not a soul can I see. After hours of anxious suspense I see a single rebel winding his way back from the firing and around to our side of the mountain.

I announce to the crowd of Generals standing around: "There goes a straggler!" and in an instant everybody's glass is to his eye, but no more stragglers are seen, still the battle rages, and the little gleam of hope, that solitary straggler raised in our breasts, dies out. Minutes drag like hours, the suspense is awful, but look! look! Here comes a crowd of stragglers! here they come by hundreds, yes by thousands! The mountain is covered with them! They are broken, running! There comes our flag around the point of the mountain! There comes one of our regiments on the double quick! Oh! such a cheer as then went up in the valley! Manly cheeks were wet with tears of joy, our bands played "Hail to the Chief," and 50 brazen throated cannon, in the very wantonness of joy, thundered out from the fortifications of Chattanooga, a salute to the old flag which was then on the mountain top. The work was done. Lookout was ours, never again to be used as a perch by rebel vultures. Didn't we of the old Army of the Cumberland feel proud though? It was one of the regiments that fought at Chickamauga that carried that first flag to the mountain top. It was a brigade of the old Chickamauga army that led the storming party up the mountain. A straggling skirmish fire was kept up along our (the eastern) side of the mountain, which we could trace by the flashes of the guns, until 11 o'clock at night, but then all became quiet, and again we passed the night in line of battle, sleeping on our arms.

Bragg, no doubt, thought Hooker would continue to press

forward across the valley from Lookout and attack his left on
Mission Ridge in the morning, so he prepared for that during
the night, by moving troops from his right to his left, to meet
the anticipated attack of the morning, but Sherman, with his
Vicksburg veterans, had all this time been lying concealed behind the hills on the north side of the Tenessee river, just
north of the northern end of Mission Ridge, where Bragg's
right was, awaiting the proper moment to commence his part
of the stupendous plan. The time was now come. Lookout was
ours; now for Mission Ridge! Before daylight of Wednesday
Nov. 25th, Sherman had his pontoons across the river, about
3 miles north of Chattanooga, and under cover of a dense fog,
crossed his whole Corps and took possession of the northern
extremity of Mission Ridge, finding nothing there but a few
pickets, and there he fell to work fortifying. By this time Bragg
saw his mistake. The attack of Wednesday was to be on his
right, at the North end of Mission Ridge, instead of his left
at the South end of the Ridge, so he hurriedly countermarched
his troops back from his left to his right. When the fog rose,
about ten o'clock in the morning, Sherman attempted to carry
the summit of the Ridge but was repulsed; again he tried it
but was again repulsed, still again he tried it and was repulsed.

This time the fighting was all to the left of where we were
instead of to the right, as it had been the day before. Sherman,
after terrible fighting, had been repulsed in three successive
efforts to crush the enemy's right on the top of the Ridge, and
an order came for our Division to move up the river to his
support. We started. The enemy could see us from the top of
the Ridge, and quickly understood (or thought they did) our
design, so they commenced shelling us, as our long line of 20
regiments filed along, but we moved along until we came to
where a thin strip of woodland intervened between us and the
Ridge. Sheridan's Division followed us and did the same.
The enemy supposed of course that we were moving on up

the river to the support of Sherman, but we were not; we halted and formed line of battle in that strip of woodland, facing Mission Ridge. This, I confess, staggered me; I couldn't understand it; it looked as though we were going to assault the Ridge, and try to carry it by storm, lined and ribbed as it was with rifle pits, and its topmost verge crowded with rebel lines, and at least 40 cannon in our immediate front frowning down on us; we never could live a moment in the open spaces of 600 yards between the strip of woods in which we were formed, and the line of rifle pits at the base of the mountain, exposed as we would be to the fire of the 40 cannon massed, and from five to eight hundred feet immediately above us, also to the infantry fire from the rifle pits.

I rode down along the line of our Division, and there I found Woods Division formed on our right and facing the Ridge just as we were; I rode on and came to Sheridan's Division formed on Woods right and facing the same. Here was a line of veteran troops nearly two miles long, all facing Mission Ridge, and out of sight of the enemy. The purpose at once became plain to me, and I hurried back to my own Division, and on asking Gen. [Baird] he replied: "When 6 guns are fired in quick succession from Fort Wood, the line advances to storm the heights and carry the Ridge if possible. Take that order to Col. [Edward H. Phelps]" (commanding the third brigade of our Division) "and tell him to move forward rapidly when he hears the signal." I communicated the order at once and that was the last I saw of the brigade commander, for he was killed just as he reached the summit of the Ridge.

A few moments elapse, it is about half past three o'clock P. M., when suddenly, 6 guns are rapidly fired from Fort Wood. "Forward!" rings out along that long line of men, and forward they go, through the strip of woods, we reach the open space, say 600 yards, between the edge of the woods and the rifle pits at the foot of the Ridge. "Charge!" is shouted wildly from hundreds of throats, and with a yell such as that valley never heard before, the three Divisions (60 regiments) rushed forward; the rebels are silent a moment, but then the batteries on top of the Ridge, open all at once, and the very heavens above us seemed to be rent asunder; shells go screaming over our heads, bursting above and behind us, but they hurt nobody and the men don't notice them; about midway of the open space a shell bursts directly over my head, and so near as to make my horse frantic and almost unmanageable; he plunges and bursts breast strap and girth and off I tumble with the saddle between my legs. My orderly catches my horse at once, throws the blanket and saddle on him, gives me a "leg lift" and I am mounted again, without girth, but I hold on with my knees and catch up with our madcaps at the first rifle pits, over these we go to the second line of pits, over these we go, some of the rebels lying down to be run over, others scrambling up the hill which is becoming too steep for horses, and the General and staff are forced to abandon the direct ascent at about the second line of rifle pits; the long line of men reach the steepest part of the mountain, and they must crawl up the best way they can 150 feet more before they reach the summit, and when they do reach it, can they hold it? The rebels are there in thousands, behind breastworks, ready to hurl our brave boys back as they reach their works.

One flag bearer, on hands and knees, is seen away in advance of the whole line; he crawls and climbs toward a rebel flag he sees waving above him, he gets within a few feet of it and hides behind a fallen log while he waves his flag defiantly until it almost touches the rebel flag; his regiment follows him as fast as it can; in a few moments another flag bearer gets just as near the summit at another point, and his regiment soon gets to him, but these two regiments dare not go the next twenty feet or they would be annihilated, so they crouch there and are safe from the rebels above them, who would have to rise up, to fire down at them, and so expose themselves to the fire of our fellows who are climbing up the mountain.

The suspense is greater, if possible, than that with which we viewed the storming of Lookout. If we can gain that Ridge; if we can scale those breastworks, the rebel army is routed, everything is lost for them, but if we cannot scale the works few of us will get down this mountain side and back to the shelter of the woods. But a third flag and regiment reaches the other two; all eyes are turned there; the men away above us look like great ants crawling up, crouching on the outside of the rebel breastworks. One of our flags seems to be moving; look! look! look! Up! Up! Up! it goes and is planted on the rebel works; in a twinkling the crouching soldiers are up and over the works; apparently quicker than I can write it the 3 flags and 3 regiments are up, the close fighting is terrific; other flags go up and over at different points along the mountain top—the batteries have ceased, for friend and foe are mixed in a surging mass; in a few moments the flags of 60 Yankee regiments float along Mission Ridge from one end to the other, the enemy are plunging down the eastern slope of the Ridge and our men in hot pursuit, but darkness comes too soon and the pursuit must cease; we go back to the summit of the Ridge and there behold our trophies—dead and wounded rebels under our feet by hundreds, cannon by scores scattered up and down the Ridge with yelling soldiers astraddle them, rebel flags lying around in profusion, and soldiers and officers completely and frantically drunk with excitement. Four hours more of daylight, after we gained that Ridge would not have left two whole pieces of Bragg's army together.

Our men, stirred by the same memories, shouted "Chickamauga!" as they scaled the works at the summit, and amid the din of battle the cry "Chickamauga!" "Chickamauga!" could be heard. That is not *fancy* it is *fact*. Indeed the plain unvarnished facts of the storming of Mission Ridge are more like romance to me now than any I have ever read in Dumas, Scott or Cooper. On that night I lay down upon the ground without blankets and slept soundly, without inquiring whether my neighbors were dead or alive, but, on waking found I was sleeping among bunches of dead rebels and Federals, and within a few rods of where Bragg slept the night before, if he slept at all.

You must not think that the General and staff remained at the second line of rifle pits on the side of the mountain, where I left them a few pages back, until the fight was over. The steepness of the mountain compelled us to zigzag back and forth, ascending a little with every zigzag until we reached the summit while the hand to hand melee was going on, before the rebels broke away down the eastern slope.

Early next morning I rode back to my quarters in the city, where I am now writing, got a new saddle girth and wrote you a brief letter, just to let you know I was safe. That was Nov. 26th, Thanksgiving Day in the United States, I believe, and it was the same with me, though my "Thanksgiving Dinner" was hard tack and raw bacon, but it was toothsome as turkey, for hunger makes fine sauce, you know. You wrote me that same day. After writing my hasty letter to you I hurried back to the Ridge and found my Division gone in pursuit of Bragg, but I soon overtook it, and we bivouacked for the night without having overtaken the enemy. On that night (26th) I rolled up in my saddle blanket and slept on the ground soundly. We started at two o'clock, on the morning of the 27th, and reached Chickamauga Creek, the bridge over which the rebels had burned in their retreat, and by daylight we had a bridge over it and marched to Greyville, where we met Davis' Division, which had moved by a different road and had captured a battery of 300 rebels in a fight there that morning. Davis had moved by a shorter road and arrived there ahead of us. I wasn't *very* sorry for it, for by him getting there before us he saved

us a fight, and I like to dodge fights, but appear to have poor
success at it, and a fellow stands a chance of getting just as
badly hurt in a little fight as in a big one.

After halting a few moments at Greyville we started in a
Southeasterly direction, toward Ringgold, where we heard the
sound of a battle going on, and Gen. [Palmer], our Corps
Commander, rightly supposed that Hooker, who had taken
that road, had come up with the enemy. After marching ten
miles very rapidly we reached Hooker and found him hotly
engaged with the enemy; our Division was soon in line and
ready for the word to "go in" but the rebels withdrew, and
fell back to Dalton. We bivouacked at Ringgold on that night
(27th) and the next day one brigade of our Division was
sent down the railroad toward Dalton to destroy the railroad
bridges. I asked leave to accompany this brigade, as I had been
over the road with [Wilder's] brigade of mounted infantry,
before the battle of Chickamauga, and knew the country and
location of the railroad bridges. The General gave me leave
to go and direct the expedition, so I went along. We burned
5 railroad bridges, tore up and burned the ties of a mile of the
track, took some prisoners, one of them a lieutenant on the
staff of Gen. Joe Johnston, and found the houses along the road
filled with dead and wounded rebels, whom we left as we
found. We got back to Ringgold, in the rain, before dark, and
bivouacked for the night, (28th). Gen. Turchin, who had a
couple of tents along in a wagon which he had brought with
him, loaned us a tent, and we all, General and staff, rolled
up in our saddle blankets and slept together under that tent.
I enclose a rough pencil sketch, made by one of our staff
officers, depicting a portion of our staff that night just before
we got any supper. Gen. [Baird], you see, is making desperate
efforts to fry his own supper, consisting entirely of fresh pork.
The African, with frying pan is endeavoring to provide something for the rest of us.

No other incidents of note occurred until we returned to Chattanooga, except, as we were returning, I was riding through the woods in company with Gen. [Palmer], our Corps commander, and his staff, when we came across a caisson, loaded with shells, which the rebels had abandoned.

Gen. [Palmer] ordered me to find my Division commander and have him bring the caisson in to Chattanooga. I couldn't find my Division commander nor any team that could haul it in, so I went to work with the assistance of my orderly, and knocked some weatherboards off an old church near by, and built a rousing fire under the caisson, but had to hurry away from it after I got my fire well started, and hadn't gone far until the fire reached the powder, and then I had the fun of hearing 90 rebel shells explode together, and I tell you, it made something of a racket in those old Georgia woods. I am glad now that I didn't ask for leave of absence before the fight, for I should have missed it, and should always have regretted it. I shall now get one as soon as I can. Gen. Reynolds has gone to New Orleans to take command there. I should have been glad to go with him, but if I did I wouldn't have got home until the close of the war, and I couldn't think of that. There are many things I intended to write about when I began this, which I have omitted, but this is long enough, and I'll quit. . . .

Your husband.

Chattanooga, Dec. 9, 1863.

Dear wife:

I received, to-day, your letter of 28th ult. It is a good one, well and spicily written, and was full of little items decidedly interesting.

Dec. 10. Just as I had written the word "interesting" in the line above, a party of friends came into my tent and that ended my letter writing for the night. Calls are often made at inopportune times, as you have no doubt discovered, but one must do as he is advised to do at the picture gallery, "look pleasant." I was in good humor last night and was sorry to be interrupted, but I can't say I'm in bad humor now, so I think I will try and finish the letter. On reading your remarks relative to "Vic" my mind ran back to certain "Lines to Vic," in "The Commercial" of long since, and I had a quiet little laugh all to myself. What funny pranks Time plays with the bright little romances of our "girl and boy" days. The romantic poetaster of a very few years since, now sits, solitary, in his muslin house on the bank of the Tennessee and thanks his stars that he has an assurance of plenty of pork and hard tack for his morrow's breakfast, while she, for whom he racked his brains to find jingling rhymes, has settled down into a quiet, steady materfamilias. Why the mischief don't Major ──────── marry somebody? He has fought, fled and flickered for his country; he's an old soldier, and ought to have the blessings of a helpmate to brighten his declining years. But here am I, talking about the blessings of a helpmate, just as if I knew anything about it; I guess I had better wait until I can speak with more experience.

I sometimes think that when I do get home it will require the services of another clerical gentleman to convince us we are within Hymen's dominions. I told Gen. [Baird], a couple of days since, that I was going home soon if I had to have a fight for it, and he said that after the troops get back from Knoxville that had gone there to reinforce Burnside, he would fix it so I could get home. Good for him! I am having the easiest time now I have ever had in the service. I see that the pickets are properly posted and instructed every morning and inspect Government property in this Division. I have a clerk who prepares all my official papers and an orderly who does my errands; have a wall tent for myself and one for my office, which my clerk occupies. All this is very nice, but I don't

feel that I am earning what the government pays me. I could
do ten times as much official work as I have to do, and it seems
like waste. There are too many staff officers in our army,
lounging around, doing little or nothing. I have been accustomed
to something different—hard work in the field day after day,
continually, for weeks at a time, and I then felt happy and
contented. After all a little spice of danger, every day, is an
excellent thing; it drives away the blues and gives to the
soldier's life that dash of romance which makes pictures on
the memory that never fade, but will return

  "In the night time of sorrow and care
  To bring back the features that joy used to wear."

But I've learned enough about soldiering to know that it's
not worth one's while to go out to hunt up danger just for
the sake of laying up a stock of romance; one gets enough of
it in the ordinary course of events. I have not answered that
Mt. Vernon letter yet. I have been a careless fellow about
writing, and have spent many an hour sleeping that I might
have well used in writing to my friends, but whenever I take
a notion to punish any one with a letter you are generally the
victim decided on. When I get to thinking about the way I
am spending my time, I feel just as I used to during the long
vacation, and I think, "My boy you've got to buckle down to
your books and study hard in return for these idle days you
are passing." It sometimes seems to me that when I get
home I shall have forgotten what little I ever did know, and
have to learn everything over again. I actually feel that I have
lost a great deal of valuable time *"patrioting"* up and down and
over and through the lines of this rebellious Confederacy, and
I don't see how I'm going to make it up. Some one, though,
consoles me by telling me: "You are doing your duty to your
country." That's all very fine, but when I, and thousands of
others like me, risk neck and everything else, to run down

such villains as John Morgan,[2] you stay-at-home patriots are too intent on making money to take care of them, but turn them loose to harass us again.

Ohio is a poor stick—she permits traitors to run as candidates for Governor, and opens the doors of her penitentiary to turn loose a band of cutthroats to prey upon her sons in the field. Shame! Shame! upon Ohio. John Morgan will never be turned over to her again, to hold as a prisoner; she can't be trusted. Aren't you sorry you belong in Ohio? If to-morrow is a clear day I'm going to ride up to the top of Lookout Mountain. It is said one can see seven states from its summit. Some of these days we'll go up there together. I sent some money, some time since, by an acquaintance who was going North, to get me a uniform coat, and sent the measure by him. It seems he bought the biggest coat he could get for my money, for he brought me one big enough for myself and *all my family.* I sold it at a loss of ten dollars and gave myself credit for ten dollars worth of experience. I also had a jolly time "cussin" over it, for you should know that relieves one's feelings very much, at times when nothing else will do it. . . .

Your husband.

2. On July 8, 1863, Brig. Gen. John Hunt Morgan, with 3,000 horsemen, crossed the Ohio River below Louisville and started on a meaningless raid through Indiana and Ohio. Morgan and the remnant of his command were captured in eastern Ohio three weeks later. The soldiers were sent to prison camps, the officers confined in the Ohio penitentiary. Morgan and six others escaped on the night of November 27, 1863.

A Period of Preparing

LATE in December, 1863, Connolly obtained a leave and spent several weeks with his wife at Mt. Gilead. On February 9, 1864, he reported for duty at Chattanooga. There he remained until February 22, when Thomas, on Grant's order, sent Baird's division and three others to seize the town of Dalton, Georgia, an important railroad junction. But the Confederate defenders, now commanded by General Joseph E. Johnston, proved to be too numerous and too well posted. The Union forces drew back, Baird's division to Ringgold, where it remained until May.

Chattanooga, Feb. 9, 1864.

Dear wife:

Arrived here at one o'clock this afternoon, after a series of most annoying detentions. I was detained 8 hours at Cincinnati, 16 hours at Seymour, 12 hours at Louisville, 21 hours at Nashville and 24 hours on the road from Nashville to Chattanooga. Could have made the trip nearly as soon, and quite as comfortably, on my horse.

I gave Gen. [Baird] that big apple you forced me to bring along. He appreciated it for it was a fine one and even poor ones are a rarity here. Everything is quiet here, but Chattanooga is much more lively than it was before the cars ran through. It seemed odd to me, to-day, to whisk along in a railroad train around Lookout Mountain, and over the very same ground where I cautiously stationed pickets but a few weeks ago. Now that I am back here I think of a thousand things I might have told you that would have interested you, but, somehow I couldn't think of them while there. It seems to me I was not at home more than a day. I bought "David Copperfield" at Cincinnati, and have reached the chapter on "Good and bad Angels" so if you don't hurry up I'll finish before you yet. I found my horse in very good condition, but my servant, during my absence, closed out my slender stock of camp "fixin's," such as water bucket, wash basin, blacking brush, curry comb, brush &c &c at "ruinous sacrifice," I suppose, and decamped for the North with the proceeds. It is rather cold here tonight, but I have a good fire in my tent, and am feeling first rate, but sleepy, so will make this short and shut up shop.

Your husband.

Chattanooga, Feb. 14, 1864.

Dear wife:

Although this is Sunday, yet it has not been a day of rest for me, but just before supper I came in and cleaned up, put on my best suit and fixed up generally, just as if I were preparing to accompany you to church, then I ate supper and returned to my tent, content to sit before my cheerful fireplace and feel that I had paid some respect to the Sabbath day by "dressing up."

As I sat there looking at the embers and blaze and curling smoke of my fireplace, I fell to thinking of David Copperfield, whose veritable history I finished last night. I sympathised with him in his struggles for fame, fortune and a wife, but I reproached him for his folly in taking for wife the "Little Blossom," Dora, while so pure, so loving and so gentle a being as Agnes, was silently waiting and watching on the margin of Life's stream, for the moment when his wayward heart should be turned to her. I was not happy when he married Dora. I didn't like her during the courtship; she pouted too much, and too often refused to look Life in the face, so I was sorry at the wedding of David and Dora; but I always liked Agnes, and when "Heep" was plotting to win her I wished him drowned, hung or "drafted in the army," but after David's return from foreign travel I enjoyed his visits to Canterbury and Agnes quite as much as he did himself, although his obtuseness and blindness provoked me, and I felt him a great dunce for persisting in loving her as a *sister* instead of as a *lover,* for it was evident that her whole heart was his, and he ought to have seen it sooner, but when he *did* see it I was happy with him, and rejoiced as much as he did at his wedding. In my musings I also recalled "Tom Traddles" and his "Sophy"; his years of waiting, of earnest labor and of constant hopefulness; I recalled the gush of merry girl laughter that greeted Copperfield when, after long absence, he returned to visit his friend "Traddles," and found him the happy husband of the happy "Sophy," who had waited for this happiness so long, and I fancied that, some day, some friendly Copperfield would visit another happy "Traddles" and happy "Sophy" in their own happy home, "when this cruel war is over."

Sometimes I wonder whether I am not too much like Mr. Micawber, always sanguine that "something will turn up," but, I guess upon the whole, I am not at all like him, for I know very well that nothing will turn up for me except what

I "turn up" myself. See what a tangent the reading of "David Copperfield" has started me off on. I have another novel, "Con Cregan," at my elbow which I shall commence as soon as I have finished this letter. You see I must read something, or my mind would become as rusty as a boy's jack knife that has been lost in a rubbish pile for a year or two, and in the absence of anything better I devour every novel I get hold of—that is during my leisure hours, principally evenings, for since my return I have been busy as a bee every day, inspecting government property and condemning such as is worn out or otherwise unserviceable, so as to prepare for a new outfit for the coming campaign, and just now I have so many "Inventories of Public Property" stacked up on my desk as to give my office quite a formidable appearance of business and red tape.

We have had rumors, for several days, that this Division is to move to Knoxville tomorrow morning, but we will not, yet I think we will move, in some direction, in a few days, probably before you receive this, but it will not be to Knoxville. I think it will be either Ringgold, Dalton or Lafayette. If we go to Dalton we will probably have a stiff fight before we get there, but we will start with men enough to whip them. You recollect the old woman in ——— who told my fortune. She told me I would be in no more battles; I hope she was right, but from the look of things here I think she was mistaken in the man, for my chances for a fight are excellent. One thing is certain, we have the rebellion "scotched" and its being "killed" is now regarded by this army as a question of short time. We may be too sanguine.

Twenty-four freight trains per day run to Chattanooga from Nashville, and army stores are rapidly accumulating here. I saw the 15th army corps moving across Lookout Mountain today, coming from Bridgeport; they are encamped just outside of our pickets tonight; that means business in some direction, but where or what is not yet developed. Deserters in yesterday report the rebels about to fall back from Dalton. I wish they would fall back from *every place* about 24 hours before we reach there; it would make the suppression of the rebellion much less destructive to human life, and much less disturbing to human nerves.

I had almost forgotten; this is Valentine's Day. "And you shall be my Valentine," then there's a whole lot more things of that sort which I can't recall just now, but consider them all said in the customary way. . . .

Your husband.

Chattanooga, Feb. 16, 1864.

Dear wife:

It is very cold to-night—think I shall almost freeze before morning. "Sunny South," eh? ugh! I thought I should do a large amount of work to-night, but my fingers get cold and I can't half write. My official papers must be well done whether my letters are or not, so a few minutes ago I tumbled them all to one side to wait for warmer weather, and thought I would go to bed, but it's so cold I'm almost afraid to commit myself to "the arms of Morpheus" lest I should awake in the embrace of Mr. John Frost, so I have concluded to cheat both Morpheus and Frost for a while, by shiveringly writing to you. Stick a pin here until I warm my fingers. Five minutes later. Fingers warm, and fire stirred up. Have been busy out doors all day, and it was so cold as to actually make my head ache. Happened to be present at a flag presentation to-day, in the camp of the 11th Ohio. The flag was an elegant silk one, presented by the ladies of Troy, Ohio, and purchased with funds of a "Ladies Aid Society." The citizen, delegated by the ladies to present it, made a spread eagle speech. I'd rather listen to Bragg's cannonade than to a citizen urging soldiers to stand by their flag.

Gen. John Beatty has resigned and gone home. I wish your

brother Henry was out of Libby. His regiment is in this Division, and he could be Topographical Engineer on the Division staff, as there is a vacancy now. Our Top. Engineer was thrown from his horse yesterday and had his leg broken in three places, which will close his military career for a good while, and he had just returned from a leave of absence day before yesterday; he has been married a little over a year and has been in the army ever since.

I'm sorry for him but am glad it was not I who was thrown. Another pin here until I fire up again. Five minutes later. All right again. . . .

There is still some talk of this Division moving somewhere. I guess we will, but when or where I don't know. I hope we may go where there are no armed rebels, they are such unfriendly creatures to us gentlemen in blue. I have not had time to see Johnathan Wood yet. The Division to which his regiment belongs is at Rossville, about 5 miles from here. If next Sunday is a pleasant day I shall ride out there and find him. If you could save all these letters I am writing you from the army I think I would enjoy reading them myself twenty years hence, when the memory of these events, of daily occurrence, will have become blurred and faded like old daugerrotypes. Remember this letter was written with cold fingers, while one side of me froze and the other roasted. If I sleep at all to-night I shall dream of writing you a warm letter, on a sheet of ice, with an icicle for a pen.

Your husband.

Chattanooga, Feb. 21, 1864

Dear wife:

Here I am on my fourth letter to you without having heard a single word from you, but I'm sure it is not your fault. Indeed you may not have received one of those letters. We march, to-morrow morning at 7 o'clock, on the road to Dalton. The order came at dark this evening. The 14th Army Corps alone moves out. I suspect though, that another Corps, the 15th, will move toward Dalton, to-morrow, by another road, from Cleveland. If that be the case we can take Dalton, but if we try it with the 14th Corps alone I think we will fail. It is probable, though, that this is intended only for a reconnaisance, to find out just what is there, for we take but 3 days rations and 60 rounds of ammunition. Still I expect we will have some fighting; indeed I am pretty sure of it, for it's just my luck to get into a fight every time I get outside of the picket line. If I had my way about it I'd stay inside the picket line. Well, such is war; it can't be carried on without fighting, so I'll accept it as a necessity, and stop crying about it. I didn't get up until about ten o'clock this morning, just because it was Sunday morning and I was lazy. I rode out to Chickamauga Station, found Mr. Wood, and spent a couple of hours with him.

The day was beautiful, the roads fine, my horse felt well and I enjoyed the ride very much. You must see this country with me sometime for it is great, and I know you would be delighted with it. But I must be up early in the morning, so I'll turn in to my cot now, and by this time to-morrow night I'll be rolled in my saddle blanket in front of a huge log fire, if I have good luck.

Your husband.

Ringgold, Ga., Feb. 26, 1864.

Dear wife:

We moved out from Chattanooga, Monday morning, and after hard fighting part of the time, reached within 4 miles of Dalton last evening, but were compelled to fall back last night to this place, a distance of four miles. I was in the saddle at half past two o'clk yesterday morning and was in it almost continuously, from that time, during the entire day and all last night until daylight this morning.

About an hour ago I lay down to sleep, but in five minutes was aroused by an order for a forward movement again, so while the troops are getting ready I am writing you this hasty pencil note. The only blood I shed in yesterday's fight came from scratching my face in riding through a briar patch to put our troops in position. I received yours of 17th on Monday, the same day we commenced this movement.

Day before yesterday, at Tunnel Hill, Ga., where we had a little skirmish, after the fighting was over, I rode up to a house and, on entering, found the occupant to be a widow, with three little children. Our soldiers had been in and carried away everything she had to eat. She was crying and her children were hanging to her and crying as though their little hearts would break. It was more than I could stand, but what could I do to relieve them? I had no food, but I felt in honor bound to do something, so I gave her a ten dollar greenback and turned away and left her with almost as heavy a heart as the poor woman had. God help her. Last night after dark, while we were yet lying on the field of the fight, a little lamb came up to me bleating most piteously; I took it up in my arms, petted it until it fell asleep like an infant, and lay sleeping on my lap an hour. I couldn't think of leaving it there to starve, and I couldn't take it with me, so I carried it to a house, about a half mile distant, and gave it to a little girl who promised to take good care of it. These two incidents impressed me and I can't help making note of them. We start for Dalton again to-day. I expect there will be some tolerably sharp fighting, but it will be only for reconnoitering purposes. We'll get them, when we go after them in earnest.

                                        Your husband.

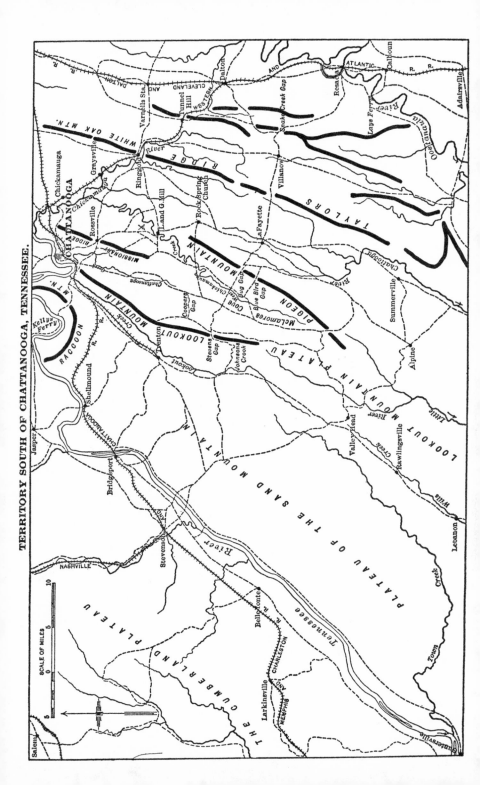

TERRITORY SOUTH OF CHATTANOOGA, TENNESSEE.

Chattanooga, March 5, 1864.

Dear wife:

It appears to me a long time since I have written you, but we have been campaigning some and that, you know, always interferes with correspondence. It turned out just as I expected, I got back from my leave just in time to be in the first fight my Division was engaged in. We were engaged with the enemy near Dalton, Ga., but you have, no doubt, learned all the particulars of our operations from the newspapers, before this time. The object of our reconnaisance was successfully accomplished, without very heavy loss on our side, and we retired about 12 miles, to Ringgold, Ga., where my Division is now stationed. We are on the extreme front, about 18 miles southeast from Chattanooga, with the rebel pickets in sight of ours. I left Ringgold yesterday, with an escort of ten men, under orders of our Division commander to inspect the roads leading from Ringgold to Chattanooga, and on reaching Chattanooga, to report to the corps Commander as to the condition of the roads and bridges. I reached here last night about 9 o'clock after a very fatiguing day's ride, and reported this morning. We will have the railroad in running order from here to Ringgold in 20 days, and then will be connected with the North once more. I think our situation at Ringgold will be very pleasant; it is quite a nice town, and had about 1,000 inhabitants before the war. All the business portion of the town was burned by our forces last fall, after the battle of Mission Ridge. Morris Baxter was killed in the battle at Ringgold. From my information something new, in the way of conducting the war, will be inaugurated within the next two months. I think your brother Henry escaped from Libby with the lot of officers who tunneled out, but fear he was recaptured, for I see that Lieut. H. C. *Duncan* was retaken, of the 10th Ky., and I suppose that means him, although the surname is not quite right.

Your husband.

Ringgold, Ga., March 10, 1864.

Dear Wife:

Some days since I received your letter, written at Massillon on Sunday, Feb. 24th. You guessed correctly, I have been in another engagement; I don't like 'em, but can't afford to miss when my command takes part. The enclosed letter, written with a pencil and dated Feb. 26th, was written hurriedly on the date it bears, that being the day after our engagement, but I had no envelope, no stamp and no opportunity to send it then, so I put it in my pocket where it has remained hidden away ever since until I discovered it this evening, and although a little stale, will enclose it and save writing the same things over again. We were just about to march when I wrote it, and I supposed we would stir up another fight before night, but we didn't and the next day we retired to Ringgold, where this Division has remained since. We are the extreme southern outpost of the army. Johnston's army is at Dalton, only 16 miles distant, supposed to be about 40,000 strong, while we are 18 miles from Chattanooga, and only about 5,000 strong. Some fine morning we may wake up to find Johnston's army all around us. Well, the worst they can do is to capture us, but I'll take care to see that our pickets are watchful and posted at every possible approach to our camp, that being my duty.

Day before yesterday morning I took the 38th Ohio regiment out to the front and put it on picket. The regiment has just returned from Ohio, having reenlisted as veterans. During the 24 hours they were on picket one of their recruits deserted to the enemy; we learn today, by conversation with some rebel officers under a flag of truce, that the deserter was one of

Morgan's officers who escaped from your Ohio penitentiary. Good for Morgan, and his men; they are sharp.

I wrote you a few days since from Chattanooga, where I had gone for the purpose of inspecting the roads between here and there. I started back here the next day after I wrote you, and on a new road. I had travelled this new road about 8 miles and was much pleased with it; thought it was the best road I had found for military purposes, and much the shortest, but after having gone that distance, I met a courier from a small cavalry force which had been guarding a pass in the mountains, and he informed me that the enemy had driven them away from the pass, and that if I went ahead I would probably meet with rebel scouting parties. I had nothing but my sword and a small pistol, my escort was only 8 mounted men armed with pistols and sabers, the enemy would probably outnumber us and be armed with carbines or Enfield rifles, so I concluded to practice Falstaff's strategy by countermarching and advancing briskly back to where I came, and I then took another and safer road to this place.

My quarters now are in a house, where our Medical Director [Surgeon F. Lloyd] and myself occupy a large pleasant room together. The furniture is not elegant but answers our purpose admirably. It consists of one cot in one corner of the room and another cot in another corner; my desk in one corner of the room and the Medical Director's in another, four split bottomed chairs, a little box filled with tan bark, for a spittoon, at my desk, a snug fireplace at one end of the room; there are three windows, two looking south toward a mountain called Taylor's ridge and one looking east upon White Oak mountain, where Morris Baxter, poor fellow, fell. Wilder's brigade of mounted infantry was the first Federal force that entered Ringgold; that was last September, and this was then a handsome town of about 1000 inhabitants, but now the scars of war mar its beauty, and, save a few scattering houses, nothing but shapeless piles of brick and lone chimneys is left to mark the site of the town of Ringgold.

All this country was occupied by the Cherokee Indians until 25 or 30 years ago; there used to be a Cherokee village here, and the house which was built by a chief of their tribe, Dick Taylor, (after whom the mountain is named) was burned here a few weeks ago by a party of our cavalry. Were it not for the prowling rebel scouts, I should like to roam around over these mountains and through these valleys, for they are filled with traces of the red man. I did venture some distance out this morning to see an Indian mound, situated in an open plain, and about 15 feet in diameter at the base, gradually sloping upward about ten feet and terminating in a point. I rode slowly around it, musing upon the many changes that valley had seen since the day when, probably, some party of Indian braves had quietly reared 'that mound as a resting place for some lost chieftain, where his spirit might encamp forever, in the midst of the hunting grounds of his tribe. What beautiful superstitions the Indian entertained; so full of poetry and of faith in a Supreme Being. Longfellow, in his "Hiawatha," beautifully alludes to that faith, when he speaks of the Indian *stretching out his hand in the darkness and touching God's right hand.* Speaking of Longfellow reminds me of the days when I used to read books, but now I rarely look inside of one unless it be a novel. What a waste of precious time!

Dear little Jennie dead! the sweet little flower transplanted to God's garden; I can well imagine how the little jewel

"Untouched by sorrow and unsoiled by sin"

is missed from that pleasant household. I can see her now, as she sat upon my knee and talked to me in her childish prattle, and it seems strange to me that those bright eyes should be forever closed in death. Present my condolences and kindest regards to the sorrowing parents, and I trust that the Christian's hope of meeting the lost darling, happy, in a fairer world, may soon remove the shadows from their hearts. There are about 200 documents, reports &c on my table, awaiting my attention, and I can't write any more until they are disposed of. Good night.

Your husband.

Ringgold, Sunday, March 13, 1864.

Dear wife:

I received a letter from you today, just as I was mounting my horse, and read it as I rode along. I'll write you one now.

"But how it may turn out, let time and chance determine;
Perhaps it may turn out a sang, perhaps turn out a sermon."

There is not much music about me just now though, so the chances are that it will not be much of a song, and as piety is a scarce article here there is not much probability of its being a sermon.

On looking again at the lines I have quoted above I find, that while writing them I was paying more attention to a conversation being carried on in the room, between two surgeons than I was to my Burns, for I have misquoted. Let me correct it:

> "But how the subject theme may gang,
> Let Time and Chance determine;
> Perhaps it may turn out a sang,
> Perhaps turn out a sermon." [1]

There, that's more creditable to "Bobby."

This is a bright, warm, sunshiny Sabbath. The birds are making the mountains and valleys vocal with their songs;

1. "Epistle to a Young Friend."

wild flowers bedeck the fields and mountain sides; the peach trees are in full bloom, and everything serves to make time pass pleasantly for us. On my ride this afternoon, after winding through several mountain gorges and climbing mountain sides by bridle paths, I found myself on top of White Oak mountain, looking down almost directly into the few remaining chimneys of Ringgold, on the one side, while on the other side, toward the East, the view stretches far away to the Cohuttah mountains, a part of the range dividing North Carolina from Tennessee. Looking to the northwest, and apparently but a few miles away, I saw Lookout looming up like a giant, and near its base, the camp fires at Chattanooga curling up. Looking southeast I saw the rebel videttes sitting on their horses in the road leading to Dalton, the smoke ascending from rebel camp fires at Tunnell Hill, between here and Dalton, and could discern every spot at which rebels are encamped in our front for many miles, by the smoke that curled up amongst the pine trees. On the top of this mountain, where they will never be disturbed by the ploughshare of the farmer, I found graves, graves of Ohio boys; fourteen of them lay there side by side, fitly sleeping their last long sleep on the mountain which their valor helped to win. They belonged to the 76th Ohio. This used to be an Indian village, and I can well imagine the pleasure of the Indian as he roamed, unrestrained, amongst these picturesque mountains and valleys and fished in these streams.

Major [Lowrie], the Adjutant General of this Division, was married in Pittsburg last November, and after his marriage, left his bride as suddenly as I did when we were married. He left the day after his marriage, but he looks so woe begone that I fear he is suffering from "nostalgia." I don't believe I ever looked as solemn about it as he does, and if I feel it I shall not let any one know it if I can help it.

There will be considerable fighting *somewhere* before long, and I think it will be an advance on Atlanta, judging from the amount of supplies being accumulated at Chattanooga. The railroad is finished half way between here and Chattanooga, and I think will be finished to this place next week. This is the extreme southern out post of this army, but we are connected with Chattanooga and the North by telegraph. Send me some postage stamps.

Your husband.

Ringgold, March 16, 1864.

Dear wife:

After tea. Yes *tea*. For be it known that I am living just now like one in civilization; I am boarding with a retired merchant, and furnishing the leading rations. The family consists of the merchant, his wife, her sister, and his two children, a little boy about 5 years old and a little girl about 8 years old. The little boy didn't like me at first—said I was a Yankee and wouldn't speak to me—didn't like Yankees "because they burned Pa's store and killed our cow," but after many promises to let him ride my horse, I have so far succeeded in overcoming his prejudice against Yankees as to induce him to sit on my lap. The retired merchant is a Mr. Whitman. When Wilder's brigade first came through here last fall, before the battle of Chickamauga, it carried away on horseback his entire stock of goods, whereupon he put the key of his store in his pocket and retired from business. Then came the battle of Chickamauga, in which we were severely handled, all because of plundering Mr. Whitman's goods, of course, but Mission Ridge followed Chickamauga, and Hooker followed Bragg as far as this place, where a battle took place and the town was burned, including Mr. Whitman's store building, so Mr. Whitman is now completely retired from business, with *nothing* left of his store but the key to the burned building. I am sorry for him, for he is a very moderate man, and a Christian, I know, for he says grace over a very scanty meal. His wife is a good woman, barring her secesh sentiments; her sister is about 5 feet in length, the same in circumference, and about half that straight through. These dimensions are not from actual measurement, and may not be strictly accurate. There is a piano in the house and if the sister plays for us I shall deduct two or three feet from her circumference and add a cubit or two to her height. Really, and in sober earnest, I am living more comfortably now than I have since I've been in the service, and would be content to do the rest of my soldiering in Ringgold, but I don't expect to do it all here by any means. I have only 17 months more to serve, anyhow, and that is some consolation. . . .

Your husband.

Ringgold, March 20, 1864.

Dear wife:

It is Sunday night. I have just finished a letter to the Adjutant of my regiment, and it is late, but I can't think of retiring without a brief talk with you. Day before yesterday, I received three letters from you; one written at Mt. Gilead, Sept. 17, 1863, one at Mansfield, Oct. 8th and the third at Mt. Gilead, Oct. 26th. I wonder if my letters to you get hung up that way? They were a little old, that's true, but I was glad to get them. . . .

March weather is pretty much the same everywhere, I guess. Some days are like summer here, with trees and flowers blooming and birds singing; then this is followed by wintry blasts fit for the shores of Hudson's Bay. We have small pox and measles here in abundance, and, about tomorrow, I shall indulge in the luxury of vaccination.

Then I expect I'll have a jolly time for a few days. I was vaccinated once in "happier days" as Wilkins Micawber, the "Fallen Tower" would say, but for fear the *virtue* of the *virus* has been lost I'll take another dose of patent small pox. Tomorrow, after getting my small pox started, I shall go out and shoot some squirrels, if it is a pleasant day. As soon as our fishing season opens I shall have fine sport fishing here in the Chickamauga, provided we don't move. If I were where I could vote next fall I should vote for Lincoln, if he is to be a candidate, and he ought to be. I am afraid our late defeat in Florida is attributable to a desire to get possession of the State Capital, organize some kind of a State government, and thus get control of two or three electoral votes next fall. I don't like that kind of work, even if the end sought is good.

The first train from Chattanooga reached here about noon today, and on reaching here the whistle was blown loud and long, and, no doubt, before this time, the telegraph has announced to Jeff Davis, in Richmond, that the Yankees have completed the railroad to Ringgold, on learning which he will conclude that the Yankees are preparing to move on Dalton. It does look a little that way, but about that time Jeff may look for movements on many other points. . . .

Your husband.

Ringgold, March 22, 1864.

Dear wife:

. . . It has been snowing hard all day. Think of it! Snow in Georgia in the latter part of March! It commenced snowing last night about eleven o'clock and snowed steadily until nearly dark this evening, and the snow is now over six inches deep. I had to go out to the front this morning at seven o'clock, and post two regiments on picket, in the midst of as hard a snow storm as I ever saw in the North, and I discharged that duty as rapidly as possible, and was back in my comfortable quarters before the rest of the staff were up. The snow storm has ceased, the moon is shining beautifully, and the surrounding mountains are grand, robed in snowy mantles which glitter like silver in the moonlight. . . . Uncle Sam is indebted to me over five dollars for what I've done today, but really, I have not honestly earned one cent. I have done nothing for myself or anybody else, and today is a type of many, many days I've spent in the army. Every day thus spent incrusts the mind with a rust that will take two days to remove, and yet I go on permitting this rust to accumulate, trusting to the future to remove it. I know it is wrong but I guess I'm too lazy to do otherwise.

This is an odd strain of reflection for me to fall into, just because it snowed today and compelled me to lounge lazily by my fire, but I'd better thank my stars that I had a fire to lounge by, instead of being out in the snow with the men I placed on picket this morning. I wish the weather was settled so that the spring campaign might open in earnest; I am growing impatient; we have a certain amount of whipping to give the rebels this summer, and I am anxious to see the army getting at it. The Medical Director, who is sitting in the room with me, is so much inclined to talk this evening, and bothers me so much, that I have been compelled to write thus far by catching quiet moments between his questions and funny stories, so I guess I'll quit. He'd better be writing to *his* wife, and I've just told him so, but he says: "Oh, she don't expect me to write very often."

Your husband.

Ringgold, March 28, 1864.

Dear wife:

This is a very dark, muddy, March night, but I have brightened it somewhat by re-reading your last letter, and I propose to spend the rest of the evening, until bed time, talking to you. March 29th. Just as I had written the above there came a knock on my door; "Come in," and in came the General and Captain [Buttrick], aide de camp; the General proposed a game of whist, and of course, the Doctor and I were bound by the rules of hospitality, to accede to the wishes of our visitors, so this letter was laid aside and the Captain and myself seated ourselves as partners, for a rubber of whist with the General and the Doctor, and we beat them every game; we drank one bottle of sparkling Isabella wine during the evening, and our visitors withdrew about half past eleven; it was then too late for me to finish this letter so I concluded to defer it until, perhaps, tonight, but it is now about noon, and for fear something should occur again this evening to prevent me from writing, I have determined to write some now.

Five o'clock P.M.

At the above point the "thread of my discourse" was broken again, by an officer entering, who informed me that the General and staff would ride out to see the artillery practice at target firing. Being an ornamental member of the staff, it would never do for me to remain behind, so down went my pen, into the drawer went this letter, and in a few minutes I was booted, belted, buckled and spurred, mounted and dashing away with the General and staff, scattering mud over everybody that didn't keep at respectful distance, and receiving in return, no doubt, the hearty curses of pedestrians. Well, the artillerists fired their big guns, and didn't hit anything but the side of the mountain; our horses curveted, capered and pranced at the sound of the big guns, scattered lots of mud, and we all returned in a couple of hours, to eat cold dinners, and criticise the artillery practice.

After dinner I went out and inspected a few hundred cavalry equipments, such as sabers, carbines, revolvers, saddles, bridles, &c., &c., concluded to condemn the whole lot as worthless, came back, took a snooze, got up a little while ago because it's drawing near supper time, and, for fear something should turn up this evening, determined to proceed with this letter and get it as nearly finished before supper as possible. P'shaw! Here come some fellows, and I'll have to quit until after supper.

After supper. . . . I wrote to Andrew yesterday, and your letter containing stamps was handed me just as I had finished my letter to him, and I was sitting there, thinking where I could get some stamps, for I hadn't one to put on it; I had used my last one the day before. Yours came so opportunely that, as I opened it and saw them, I turned to the Doctor and said "Doctor who wouldn't have a wife? See, my wife has just sent me a lot of stamps, just what I needed most." "By George!" said the Doctor, "give me one Major, and I'll write to *my* wife to send *me* some, for I'm out," and thereupon he sat down and wrote to *his* wife, something he hadn't done before for many weeks. . . .

Your husband.

Ringgold, April 5, 1864.

Dear wife:

It has been quite a while since I've had a letter from you. Day after day I watched for the coming mail bag, only to be disappointed. I have speculated about misdirected letters, captured mails and everything else that could interfere with my mail, and then fell to thinking perhaps you are waiting and watching for letters from me, only to be disappointed the same as I am, so I determined to drop everything and write you this very afternoon.

A few days since I started out with a small cavalry escort and a Topographical Engineer, to examine and get a map of a certain road. As we rode along the Engineer asked me if I was married. I told him I was. He asked me my wife's maiden name, and I told him; he then said his wife is your cousin. On further inquiry I learned that he was Lieutenant McAbee, 11th Ohio and Top. Eng. on General Turchin's staff; that he is an artist by profession, his wife's maiden name was Bechtel, that she is at her father's near Massillon, and that they lived in New York for some time before he entered the army. I then remembered you telling me of a cousin who had married an artist and gone to New York to live, and concluded this must be the man. He is a nice fellow and a competent Engineer.

As we were riding along talking, I discovered a Johnnie off

to the left of the road, about a quarter of a mile distant, dodging along behind a fence, and running toward the mountain: spurring my horse over a low place in the fence by the roadside, and followed by a couple of the escort, we went tearing off over the fields at a rapid rate. The reb soon found it was no use to run, so he stopped; I reached him first, and he stretched out his hand as if to shake hands with me, the color was gone from his face, he shook as with an ague, and he couldn't utter a word. He had slipped away from his regiment near Tunnel Hill the night before, and had come home to see his wife, and had started back to his regiment when I caught him. He was mounted behind one of my men and we went by where his wife lived, so that she might see he was unharmed and bid him good bye. Poor woman, I felt sorry for her, and her four little children, as she and they stood around me in tears, entreating me to leave the husband and father with his helpless family, and promising that they would all go with him, tomorrow, within our lines, and that he would then give himself up as a prisoner, but I had to refuse and turn away with my captive, leaving that little family alone among the frowning mountains, for grim Despair to assume the husband's place by that wife's side, and gaunt hunger to pinch the cheeks and chill the blood of those innocent children, and as I write these lines, are the prayers of that lonely wife for her captive husband, stealing out from that lowly dwelling, creeping up that rugged mountain side and winging their way to heaven, or are the cries of the helpless famishing children rising from that broken home and reaching to the Throne above, there to be recorded against me? These are the little tragedies of war more dreadful to me than the larger ones. You have probably seen, by the papers, that [Charleston], Ill., has had its own little war.[2] Quite a "tempest

2. On March 28, 1864, a riot took place in Charleston between Union soldiers home on leave and Copperheads, of whom there were many in this part of the state. Nine men were killed and twelve wounded in the fighting.

in a teapot." I have no doubt John Barleycorn is responsible for that rebellion. The telegraph made it an extensive affair. The story of them being 1,000 strong, entrenched at [Cook's] Mills, &c., &c., is all a humbug, I'm sure. Some of those Illinois copperheads need killing *just a little,* but I want the killing done before I get home. There is but little encouragement to write letters when I can't be certain you will ever get them, so a short one will do as well as a long one and I'll quit here.

Your husband.

Ringgold, April 10, 1864.

Dear wife:

Just as I was about beginning this letter the mail carrier handed me your letter of April 4th. We had a grand review here yesterday; our Division was reviewed by Gen. Thomas. There were present at the review Gens. Thomas, Hooker, Palmer, Elliot, Geary, Brannan, Baird, Turchin, with their staffs; the day was splendid and we had a gala time; the Division made a fine appearance. It begins to look as though the Army of the Cumberland was to do the reviewing and *fancy* soldiering this summer while the Potomac Army will do the hard work, and if that's the arrangement I am perfectly satisfied.

I send you today a list of "Countersigns" and "Paroles" for the Army of the Cumberland, also a rebel order for retreat, which I picked up in Columbia, Tenn., last summer, and have carried in my pocket ever since. I thought they might be interesting, hereafter, as relics of the rebellion, and worth being preserved. If I should keep them here I would wear them out carrying them in my pocket.

I must go and call on Mrs. Gen. Turchin this afternoon. She sent me word that she wants me to call and post her in regard to that "rebellion" at [Charleston] Illinois. She is a great politician, keeps well informed on the current events of the war, has been in the field with the Gen. now nearly three years, and utterly detests copperheads. She is fine looking, intelligent and a thoroughly womanly woman. So General Sam [Beatty] thinks his namesake, Gen. John [Beatty] will now run for Congress. That shows where Gen. Sam's heart is fixed; he evidently aspires to Congress himself, and I suppose he would do for a member of Congress, even if he *does* spell Regiment, "Ridgement." [3] Teachers ought to know how to spell but soldiers and members of Congress don't need to. Even Washington and Jackson were poor spellers according to present standards. I am called away now and will close this or it may remain unfinished two or three days.

Your husband.

Ringgold, April 15, 1864.

Dear wife:

This is Friday evening. Thought I would have a letter from you today but am disappointed, so I'll get even with you by writing one to you. I have quit boarding with the retired merchant and have joined the mess of our Adjutant General and Medical Director, and we have white table cloths, napkins, &c, &c, and live well. I left my boarding place because they took a Sanitary Commission Agent and a telegraph operator to board without saying a word to me, and I preferred selecting my own company; they regretted my leaving very much, and entreated me to remain, but I declined.

I have done a good deal of work today, but the soldier who carries his musket all day would only call it sport, if he had done it. I am really getting quite tired of this kind of soldiering. I used to think, last summer, when skirmishing, marching and fighting was a daily business, that a staff position, with shiny

3. General John Beatty, Connolly's friend, resigned his commission on January 28, 1864, and returned to Cardington, Ohio, so that his brother William might have a chance to serve. Brigadier General Samuel Beatty, of Jackson, Ohio, had served two terms as county sheriff, and may well have had, as Connolly surmised, political aspirations.

boots, sleek horses, clean clothes, and plenty of ease and idleness, would be very fine, but I have tried both now, and must say that the wild, free, dashing life of last summer was preferable to this pompous ease and stylish dignity. In a few days, May, the Queen of the year, will come with her sunshine and flowers, and I expect this country will be beautiful, but the sunshine will come to glisten on the burnished armor of thousands of soldier boys marching to their graves, and the May flowers will come to form the dying beds of many heros, but better thus than that the sunshine and the flowers should, in the long years to come, shine on and garnish a Nation's tomb. I clip the enclosed slip from the Chattanooga Gazette of today. The lines struck me as being beautiful, and as I read them I fancied I could see that Swiss mother, in her Alpine home, looking out upon the same stars that watched her son in his lonely picket vigil, praying for his safety, and I could see her, as with kindling eye and glowing cheek she spoke of her son in Freedom's Army. And the soldier son too, I could see, as he paced his midnight round, watching the stars his mother watched, humming some song of freedom that his mother taught him in his childhood, in the land of Tell.

I pin the slip, with the caption "A Swiss mother's gift to the New York Sanitary Fair," hereto.

Your husband.

Ringgold, April 17, 1864.

Dear wife:

It is Sunday night, and I have just said: "Now Doctor stop your foolishness, and don't bother me until I've written my letter." This has been quite a pleasant day; the sun shone brightly, but the air was rather cool; apple trees are beginning to bloom, wild plum trees are wrapped in a white cloud of blossoms, and in a few days more summer will be upon us. I was up a little before sunrise this morning; my servant brought

into my room a tub of tepid water and I got out of bed into
the tub and had a good bath, dressed and stepped out on the
porch just in time to see the sun rise above White Oak Mountain, and apparently linger there a moment, as if to brighten
the graves of the fourteen Ohio boys, on the very mountain
top, just in front of, and east of my door. The morning air was
bracing. I wish it was as comfortable to get up with the sun
every morning as it is to lie in bed; then I could be an early
riser. On my return home which shall we do, board a while
or go to housekeeping at once? I don't know and I must ask
somebody. You ought to know. I am very well arranged now
for housekeeping *by myself;* I have a pillow, two pillow cases,
four blankets which I occasionally reinforce with a good heavy
saddle blanket, a cot, two split bottomed chairs, a table, a wash
basin and four crash towels. So far as everything goes except
the cot and pillow cases I have enough for *the whole family,*
so it is well enough to have a fair understanding as early as
possible. I can't find any books on the subject to read; the
"Army Regulations" or the "Infantry Tactics" don't discuss
the question, and the two great political parties have omitted
to say a word about it in their platforms, so how the mischief
is a body to decide the question? Do enlighten me on the subject.
If I had an "Aladdin" lamp to rub I might get some light on
the subject, but such lamps are not in use in this army.

It is raining a little this evening. Just now a dispatch has
come saying that Forrest has captured Fort Pillow on the
Mississippi, and massacred some 300 black soldiers who were
a part of the garrison.[4] If that be true it will create a hundred

4. On the early morning of April 12, 1864, Forrest pounced on Fort
Pillow, Tennessee, garrisoned by both white and colored Union troops.
Though facing hopeless odds, the Union commander refused to surrender, and
Forrest carried the fort by storm. Almost two-thirds of the defenders were
killed. In the North, it was widely believed that the Confederates, infuriated
by their contact with colored troops, had massacred the Negroes. The weight
of the evidence indicates that the very heavy loss of life was due to the stub-
bornness and incapacity of the Union commander.

fold more sympathy in the army for the negro than ever existed before, and will insure Forrest "a strong rope and short shrift" if he ever falls into the hands of negro soldiers. The Doctor says he has just thought of a funny story so I know I'll have to quit. Good night.

Your husband.

Ringgold, April 18, 1864.

Dear wife:

I didn't get up until eight this morning, simply because I didn't have to. At ten o'clock I inspected the General's escort, which occupied only half an hour, then I dropped into his room, and received an order to get a lot of picks, shovels and axes out to the picket reserve on top of Taylor's Ridge, select the ground for entrenchments and set the men at work fortifying. Taken somewhat aback at this order, I withdrew to my own room, lay down on my cot and began to inquire of myself what I knew about engineering, fortifying, entrenching &c, &c, and after a good deal of cogitation, concluded I didn't know anything worth while about such things. I thought of Gen. Pillow's famous fortifications in Mexico, wherein it was charged, he dug his ditch on the wrong side of the breastworks, and got himself laughed at by the country, for his blunder. I'll not make that same mistake, but may make some other. I got Cullum's "Art of War" and read a few pages on military engineering, laid it down in despair, went to sleep and slept until dinner; after dinner I started on my engineering expedition, selected the ground and commenced the work. Since returning this evening I think I didn't get the best ground, and I've a good mind to go out to-morrow and undo what I've done to-day. I think I shall.

We had another April shower this afternoon; it rained quite hard for a few minutes, then the sun came out hot and in a few minutes the rain was stealing away again to the clouds, like a bashful lover, after having kissed all the little flowers and caused them to blush scarlet; but the little flowers, like maidens —human flowers in God's garden—were evidently proud of the kiss, for, although they blushed and dropped their heads at first, yet they soon raised their heads and looked brighter and gayer all the afternoon.

In one of my letters not long since I told you that the small pox was prevailing here and that I intended to be vaccinated, but have never since thought of "reporting progress." I was vaccinated and expected to be sick, but having been vaccinated when a child, it wouldn't take this time, so the Doctor pronounces me "iron clad" with the *patent small pox*. I wish some Yankee "medicine man" would invent a method of vaccinating to prevent an attack of *bullets;* I would try it at once. We have no sensations here except an occasional deserter coming in, but that has become so common as to excite but little remark. If I had an industrious room mate I could do a good deal of reading and writing these days, but the Doctor is a good genial companion, not a bit industrious, will neither read nor write himself, and always has something to say or do to prevent me from writing, but "With all his faults I love him still." We heard something like heavy skirmishing northeast of here to-day, about ten o'clock; it continued about ten minutes, but up to this hour have not heard what it was.

Your husband.

Ringgold, April 19, 1864.

Dear wife:

It is night again; my routine duties for the day are done. Concluded my entrenchments were all right, so made no changes in them to-day. I've spent a very pleasant day, riding around wherever I pleased, inside and outside the picket lines, making calls &c. Called on Col. [Walker], of the [31st] Ohio. He was commanding a brigade until a few days before the battle of Chickamauga, when he was placed under arrest, charged with speculating in government horses, was deprived of his command, and his brigade placed under command of Col. [Phelps] of the [38th] Ohio, who had preferred the charges, but notwithstanding his being under arrest, he managed to get himself wounded at the battle, had his trial after the battle, and was acquitted, went home on leave and just got back a few days ago. Col. [Phelps] who preferred the charges was killed at Mission Ridge, so they will not quarrel any more.[5] One of our brigades had brigade drill this afternoon.

While I was wandering off down the mountain, a flag of truce came, and Miss Kate Sharp, with a pass from President Lincoln, came into our lines. I missed going out to meet the flag by being away from my quarters at the time.

Your husband.

Ringgold, April 20, 1864.

Dear wife:

It is night again. I think I am adhering pretty well to my resolution to write you every day. But I'm afraid you will get

5. The report of Brig. Gen. J. M. Brannan, commanding the Third Division, throws light on this episode: "Col. M. B. Walker, Thirty-first Ohio Volunteer Infantry, joined me shortly after we fell back to the ridge, and offered his services to me, as being in arrest he had no command. Being short of staff officers I accepted Colonel Walker's services, and well he served me and his country, rallying and collecting the men and encouraging them to stand by his energy and personal courage. I am much indebted to him." *Official Records,* Series I, Vol. XXX, Pt. 1, p. 404.

Connolly's letter does not quite square with the records. While Walker commanded a brigade until a short time before Chickamauga, Phelps did not take his place in that battle. In fact Phelps, the only Ohio colonel killed at Missionary Ridge, took no part in the Battle of Chickamauga. On that point Brannan's report is convincing: "The Thirty-eighth Ohio Volunteer Infantry (Colonel Phelps commanding), of the First Brigade, was detailed on the 18th as guard to the supply and general train of the division, and being subsequently ordered across the river by General Rosecrans, was unable to participate in the engagements of either day. The unavoidable absence of this splendid regiment is much to be regretted." *Ibid.,* pp. 404–05.

into the habit of expecting a daily letter from me, and after a while days will come when I can't write and then you'll be disappointed; still, "sufficient unto the day is the evil thereof." I'll write as often as I can, and when I can't you'll have to turn back and read the old ones. This has been a very fine day and I have ridden around most of the day, reconnoitering the surrounding country for the purpose of establishing a new picket line. Before starting out I provided myself with a map, made by Lieut. McAbee, of whom I have written you. A new regiment has been assigned to this Division, the [92nd] Illinois. It was mounted last July and assigned to a brigade of mounted infantry but now it seems to be dismounted and returned to the infantry. I suppose such details of army matters are not interesting to you, but in writing every day I have to mention such things in order to make a letter, for matters of news don't grow up very rapidly here within our picket lines. Don't think this army will move very soon although there is a constant stir of preparation; new clothing and camp and garrison equipment is being supplied to the men, new arms, ammunition &c, but if the authorities become satisfied that Johnston's army, in our front, is materially weakened, we will undoubtedly move out on him at Dalton soon. Judging from the time your letters are on the way, I suppose it takes my letters from 5 to 8 days to reach you so all my news is stale before you get it, except such trifles as are too small for the newspapers to pick up. . . .

Your husband.

Ringgold, April 22, 1864.
Dear wife:

I received two letters from you to-day, one written the 13th the other the 15th. . . .

We are all on the *qui vive* now; we begin to believe that we will move before the Potomac army, and although nothing is known positively, still it appears probable that the rebel army in our front is being weakened and that we will move out against them to take advantage of their weakness. Well I am ready at any time and all the time, on ten minutes notice, to move out. I received a letter from the adjutant of my regiment yesterday; from him I learn that almost every one of the original officers of my regiment is either dead or has resigned, and that the Lieut. Col. commanding, tendered his resignation a few days since, but afterwards withdrew it.[6] I don't want him to resign for then I would have to go and take command, and I don't care about doing that now. . . .

Your husband.

Ringgold, April 24, 1864.

Dear wife:

I received another letter from you to-day written at Massillon on the 18th. You can't fully understand how the wanderer appreciates these little messengers from home telling of scenes of peace and quiet among friends and kin. This was a beautiful morning; it rained last night and this morning, when I went out, the mountains and valleys were robed in fresh green, the atmosphere pure, the sun shone in a cloudless sky and I never felt better in my life than I did when I stepped out on the porch before breakfast. *Don't* you wish you were here to enjoy some of these magnificent mornings? I do.

The question of an early move is being extensively agitated now, and all things indicate that we will soon be on the war path. We are all anxious to enter Atlanta, and don't care how soon we move out.

My time for letter writing is evidently getting short, for when we move my chance of writing will not be good. If you see Gen. Beatty give him my compliments and tell him I'm still on my

6. Lieutenant Colonel Jonathan Biggs of Mattoon, who succeeded to the command of the 123rd Illinois upon Colonel Monroe's death. Biggs stayed with the regiment until it was mustered out.

way to Atlanta, although not much advanced beyond where he
left me.

                              Your husband.

                              Ringgold, April 26, 1864.
Dear wife:
   I didn't write you last night because I got in after dark, very
tired, having been in the saddle all day in command of a detachment of cavalry on a scout in search of rebels. We got up quite
a scare here yesterday morning by some scouts coming in and
reporting that the enemy were in strong force between us and
Chattanooga, and about the same time a dispatch from Gen.
Thomas at Chattanooga came reporting the same thing. The
General immediately ordered me to take 50 cavalry, and "go
out and find the enemy and see what they are and what they
are doing." I was soon off, and after a couple of hours careful
marching and reconnoitering found myself at "Parker's Gap,"
where the enemy had been reported in heavy force, without
having seen a rebel, or hearing of but very few.
   Despatching a courier from there to the General, I started off
eastward toward the line of railroad from Cleveland to Dalton,
and after traveling 6 or 7 miles, over byroads and bridle paths
without seeing a rebel, I began to hear of rebels in front of us,
to the right of us, the left of us and behind us, and worst of
all the roads were all unknown to me, never having been in
that locality before. I've been considerably scared many a time
since I've been in the army, and I was this time, but didn't
say anything about it, kept on, diligently inquiring about roads
and rebels at every house I came to, and uncertain all the time
whether I could reach Ringgold by the obscure little bridle paths
that the citizens kept telling me about. I began to think the
road was very long—that my horse traveled very slowly—that
the sun was declining very rapidly, and that perhaps I might
run into the enemy's lines with my little bunch of 50 men

and be gobbled up, and no one to blame but myself. I began to feel as I used to when a small boy, hurrying to get home before dark to avoid the "spooks," and a little uncertain which way home was, but to my great relief, just about dark I struck a gap in the mountain which led me into a road which I knew, and I was "all right," and pushed ahead at a gallop, but on approaching our own pickets, it being quite dark, they mistook us for rebels, and a half dozen shots brought us to a very sudden halt; the alarm of the pickets was soon quieted and we were safe inside our lines.

Right glad was I to find myself home again for I had gone much further than the General expected me to go, and if I had been gobbled I should have been severely censured, at least, but as it turned out my expedition was a success and the General was satisfied. See how much depends on luck in war, as in everything else! I haven't admitted to anybody here that I was lost, and may be I was not lost, but I *thought* I was, and *still think* I was, and that answers my purpose just as well as if I actually *was,* for, even if I was commanding only 50 men, still I can no better afford to admit a mistake than if I was commanding 50,000 men, that being one of the settled rules of war —never acknowledge a mistake.

I wore a linen coat to-day; is it warm enough for such drapery at home? The forest trees are putting out leaves and the woods begin to look green; flowers bespangle the green carpet of the valleys, and the white dogwood blossoms are hung in clusters of beauty on the bright green drapery of the mountain side. Gen. Kilpatrick came here to-day on the train. I don't know what his business is here, but I suppose he came down to look at the cavalry here, as it is to be a part of his command.[7] I feel

7. Major General Hugh Judson Kilpatrick, transferred in the spring of 1864 from the Army of the Potomac, where he had rendered distinguished service, to the Army of the Cumberland, in which he commanded the Third Cavalry Division until the end of the war.

quite certain we shall move by the 5th of May, if the weather continues pleasant, and when we do move I don't see how the rebels are to resist us, for this army is nearly twice as strong as it was before. The general opinion appears to be that there will be very little fighting until we reach Atlanta. I doubt the correctness of that opinion, but hope it is correct, for I am not "spoiling for a fight," yet I would rather chance a fight than to see the summer wasted. Sorry our letters are so much delayed, but shall not be surprised, soon, to hear of an order prohibiting all mail communication, so if there should be a long gap between letters soon, don't be alarmed but charge it to "military necessity."

Your husband.

Ringgold, April 28, 1864.

Dear wife:

Yours of 23rd received to-day. That's good time from Massillon. Weather splendid. It is now near eleven o'clock at night and I am very comfortable with a linen coat on and all the windows of my room open. This is a beautiful starlit night, and a splendid brass band is serenading General [Baird] next door. I have been sitting here idly, for an hour, listening to the music. I was aroused at three o'clock this morning by a knock on my door and some one calling out: "Major our pickets are attacked," which brought me to a perpendicular very suddenly, for the pickets are especially under my charge, and any neglect or mistake on my part would be fatal to me, but I soon learned that the attack was on the cavalry pickets, and that a post of seven men had been gobbled, and that relieved me, for the cavalry pickets are not under my charge and I am not responsible for their remissness, still, for fear the attack might be followed up against the Infantry pickets, for which I am responsible, I got up by half past three and was off for our picket lines.

The day came in beauty, and I was fully repaid for my four hours of lost sleep.

I must be up at half past two to-morrow morning, for the famous Kilpatrick of "Richmond Raid" notoriety, makes a raid, starting before daylight to-morrow morning, and I am to accompany him as aide de camp, "guide, philosopher and friend." I learned the roads he wishes to travel while with the brigade of mounted infantry last summer, and can, therefore be particularly useful on this expedition. I don't suppose we shall go very far or fight very much, but we must fight some, for the object is to make the enemy develop his lines, for the purpose of ascertaining his force, and with a view to subsequent operations. I might possibly be gobbled (that's a standard word in the army), and if I should be address me Major [James A. Connolly] Libby Prison, Richmond, Va., care Lieut. Gen. Grant, who is supposed, at the present writing, to be packing his trunk for a visit there himself. If I'm not too tired, and get back to-morrow evening in time, I'll give you a "written statement" of the day's proceedings. My last stamp goes with this letter.

Your husband.

Ringgold, May 3, 1864.

Dear wife:

I have been waiting several days to write you, thinking I might be able to give you some definite statement about what is to be done, but I can't wait any longer. The whole 14th Army Corps came here to-day. Gens. Palmer, Davis and Johnson are here now, Gen. Thomas will make his headquarters here to-morrow, and Gen. Sherman next day, probably. We will surely move, very soon right into the heart of Dixie.

I have been out with Gen. Kilpatrick on two cavalry expeditions. He is a dashing fellow, more so than any cavalry officer I have met.

I have been very busy night and day for five days past, but

think I will have it more quiet for a few days now, until the general movement takes place. Gen. [Baird] told me this evening that he thought a part of this Division would be left here as a garrison, for a while, so we may not get into the fight after all, and I hope not.

Your husband.

The Atlanta Campaign

In the spring of 1864 Grant went East to assume command of all Union armies. Before leaving, he turned over the western command to the brilliant, irascible William Tecumseh Sherman, who had commanded the Army of the Tennessee since October, 1863.

The battle plan for 1864 called for an advance by the Army of the Potomac against Lee and Richmond and a simultaneous movement by the three armies under Sherman's command— the Army of the Cumberland, the Army of the Tennessee, and the Army of the Ohio—against Johnston and Atlanta.

The Army of the Cumberland moved on May 7. For the next five months Connolly would be in the thick of one of the most intensive military campaigns of all time, yet he would find time to write to his wife every few days.

Ringgold, May 6, 1864.

Dear wife:

Half an hour since the General said to me "Major be ready to march at daybreak to-morrow." I never saw so large an army before as we have gathered here now. Last night, from the mountain top, I looked down on the camp fires of 80,000 men in the valley below me.

I went with General Sherman this morning, to guide him to General Howard's headquarters. Hooker and Sickles rode by a few minutes ago. Thomas, Butterfield, Barry, Palmer, Willich, Cruft, Davis, Johnson in fact *everybody* is here, and within three days we will be in Dalton, or badly whipped. The army is in fine fighting condition, and undoubtedly, before you read this its mettle will have been tried. I think Howard's Corps is expected to reach Dalton first, by flanking the rebel right; our Corps moves in the centre, directly against the front of the rebel position, and Hooker moves on our right—the rebel left.

I think Howard moves first because Sherman went to his headquarters this morning, and because most of the army correspondents are with him. But what's the use of me writing these conjectures? You will read in the papers how the move *was* made, and its results, long before you read these conjectures as to how *it is to be* made, and what the results probably will be. I presume the Potomac Army is in motion, or will be by to-morrow, and so will this one, so the great debate of arms must soon commence. May success be ours! General Sherman looks very much like his brother John at Mansfield, but more seamed and weather-beaten.[1] I was introduced to him this morning. My goodness! I do dread starting out in the dust and hot sun, after such a long period of ease, but the rebels must be whipped, and since we can't do it sitting in the house, I suppose we must content ourselves with going out after them. Everybody about me is bustling and hurrying, but I am trying very hard to keep cool until I get this finished. I don't know

1. William Tecumseh Sherman, born on February 8, 1820, was three years and three months older than his brother John, then United States Senator from Ohio.

when I can write you again, but hope it may be very soon, probably from Dalton. Address me as before and I'll get your letters *somewhere, sometime.*

> Your husband.

> In the field, May 9, 1864.

Dear wife:

It is about 7 o'clock in the morning. I have been up over two hours, had breakfast long ago, and having an opportunity of sending a letter back to be mailed, I *embrace* it. We had some little fighting yesterday and day before, but have had no heavy fighting yet, and if Johnston hasn't over 50,000 men we wont have any heavy fighting, for as soon as our army is in position, which will be sometime to-day, Johnston will find himself overwhelmed as badly and as suddenly as his predecessor, Bragg, was at Mission Ridge. We have been in line of battle now, two days, and are all tired waiting, but I think, before the sun sets, "Linden" will see "another sight." We received despatches yesterday, on the field, announcing some success to our arms, on the Potomac, but we have heard such despatches so often during the past three years, that I begin to think they are like Rory O. More's dreams, and "go by contraries my dear." We have but one mountain range between our front lines and Dalton; that range is occupied by the rebels, and I don't know exactly how we are to get them off it, but am sure we *will* get them off, and that by to-morrow, Tuesday, we will occupy Dalton. An immense light was seen in the direction of Dalton last night and it may be that our misguided Southern brethren have concluded they can't make a good "last ditch" at Dalton, and have taken up "Bragg's Quickstep" for remoter parts of Dixie. This will be a hot day and if we have many wounded they will suffer very much. I received a letter from you yesterday while under fire. How odd. I always get a letter from you while on the battle field—at Perryville—at Milton—at Chick-

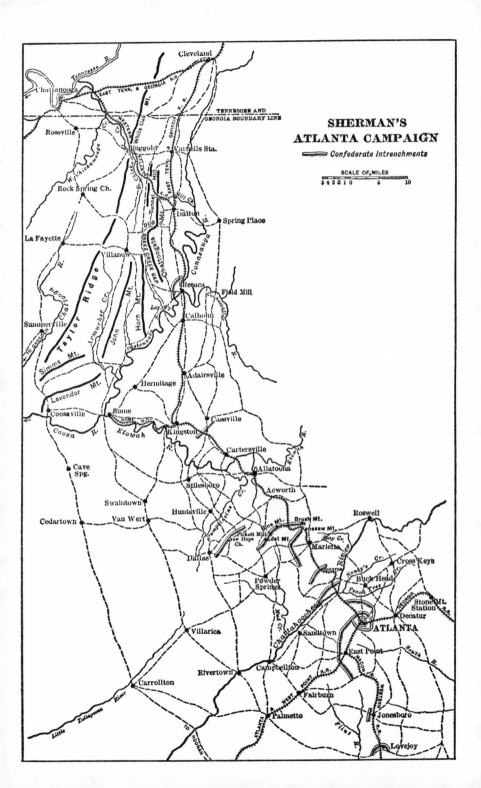

amauga—at Mission Ridge, each time the little messenger of peace came to me on the battle field.

I am writing this with a pencil and my saddle skirt for a table, so you may have some trouble in deciphering it, but no more than I've had in *ciphering* it. Good bye for to-day.

Your husband.

Near Buzzard Roost, Ga., May 10, 1864.

Dear wife:

Seven o'clock in the morning; we are saddled and awaiting orders to go forward to where the skirmish fire is arousing the echoes with its lively popping. An order relative to Grant's success in Virginia is being read to the troops, by Sherman's order, and that indicates we may open the ball to-day, but may be not. I am well, and think we can whip Johnston although he has the strongest natural position I ever saw.

Your husband.

Headquarters, May 11, 1864.

Dear wife:

We are just where we were when I wrote you yesterday morning, but an order has just come for us to move south and join McPherson and Hooker below Dalton. We take ten days rations, so I suppose we are to go to Atlanta without stopping if we can. It rained very hard last night. The skirmishing has been very heavy this morning, and I notice, as I am writing this, that the fire is increasing and artillery is opening, so we may possibly get up a fight here that will prevent us from moving south to join McPherson. It is quite cool and promises a fine day for either marching or fighting. Will write you from Atlanta, and as much sooner as I can.

Your husband.

Near Resaca, Ga., May 15, 1864.

Dear wife:

Just as I had written the date above, I said: "Hello, the enemy are shelling us." This exclamation was called out by the fact of a shell from the enemy's battery exploding very near our headquarters. It is now about nine o'clock at night, the moon is shining with a misty light through the battle smoke that is slowly settling down like a curtain, over these hills and valleys; the mournful notes of a whippoorwill, near by, mingle in strange contrast with the exultant shouts of our soldiers—the answering yells of the rebels—the rattling fire of the skirmish line, and the occasional bursting of a shell. To-day we have done nothing but shift positions and keep up a heavy skirmish fire. Yesterday our Division and Judah's Division of Scofield's Corps, had some hard fighting. We drove the enemy about a mile and entirely within his fortifications, several of our regiments planting their colors on his fortifications, but were compelled to withdraw under a terrible fire. We, however, fell back but a short distance to the cover of the woods, where we still are, and the enemy have not ventured outside their works since. A report has just reached us that Hooker drove the enemy about a mile to-day. We will probably be engaged to-morrow, and we may be engaged yet to-night, for the enemy may take a notion to come out of his works under cover of the darkness, and attack us. I hope he wont for I don't want to be disturbed after I get to sleep, and then I don't like fighting in the night anyhow. We have men enough here to whip Johnston, and if he don't escape pretty soon he never will.

I presume "you all," as the Southern people say, feel very much elated over Grant's success. Well, you will hear something from this army, some of these days that will be a full match for anything Grant or any other man can do with the Potomac

army, and I begin to have hope that the only large armies of
the rebellion will be shattered, if not destroyed, by the 4th of
July. We have the railroad in running order to Tilton, which
is several miles south of Dalton, and are having no trouble
about supplies. The weather is fine, the roads fairly good, our
men flushed with success, and I hope we push right on, day and
night, though we be ragged, dirty, tired and hungry, until we
exterminate these battalions of treason. Good night.

Your husband.

Kingston, Ga., May 20, 1864.

Dear wife:

If you will look at a map you will see that "we all" are still
pushing southward, but a look at the map will give you little
idea of the country we are passing through—will fail to point
out to you the fields that are being reddened by the blood of
our soldiers, and the hundreds of little mounds that are rising
by the wayside day by day, as if to mark the footprints of
the God of War as he stalks along through this beautiful
country. This point is where the railroad from Rome forms a
junction with the main line from Chattanooga to Atlanta.
Rome is in our possession, and such has been the extraor-
dinary rapidity with which the railroad has been repaired, as
we have pushed along, that a train from Chattanooga ran into
Kingston this morning about daylight, while at the same time
a rebel train from Atlanta was whistling on the same road,
and only two miles distant, but it is now about 9 o'clock in
the morning, and the last whistle of the rebel train, north of
the Etowah River, sounded some hours ago, the last rebel has
undoubtedly crossed the river, the bridge across the river has
been burned, I suppose, and the rebel army is wending its way,
weary and dispirited, toward that mythical ditch of which we
have heard so much.

Two hours later. Just at this point in this pencilled letter, about two hours ago I was interrupted, and the whole Division startled, by a cavalryman rushing up to headquarters, his horse covered with foam, and reporting that he had just seen the rebels, in line of battle, about one fourth of a mile distant, and advancing on us. In a jiffy this unfinished letter was thrust in my pocket, my horse saddled, and I was ordered by the General to go back with the cavalryman the way he had come, and ascertain the truth of his report, for cavalry reports are much like rebel money—don't pass at their face value. I went out through our pickets and cautiously moved along until I had gone about a mile to the front when I came to a strong line of breastworks, constructed by the rebels last night, but this morning they are deserted. I crossed these breastworks and went on until I came to another line of works, but they too are deserted. this morning. I crossed this second line and went on a short distance, when I saw some mounted rebels ahead and they saw me; they fired a couple of shots which fell far short, and seeing I was out of their reach, I stood still with my cavalryman, but the rebs started toward me, and, not wishing to have a difficulty with them, I "fell back in good order" until they fired again, set up a yell and started after me on a run when I accelerated the pace of my "Rosinante" and *advanced to the rear* at a rapid pace and got safely inside our picket line; the cavalryman who accompanied me dodged off to one side and hid in the brush when the chase began. He came in a few moments ago, all right, but is not able to explain why he made his scare report. I reported to the General and all is quiet again, but if you find this letter all crumpled up, remember I had it in its unfinished state in my pocket during that chase, and as I can't get at my desk, paper is scarce, and I can't afford to begin it again. Beautiful country, beautiful weather, and everything going well with the Yankees in Georgia. You may still address me at Ringgold.

Your husband.

Kingston, Ga., May 22, 1864.

Dear wife:

This is Sunday, a bright, sultry, lazy day; scarce a breath of air stirring, and mules, negroes, soldiers, everybody is lolling in the shade, making as much as possible out of the remaining hours of rest that are left us before resuming our forward march, still further into the Confederacy, for Sherman has said we must start again to-morrow morning, with 20 days rations. Just at this point a letter from you, postmarked May 17th, is laid on my table, so I shall lay down my pen and read it. You see I got out my desk and am writing with pen and ink for the first in quite a while. . . .

I wonder where I shall be when your next letter reaches me? Possibly sitting in the shade of a fence corner, begrimed with the dust and sweat of a hard march, possibly on the battlefield, amid the roar of artillery and rattle of musketry, possibly toiling over the narrow range of mountains that separates us from the fertile plains of middle Georgia, following, perchance, some of the same paths threaded by the adventurous De Soto, in his perilous march from the coast of Florida to the Mississippi, beneath whose waters the bold Spaniard found a grave, but wherever I may be, your letters, little white winged messengers from home, will surely find me and bring me happiness.

One of the regiments of this Division, the 9th Ohio, started from here yesterday afternoon, on its homeward journey, having served its full three years. Day before yesterday it was skirmishing with the enemy and, fortunately not one of its number was hurt. It is a German regiment; its Colonel, Kaemmerling, has been promoted to Brigadier General, but he declines to accept the promotion until he leads his old regiment home to Cincinnati. As the brave sturdy Germans filed out from our camps, their old, tattered, battle worn flags fluttering like rags, their step was proud and soldierly, for their work was well done, their comrades knew it, and their thoughts were of home, wives, children, friends; but they had thoughts, too, of their comrades in arms, to whom they were bidding a final adieu, and their bronzed cheeks were wet with tears, and we all felt sad at parting with them. Brave fellows! they have fought long and well for their adopted country, and are worthy of Cincinnati's, yes of Ohio's proudest reception. If I can go home with duty as well done as theirs I shall be content.

So ——— has hired a substitute! What cravens, to hire poor men, cripples, convicts and the riff raff of society to do their fighting for them. Such men are not worth protection either in life, liberty or property. I see that Col. Vance was severely wounded in Banks' disastrous battle near Shreveport. Has anything been heard of his fate? I am anxious to know, for I esteemed him highly as you know. I hope his life is saved.

This country from Dalton south begins to look more like our northern farming country than any section of the South I have seen. The farm houses look neat and comfortable; the barns are well built and capacious; the farms have a clean, thrifty, Yankeeish look, and the women no longer have that yellow, smoky, snuff dipping appearance that characterized so many of those of Tennessee and northern Georgia.

At this point I was compelled to stop to attend religious services at our headquarters. Rev. [Lowrie] of Pittsburg, a brother of our adjutant general, was the officiating clergyman. He is here visiting his brother; he has been eating at our mess for two days past, and we have napkins and grace before each meal. Quite civilized are we "away down south in Dixie." I suppose he will preach about the godly soldiers of Sherman's army when he goes home. There are many speculations going the rounds among the officers and men in the camps, concerning our future movements, but no one can guess what Sherman will do. I am very anxious to see Atlanta, Savannah, Milledgeville, Macon and Mobile, but am afraid I will hardly see all of these places this summer, but I shall see some of them.

My duties, in the field, as Inspector, give me facilities for finding out more about the country than I otherwise would. I am expected to find out all about the roads we travel on and the cross roads we pass—where they run to—in what direction they run—whether they are good or bad—what streams they cross—something about the feelings of the citizens who live on our line of march &c &c, besides placing the pickets on our front when we stop for the night, and connecting our pickets on the right and left with those of other Divisions, so as to make the picket lines continuous. This picketing is sometimes very difficult when we march after dark, and have to put out pickets in the woods, in a strange country, and Inspectors, under such circumstances, sometimes lose their way and wander into the enemy's lines, when they think they are going into their own. I know of one Inspector who has been captured that way since this advance began.

Somehow I feel safe in the woods at night, and have no fear of being lost. When the General has to ride around through the woods after night, where there are no roads, he always takes me with him, and trusts to my guidance, and I have never lost him yet, but came very near it a few nights since, when it was very dark and the stars were obscured, but by using a pocket compass of the Generals and lighting a match we ascertained where North was, and so got safe within our lines again, but next morning I discovered that we had been a long way outside our lines. I am out of postage stamps and wish you would send me twenty in your next letter. . . .

Your husband.

In the woods, near Dallas, Georgia, May 28, '64.
Dear wife:
I have just sat down with my back to a sapling, to write this with pencil, on this soiled piece of paper, with a shingle on my lap, for writing desk. The adjutant of my regiment got into the enemy's lines, by some kind of mistake, a few days

since, and was captured. If you look at one of "Loyds Map of the Southern States" I guess you can find about where I am. I have to look at a map myself to ascertain my whereabouts. For several days our Division has not been in the front, and I have only heard the enemy's guns in the distance. The day after I wrote you my last letter from Kingston, the enemy came in our rear and burnt 40 wagons of the 23rd Army Corps. This Division was immediately ordered to cover the rear of the wagon trains for the entire army, and we are jogging along now at the rate of about 8 miles a day. Last night our headquarters were at a citizen's house, and before retiring we had "family prayers", singing of hymns, &c. The weather is delightful for campaigning, and I am quite sure we will be in Atlanta by the middle of June, and we are all strongly in hope of celebrating the 4th of July at the "last ditch" of the rebellion. Some of the half hearted in our army (for we have such) are gloomy because, they say, Grant can't whip Lee, and point to the fact that gold has been rising in value ever since Grant first engaged Lee. I don't know how you folks at home feel about it, but I feel sure Grant *will* defeat Lee and that we will defeat Johnston, and that our flag will float over Richmond and Atlanta by the 4th of July, but if not by that time it will *sometime*.

We passed about 200 rebel prisoners going to the rear, this morning. They were captured in a sharp engagement last evening. We are now in the region of the Georgia gold mines, and I am told that the cripples and poor men who have not been conscripted, are out gold washing among the mountain streams, to get gold dust enough to buy corn with. If my almanac is right I believe to-morrow is Sunday, and if I have time I will write you instead of going to church. I have a chance of sending this back to Kingston by our adjutant general, who has resigned and starts home to-day.

Your husband.

In the woods near Dallas, Ga., June 1, '64.

Dear wife:

Lieut. McAbee starts to the rear to rejoin his regiment and go home with it to-morrow or next day, and as we are just ordered to the front I shall probably not see him again, so I "embrace the opportunity" to send a line out to be mailed by him. We have not had any heavy fighting yet, that is, this Division, but the losses in the whole army have been considerable. I supposed we should be in Atlanta by the middle of this month, but we must move faster than we have for a few days past, or we shall not get there by that time. Wouldn't it be glorious if my three years were as near up as McAbee's?

I am begging postage stamps and anxiously awaiting a supply from you. Weather very hot during the day but the nights are cool and pleasant, splendid weather for campaigning. I see a man coming with papers for sale, and I must stop writing to get a paper, so that I may know what is doing in the world outside our picket lines. I am in excellent health and burning black as an African in this hot sun.

Your husband.

Near Acworth, Ga., June 8, 1864.

Dear wife:

After a week of continual skirmishing and fighting, the enemy have run from us again, and I have an opportunity of writing you without the annoyance of being compelled to duck down my head every few minutes, to let a straggling bullet whistle along.

A few days since Major Norton, a friend of mine, who was Inspector General of this Corps, was shot dead while walking around my line, and the following day I was riding around the same line and a bullet whistled so near me that I was scared out of a year's growth. Bullets that come so near don't hurt

I know, but they scare tremendously, so I have made up my mind that there is no necessity for me to ride around my line any more while so very near the enemy. We are now within about ten miles of Marietta, on the railroad, and will be compelled to rest here a few days until the railroad can be completed and rations brought forward, before resuming our march on Atlanta. The Chattahoochee River still stretches between us and Atlanta, and, once across that River, Atlanta must be ours. It has rained some every day for the past six days. Crops are very poor this year in this part of Georgia, and I don't know that they are ever very good.

Wheat is beginning to change color a little, and corn is about 8 inches high. I made my bed, last night, on the front porch of the house in which I am writing this letter, and the first thing I did this morning, after getting up, was to climb a mulberry tree in the dooryard and get a fine mess of nice ripe mulberries. Apples and peaches will soon be ripe and then we can live better than we do now; another week will fully ripen the cherries, so while you are sitting around your fires, or shivering in the cold blasts, you can imagine me, under the shade of a peach or cherry tree, plucking and eating the choice fruit; but on the other hand, when you retire to your couch, you can imagine me tumbling down at the roots of a tree to sleep, with a stone for a pillow, and Georgia lizards crawling down my boot legs and playing hide and seek in my pockets. Our soldiers, by some means, feel authorized to live on the country, and their living on the country has degenerated into the most outrageous pillaging, but not in the presence of officers, families being left without a morsel of food; I don't know how the poor creatures are to live, but Sherman wont let them starve.

I learn this morning that Fremont has been nominated for President, by the Cleveland convention.[2] I hope he stands no

2. John C. Frémont, first Republican candidate for the Presidency (1856) and a gaudy failure as a major general during the first year of the war,

show for election, but don't know whether he does or not. I want Abraham Lincoln for President, and think he will be, but we in the army are ignorant of what the politicians are doing or can do, and we Illinoisans in the army amount to no more than so many negroes, in the election, for we are disfranchised. I have received four letters from you in the past six days. The last was mailed May 30 and I received it yesterday, so you see your letters come through in good time.

Mail starts from our headquarters in a few minutes and I must close so as to get this off in it. I'll have to beg a stamp for this.

Your husband.

Near Acworth, Ga., June 9, 1864.

Dear wife:

A few minutes ago I was told our mail would go out at 9 this morning, and as it is now about 8 I shall spend that hour in talking to you. It rained a little last night and this morning is refreshingly cool, but the sun is shining brightly and gives promise of warming us up immoderately before night. I am sitting in the door yard of a "Georgia planter," under the shade of his mulberry trees, the ripe fruit hanging above me. Think I shall climb the tree and eat some of it after finishing this. Brass bands are playing in every direction, and the mocking bird is making the leafy shade vocal with his attempts to imitate the brass music of "Dixie," "Star Spangled Banner" &c &c. Take it altogether, I have enjoyed this campaign very much, and I like what I've seen of Georgia better than any Southern state I've been in. When relieved of its incubus of slavery it ought to take good rank among the states of the Union. Its farm homes are very much like our Northern farmers homes, and the people are more like our home people. There appears to
_____
was nominated for President by a convention of Radical Republicans meeting at Cleveland on May 31, 1864.

be a "middle class" here, something I have not found in any other Southern state. This is the third day we have remained at this camp. We had orders to march early this morning, but the official order to march has not been received, and I don't suppose we will move from here until to-morrow. Our campaign, thus far, has been very successful, but I think we ought to have captured a large part of Johnston's army at Resaca, if McPherson had succeeded in doing what Sherman ordered him to do.

We have flanked them and driven them from one strong position to another until they are now pushed back to the Chattahoochee, and we find ourselves, an enormous army, well fed, clad and armed, in the very heart of Dixie. We will not get Atlanta by the middle of June, as I predicted some time ago, but I think it safe to predict that our National colors will fly over Richmond and Atlanta by the 4th of July, and that will satisfy us. I presume the Baltimore Convention is in session now, and possibly, this very day, will make its nomination.[3] I see, by the papers, that *my* state was represented in the Cleveland convention, and am ashamed that the state had a delegate in it.

Being tired of the inactivity of camp, I asked permission of the General yesterday afternoon, to take the escort, and go out to the front to learn the roads, and find out where the enemy were in our front. Started about 3 o'clock, and after going about one and a half miles, came to a house where there had been ten rebels about 15 minutes before; the inmates told me the direction in which they went, and we started to follow them, but after going a short distance I became satisfied we couldn't overtake them, so we turned back and resumed our

3. Many Americans have forgotten, if they ever knew, that Lincoln was nominated in 1864 by the Union Party rather than the Republican Party. The Union Party was basically Republican, yet it included many Democrats who were in favor of prosecuting the war vigorously. It met at Baltimore on June 7 and on the following day nominated Lincoln and his running mate, Andrew Johnson of Tennessee.

original line of march; after going about three quarters of a mile farther in our original direction, I saw a rebel about 200 yards ahead in the road, his gun slung by the strap over his shoulder and riding directly toward us. I knew he hadn't seen us yet, so I turned my men into the edge of the woods, pistols were out and cocked in silence, for I didn't know how many rebels might be following him, and we awaited his approach; in a few minutes he rode up within six feet of me, and he never saw me until my summons to halt, given in a low tone, with pistol leveled on him, aroused him from his fancied security, and he discovered himself confronted by twenty boys in blue; of course he made no resistance, but quietly unslung his gun and handed it over; on inquiry I learned that his company of twenty men were on picket just then within about 250 yards of us, and that they had no idea we were about, so I determined to surprise and capture the whole party, and ordering my men to keep concealed and quiet, I dismounted and slipped along the road, dodging from tree to tree, for the purpose of seeing how the ground lay; soon I found myself within about 100 yards of three rebel pickets on horseback, but while reconnoitering them from behind a tree I exposed myself too much and one of them saw me, or thought he did, for he raised his gun and called out: "What are you doing there?" Of course I made no reply, and he repeated the question, whereupon I began to withdraw quietly and he fired at me, so, being discovered, I gave up the attempt at surprise, and returned to camp with but one prisoner, and on reporting to the General he gave the horse to me for my own use. Mail is just about ready to start and I must close.

Your husband.

In the field, near Big Shanty, Ga., June 14 '64.
Dear wife:
I am tired, very tired to-night, but thankful to find myself *all in* one piece and able to write you even a hasty note. Pardon

me, if after making you wait so long, I only send you a brief note now, for it requires an immense effort for me to do anything but go to bed to-night. We commenced to advance our lines this morning, and during the whole day these headquarters have been under fire and are now. Our Division has lost a good many men to-day, but we have held every inch of ground over which we advanced since morning. It is now about two hours after dark; the artillery fire has ceased, and the musketry fire is now confined to a few dropping shots by the skirmishers.[4] Everybody, rebel as well as Federal, is tired, I guess, and we will all sleep soundly until the dawn awakes us again to the bloody carnival. I dislike this early rising, and I promise you that when I get home I shall issue a "General Order" prohibiting early rising in my "department."

I received to-day, your letter mailed June 6th, and, putting a large oak tree between myself and the rebel bullets, I read it with great pleasure. It did me a "power of good." I have not seen the platform of the Baltimore Convention yet, but it doesn't make much difference to me what it is, for I find "lines of battle" are much more potent than lines of platform. I expect the platform is a little radical on the slavery question, but not half as radical as I am myself, so I can't object to it on that ground. You say you weigh 117 pounds, and call that very light. I don't believe I weigh more than 10 pounds over that, so I don't think you ought to complain much about your weight. I don't know whether my late letters reach you or not, for we are now completely in the enemy's country, surrounded

4. General Baird, Division commander, described this action. "June 14, our whole line advanced, and my left reached the Big [Shanty] road, where it intrenched. Directly in front on the south side of the road the strongly built lines of the enemy, stretching from the base of Pine Mountain to the east, were discovered at a few hundred yards' distance. My right, nearer to the mountain, was more strongly resisted, and, although skirmishing hotly throughout the day with heavy loss, did not until dark succeed in dislodging the rebels from their rifle-pits or in gaining the road." *Official Records,* Series I, Vol. XXXVIII, Part I, p. 738.

on every side, and keep open communication with the North only by force of arms. But we will get a fair chance at this army in our front some of these days and if we don't make them think communication is opened up I will be much mistaken. Tell sister Ella I dreamed about her last night; I dreamed I had been captured and she was laughing at me about it. I must go to bed for these rascally rebs will have us awake before daylight.

Your husband.

In the field, near Marietta, Ga., June 17, 1864.

Dear wife:

I received your letter of June 9th, containing the stamps, yesterday. I wrote you night before last, after a very hard days work, and the next morning we discovered that the enemy had evacuated their works during the night and by daylight we occupied them. On that day, too, Rev. Bishop General Polk was killed on our front, by a cannon shot.[5] We are now at the foot of Kenesaw mountain, which is 3 miles north of Marietta. Every day for the past 3 or 4 days, we have seen linen coated gentlemen and gaily dressed ladies, viewing our lines from their lofty perch on the top of Kenesaw. I presume they never heard of Mission Ridge, and think we never can get over Kenesaw, so the "beauty and fashion" of Marietta take daily drives to Kenesaw's summit to look with disdain on the burrowing Yankees in the valley below. Deluded creatures! Before a week these burrowing Yankees will be proudly marching through the streets of Marietta, pursuing their rebel escorts, as they scramble in undignified haste, for the south bank of the Chattahoochee.

5. Major General Leonidas Polk, who had resigned his lieutenant's commission six months after graduating from West Point (1827) to enter the Virginia Theological Seminary. He became an Episcopal minister and later a bishop. At the outbreak of the Civil War Jefferson Davis, Polk's fellow-cadet at West Point, offered him a commission as a major general in the Confederate Army. Polk accepted.

We are to advance again this morning. Don't know whether it will bring on an engagement or not, but we'll try it anyhow. . . .

Your husband.

Foot of Kenesaw Mountain, Ga., June 20 '64.
Dear wife:

About an hour ago (it is now about 4 P. M.) I sat down to write you a hasty letter, in the midst of the most terrific cannonade I have heard during the war. I had actually written a little over a page when I heard a heavy musketry fire away off on the right, intermingling with the artillery; I wrote and listened, wrote and listened, and the musketry fire grew heavier and came rolling along from the right to the left, right toward our part of the line; in an instant the unfinished letter was torn up, sword buckled on and I was off for the front; wild cheers rose up from the depths of the gloomy forest, the musketry fire grew heavier, the artillerists plied their guns more rapidly, rebel batteries, heretofore concealed, opened on us from the mountain top; full 75 cannon, all within 3 miles of each other, were bellowing at once, and taking all things together it was the most elegant prospect for a general engagement I have seen since this campaign commenced, but the firing ceased just as suddenly as it began, leaving the rebels, no doubt, to wonder what it all meant. And now, while I am writing this letter in the valley at the foot of the mountain, the rebels on the top are speculating about what the Yankees meant by such a noisy demonstration, and I'm sure they don't know yet what it did mean, but they'll find out about to-morrow afternoon.

"We all" soon found out what it meant, and as the fire grew heavier and heavier on our right, whole Divisions of our troops, that have been lying back of the lines, in the woods, for two days, came marching through, hurriedly, toward our right, under cover of the woods, and now our right has been lengthened until it extends beyond the rebel left a mile, and has commenced moving forward to swing around the left of the rebels. As I write I can hear the cheers of the new men who went to our right.

June 21st, 3 P. M. Just as I wrote the last word above, a heavy fire of musketry and artillery broke out, and our right instantly became engaged, as it swung forward. This time I thrust this unfinished letter in my valise, hoping I could finish it last night, but the fighting on the right was protracted until after dark, and on returning to quarters was too tired to write, so I postponed it to to-day. We learn to-day, that Hooker and Scofield, who did the fighting on our right yesterday, were not successful in turning the rebel left, but gained several miles on them, with heavy loss. It has been raining almost incessantly for the past ten days, and for the same length of time our progress toward Atlanta has been very slow, but we have advanced *some* every day and taken no backward steps. Although we have had no general engagement, yet this army, or some part of it, has fought every day since we left Ringgold, 46 days ago. Sherman at one time could have forced a general engagement, but it does not seem a part of his programme to do so yet, but the time for it will come some of these days. We may have neither Richmond nor Atlanta by the 4th of July, but the situation is excellent and no such thing as failure is thought of in this army. True, we are encompassed by rebels; they cut our railroads in Kentucky, Tennessee and in Georgia; they capture our wagons between here and Chattanooga; they burn RR bridges between here and Chattanooga, and I suppose they imagine their "critter companies" are making havoc with our railroad line which supplies us with rations. But all their efforts are futile, and this army to-day, is better provisioned than the Army of the Cumberland was in its last summer campaign.

Flour, Fresh Beef, Salt Beef, Salt Pork, Ham, Bacon, Beans,

Sugar, Coffee, Hard Bread and everything necessary for the soldier we have in the greatest abundance; much better off in that respect than when we were in Chattanooga. A few days ago, while our Division lay on its arms in line of battle, our skirmishers heavily engaged with those of the enemy, and rebel bullets whistling lively about Division headquarters, the regimental quartermasters might have been seen distributing new pants, shoes and hats to the men, as they lay behind their breastworks. If the rebels could have seen this I think they would have despaired of "cutting our communications." A rebel Colonel, captured night before last, told a good story about "cutting our communications." He said that about two hours before he was captured, Gen. Cheatham and staff rode along their lines, announcing to each regiment that the Yankee railroad to Chattanooga had been destroyed by their cavalry, and that the Yankees would be compelled to retreat very soon to get something to eat. Just as Cheatham was making this announcement to this Colonel's regiment, one of our trains from Chattanooga came thundering along into our lines, whistling and screaming like an engine gone mad; the whistle and rumble of the train could be heard by this regiment almost as distinctly as by our men, and, as the Colonel said "Cheatham dried up."

The difference between this army now and a year ago is very perceptible. A year ago, when our men were marching toward a heavy musketry fire, you could see that they felt nervous, and there would be a slight shade of anxiety on most faces; their looks would be turned toward where the fire was heaviest, as if to penetrate the dense forest and see what fate had in store for them; but now our columns move toward the heaviest fire, the men laughing, singing, whistling, making jocular remarks about the Johnnies, nobody straggling, no cheeks blanched; not that our men fear *death* less than they used to, but they have learned by experience that of the hundreds of thousands of bullets that are fired, but very few hit anybody. I have not drawn any pay since January, and don't care much now whether I draw any all summer; I am out of money, we are all out of money, but we don't *need* money down here— don't need *anything* but men, muskets, ammunition, hard tack, bacon, and *letters from home*. Get "Loyd's Map of Georgia" and you can see what progress we are making through the "Confederacy."

I saw a telegram a couple of days since announcing the return of Vallandingham to Ohio, and his election as delegate to the Chicago Convention. Can this be true? I can't believe he has been permitted to return. If he should show himself along our lines here he would be shot as quick as Jeff Davis, and if the President has pardoned him, I shall not be surprised to hear that he has also given John Morgan a "permit" to steal horses, burn bridges and murder Union men, until after the election. I saw Capt. B——— on the 15th inst., but as I was just conducting some of our troops to their position I had no time to talk with him. His regiment had no fighting that day, but I think they have had since. His Division is not far from ours and I shall ride over there to-morrow and see him, if I can find time.

Save the pencilled note which I enclose, written by Col. M——— while he was "officer of the day" for the Division. When I get home, if you show it to me, it will remind me of a "story of the war" which will be interesting, but is too long to relate here. . . .

Your husband.

Foot of Kenesaw Mountain, Ga., June 26, 1864.
Dear wife:

I received yours of 18th yesterday. That is making very satisfactory speed. This is Sabbath morning, bright, beautiful and giving promise of much heat before night. I am very lazy this morning, and begin to experience, in a slight degree, the lassitude produced by this Southern heat. I am lounging at my table, head resting on hand, no coat, no vest, no collar, no socks, only slippers on my feet, and I expect I'll write you a rambling, slipshod letter. . . .

Look at some of the wives of our acquaintance who *had* husbands in the army, and were dissatisfied until they got them home. There is Mrs. Major H————. She had a husband in the army but felt she was sacrificing too much; now she has him at home. Do you suppose either of them feel satisfied? Mrs. Col. I———— had her husband in the army but soon had him home again. Do you suppose either of them now feel content with the part he played? Mrs. Major ———— had a betrothed husband in the army, just as you had, but her husband gave up his sword as well as his heart, at Hymen's altar, and now she has him home with her. Many more we know, who couldn't withstand the temptation of home, wife, society, but, now that they are compelled to sit, idly watching the stream of great events go by, they are haunted day and night, by a sense of duty unperformed, and it will be their "skeleton in the closet" from which they will shrink in future years.[6] So let us "grin and bear it," for we want no such "skeleton in our closet."

We are still at the foot of Kenesaw mountain, and have been here more than a week; the enemy appear determined to risk a battle here, and I suppose we will have to accommodate them. It is understood Sherman says he will flank no more, but will move directly on their works, so, either we, or the rebels, will have been whipped before you receive this, and I certainly hope it will not be we. I understand this Corps is to be held in reserve and not engage in the assault, and accordingly, one Division of the Corps was withdrawn from the line last night and moved off quietly toward the right, under cover of the

6. References to Ohio acquaintances who cannot now be identified.

woods and darkness. Our Division will probably withdraw and move off in the same way to-night, and the other Division will do the same to-morrow night. Being in reserve, we will only come in at the "pinch" of the engagement, if our assistance becomes necessary.

It's getting awful hot. You say it is hot in Ohio! Why Ohio is an ice house compared with Georgia in June. We have had about three weeks of almost incessant rain, but the heavens now are brass, and not so much as a tea cup full of water could be squeezed out of all the clouds we have seen for three days. The skirmishers are popping away on our front, and a few minutes ago the rebels opened on us with their artillery on the mountain top, and as their shells came screeching and howling over our headquarters, I tell you, I had a great mind to drop my pen, cram this letter in my valise and run to a big tree for safety; but they have stopped shelling now and my nerves are steady again. Kenesaw mountain is, I should think, about 700 feet high, and consists of two points or peaks, separated by a narrow gorge running across the top of the mountain. The mountain itself is entirely separated from all mountain ranges, and swells up like a great bulb from the plain. The right of the rebel army rests on that mountain, and it stretches from thence through the plain and along little ridges, in a southerly direction, almost, and probably quite, to the Chattahoochee River, a distance of nearly 12 miles, so you see the rebels are facing nearly west and we are facing nearly east.

Grant being in possession of Petersburg gives him a decided advantage, and while I can scarcely hope he will take the rebel capital so soon as the 4th of July, yet the signs are daily growing better. These two campaigns of Grant and Sherman are the most stupendous the world has ever seen going on at the same time, and I really consider myself fortunate to be engaged in one of them. They've commenced that annoying shelling again so I'll quit and prepare for dodging in the timber, for these shells are dangerous, they go to pieces so carelessly.

Your husband.

S. E. of Kenesaw, Ga., June 28, 1864.

Dear wife:

I wrote you three days ago, and told you then that we would assault the enemy's works, and probably have a severe engagement before you could receive the letter. Well, we assaulted them yesterday and were repulsed, and, as is usual in such cases, our loss was heavy.[7] This Division was in reserve and therefore lost but few, hit by stray shots and shells. Major Yager of the 121 Ohio (he was from Knox Co., Ohio) had a leg shot off and died last night. Lieut. Col. Lawrence of the same regiment, also Capt. Loyd of that regiment were wounded. Sidney Wood was wounded in the forearm, one of the bones broken, but his father says he will not lose the arm. Col. Harmon of the 125th Illinois, an Illinois acquaintance of mine, was killed. I closed his eyes on the field and laid him out decently. Gen. Harker was killed; he was a gallant officer and his death is universally regretted in this army. Col. McCook, commanding a brigade in Davis' Division, was severely wounded. Our loss in officers was fearful. The fighting continued about an hour and our loss is about 2,000. Our men gained the enemy's works, planted their colors on them, and even jumped into their trenches and fought there hand to hand, but were finally compelled to retire; they retired, however, only a short distance, and the front of this corps is now within twenty yards of the enemy's works.

The day was excessively hot and the men were exhausted

7. Sherman's frontal attack on Kenesaw Mountain was his major mistake of the campaign. Out of 16,225 Union troops engaged, 1,999 were killed and wounded. The Confederates lost 270, killed and wounded, out of 17,733.

when they reached the enemy's works, and were there compelled to fight comparatively fresh men. I heard a conversation between Sherman, Thomas, Hooker and Palmer this morning, and while I shouldn't dare to write here what I heard, yet I may say that something else will now be done, and if it's what I think it is, it will be one of the bold moves of the war. If you shouldn't receive another letter from me for three or four weeks don't be surprised, for we may have little more communication with the North for some time. I thought we would move tonight but it is deferred to tomorrow night. Just this moment heavy musketry firing has broken out on our front. I expect the rebels are trying to break our lines. Let them work away, they can't break them, and tomorrow morning they will wish they hadn't undertaken it. The firing is getting heavier and I must close.

Your husband.

S. E. of Kenesaw, Ga., June 29, 1864.

Dear wife:

It is ten o'clock at night. The General and all the staff except myself have retired, and just as I was about to retire to my "downy cot" of government blankets, an idea struck me that I couldn't sleep for an hour and that I might as well spend part of that hour in talking to you. I don't propose to write you a letter to-night, but I shall just write along until I get out of the notion, then I'll put this away in my valise, and resume, perhaps, to-morrow, unless to-morrow should chance to be one of our fighting days, and if it is, I'll not promise to write much. I sat down to write you a letter last night, but the rebels commenced so noisy an attack on our lines that it stirred us all out, and I was compelled to conclude the letter very hastily while my servant was saddling my horse. After my horse was saddled, though, and the General and staff were just about to mount the firing ceased and we didn't go out. I think it will seem very strange to me when I get away from the sound of musket firing, for I am sure I have heard it continually, during my waking hours, for the past 54 days.

I have been reading Byron all evening. I picked up an old copy of it, and of Ramsey's History of Tennessee, so you see I have something to read occasionally. When on the march I have them rolled up in my blankets, that being the only way I have to carry them safely. I happened to be reading Byron this evening for this reason; some time since I had a dispute with one of our staff, concerning the authorship and correct rendering of the following:

> "O woman! in hours of ease,
>   Uncertain, coy and hard to please;
>   When pain and sickness wring the brow,
>   A ministering angel thou,"

and I was looking through Byron for it, under the impression that he was the author, but I have not found it in him, and I begin to doubt his being the author, and incline to the opinion that it is either in Wordsworth, Cowper or Scott's "Marmion" or "Lady of the Lake." I can't get hold of any of these here, so I have to call on you to tell me who is the author. We only differ as to the rendition of the first verse or line as it is usually called. I render it:

> "O woman! in hours of ease."

He renders it:

> "O woman! in *our* hours of ease."

Now which is correct pray tell, or are we both wrong? I rather think the third verse or line should read:

> "When pain and *anguish* wring the brow,"
or: "When pain and *suffering* wring the brow." [8]

I used to be quite certain about the accuracy of my quotations, but this miserable war business has made me lose confidence in myself in such matters, and I'm going to quit it soon as I decently can, and go home and shut myself up for a while and have you teach me. If there is no move on hand to-morrow I shall try to find Sidney Wood, and see that his wounds are properly attended to. My regulation blankets now woo me to repose under their rough folds; the arms of Morpheus are outstretched to receive me, so "now I lay me down to sleep."

July 1st. "The wisest plans of mice and men gang aft aglee." Just after writing the above, night before last, I thought I had laid "me down to sleep," but I was mistaken. About one o'clock in the morning I was awakened by a furious cannonade, and shells bursting in dangerous proximity to our headquarters, but night alarms being so frequent this campaign, I didn't jump out of my blankets immediately, only sat up and listened, trying to determine what it was, and what part of the line was attacked. I didn't listen many minutes though, until the roll of musketry convinced me that it meant business, and was very near our front, so calling out: "Andrew! saddle my horse!" I dressed quickly; similar calls for horses were heard, simultaneously, from all the staff tents, and in a very few minutes we were all mounted and riding through the dense woods, as rapidly as possible, toward our Division front. The night was intensely dark, iluminated occasionally by a flash of lightning or a bursting

8. The quotation is from Scott's "Marmion" and reads as follows:
> "O woman! in our hours of ease,
> Uncertain, coy, and hard to please,
> And variable as the shade
> By the light quivering aspen made,—
> When pain and anguish wring the brow,
> A ministering angel thou!"

shell that came screaming along, but as we neared the front we could see that the musketry was not on our front, but just to our left, and the lines on either side were distinctly marked by the flashes of the guns, so that they looked like two parallel red lines, drawn across the black bosom of the night. The flurry ended with no harm done, and we got back to our blankets a little before daylight. The rebels had attempted to drive in our skirmishers, and take an advanced line, but they were completely foiled, our loss being about half a dozen, theirs unknown, but it must have been much greater.

Yesterday was not one of our fighting days, but I didn't finish this letter, for it was one of our moving days. We received an order yesterday to relieve, that is, to take the place of, Geary's Division of Hooker's Corps, and as Geary was in the front line, the change couldn't be made in daylight, without the enemy seeing it and shelling us, so it was necessary to do it last night, and with the utmost quiet, so I had to ride around Geary's line with the General yesterday, noting landmarks, and studying the position, so that I might be able to conduct our troops to their places in the darkness, for whenever we make such night changes it is my duty to conduct the troops to their new position. I got through last night about midnight, and being tired and sleepy, didn't go back to headquarters, but hitched my horse to a sapling, took off the saddle for a pillow, and spreading my gun poncho on the ground, slept soundly on it, without other bed, until the sun shone in my face this morning. We have been doing nothing to-day but riding around our new lines, and scanning our front with field glasses, to learn as much as possible about our new position before night should come; but now night has come, and with it a partial respite from the excessive heat, and the question with us now is: Will the enemy attack us to-night? Everything is remarkably quiet so far; even the skirmishers have almost ceased firing, but we may have plenty of noise before morning. I hope not, for if it gets cool enough I want to get a good sleep to-night.

July 2nd. Just at this point I had to stop last night, to send out some orders to our Brigade Inspectors, relative to a change which the General desired to have made in our picket line, and so your letter was thrust into the valise again. This letter appears to be as much "continued" as one of Sylvanus Cobb's stories, but I hope I shall be able to conclude it this afternoon. It is now about 4 o'clock; we had a fine shower about noon, which reduced the heat. I received your letter of June 24th, to-day. The heat you speak of there must be very great, when it makes letters so very small. The heat here has a different effect, as you see, and causes my letters to grow and spread like pumpkin vines. Well, we are near "Pumpkin Vine Creek," and that may account for it. I learn to-day, that Fessenden of Maine is Secretary of the Treasury *vice* Chase, resigned. Ah, Salmon P.! I had begun to have faith in you, but with all your ability you are a selfish demagogue, to abandon the government now, when the grand crisis is at hand. Chase has been so entirely identified with our national finances since the war began that I'm afraid his retirement now will have a bad effect, and will tend to complicate the Presidential question still more. I shall now expect an alliance between the Chase and Fremont factions. . . .

Day after to-morrow is the "glorious 4th," and a deserter who came into our lines last night told me that the rank and file of the rebel army in our front are firmly impressed with the belief that we intend to attack them along the whole line on the morning of the 4th and continue the fighting all day regardless of the loss, until either that army or ours is annihilated. Poor fellows! I expect they are trembling at the near approach of that fatal morning. They would, no doubt, be surprised to know that part of Sherman's army is nearer Atlanta, to-night, than the

bulk of theirs is. *I may not write what I know,* for this letter
may fall into rebel hands before to-morrow night. So General
John [Beatty] is a candidate for Congress. Glad of it. Tell him
I'll do what I can for him down here. . . .

Your husband.

At Chattahoochee River, July 12, 1864.
Dear wife:

Mine eyes have beheld the promised land! The "domes and
minarets and spires" of Atlanta are glittering in the sunlight
before us, and only 8 miles distant. On the morning of the 5th,
while riding at the extreme front with the General, and eagerly
pressing our skirmishers forward after the rapidly retreating
rebels, suddenly we came upon a high bluff overlooking the
Chattahoochee, and looking southward across the river, there
lay the beautiful "Gate City" in full view, and as the soldiers
caught the announcement that Atlanta was in sight, such a
cheer went up as must have been heard even in the entrenchments of the doomed city itself. In a very few moments Generals
Sherman and Thomas (who are always with the extreme front
when a sudden movement is taking place) were with us on the
hill top, and the two veterans, for a moment, gazed at the glittering prize in silence. I watched the two noble soldiers—
Sherman stepping nervously about, his eyes sparkling and his
face aglow—casting a single glance at Atlanta, another at the
River, and a dozen at the surrounding valley to see where he
could best cross the River, how he best could flank them.
Thomas stood there like a noble old Roman, calm, soldierly,
dignified; no trace of excitement about that grand old soldier
who had ruled the storm at Chickamauga. Turning quietly to
my General, he said: "[Baird], send up a couple of guns and
we'll throw some shells over there," pointing to some heavy
timber across the River.

In a moment I was off down the road, to the rear, to order up some artillery; the infantry column separated and opened the road, the artillery came thundering along through the long lines of men, and in fifteen minutes from the time our line of skirmishers reached that hill top, a Parrott shell went screaming from the high point, and burst beautifully on the south side of the Chattahoochee—the first since the war began. That was a glorious moment, and I felt proud that I belonged to this grand army, and that I was at the front instead of at the rear, doing "fancy duty." Many a long fatiguing day has passed since I first crossed the Ohio River as a soldier, and the Chattahoochee River then seemed a long way off; many a time since then have I almost felt like giving up in despair, confessing myself unequal to the stern requirements of my time, but fortunately better counsels prevailed, I have saved my self respect, and I know I am indebted to you for most of the fortitude that has enabled me to keep at the front for these two toilsome years. Your cheerful, hopeful spirit has encouraged and animated me, and I know you would not have me shrink from the ordeal or return home until I can do so honorably.

The greater part of this army is now across the river, and some of it must be very near Atlanta, but I do not know where it is, for this corps has been kept on the north side of the river, thus far, to hold the fords and cover our line of communication, until the rest of the army can take up a position on the other side of the river that will compel either a battle or the immediate evacuation of the city. This army is so situated now as to prevent a junction of the armies of Lee and Johnston, and they must now fight it out separately. If Grant can whip Lee, we can whip Johnston, and then Jeff Davis might as well "shut up shop." We are now out of the mountains, we have pushed the rebel army from its last mountain stronghold and it must now rely upon good luck alone. On reaching the river the left wing of the army captured about 300 women at one cotton factory, and the right wing captured about 400 at another. They have all been shipped North.

I have received your letters of June 28th and July 1st. It is very hot here now, but I don't suppose the heat troubles us any more than it does you folks at home. When you wrote last, you, as well as everybody else in the North (judging from the newspapers) were alarmed about a reported defeat of our army on the 27th of June. No wonder the North is in a continual fever of excitement. Just because Sherman telegraphed the *truth,* viz., that he had assaulted the rebel works and been repulsed with a loss of about 3000, everybody began to groan over our defeat. Why, bless you, we didn't think anything of it here, and it has ceased to be even talked about. Everybody in this army that knew anything about it, knew that it was a kind of experiment, to try the rebel works that we have been flanking so long, to see whether they were really as strong as they appeared to be. If we had succeeded in piercing the rebel line at any of the three points at which our assaulting columns were directed, it would have resulted in the almost total destruction of Johnston's army; the prize was great, and the assault was accordingly, desperate and bloody, but we couldn't pierce their line with the first trial, so our lines dropped back a little, the men wiped the sweat from their faces, and sat down to rest before trying it again, but Sherman and Thomas thought it would cost too many lives to assault again, so then the men went to work and entrenched where they were, right close to the enemy's line, ready and willing at any moment to dash forward and assault again. The repulse of those three assaulting columns appears to have troubled and frightened the North very much, but it didn't make half as much impression on this army as two days steady rain would have made. . . .

Your husband.

Chattahoochee River, July 15, 1864.

Dear wife:

I have your letter of July 5th. . . . I have been in Dixie to-day, at least I've been across the Chattahoochee, and if Dixie isn't over there it isn't anywhere I guess. We are lying very quietly here, on the bank of the river; part of the army is across, about 4 miles above here, entrenched and quietly waiting for ———— to ————, I dare not write it, for fear some rebel might read this before to-morrow night; I can say, though, that we are waiting for *somebody* to do *something,* and then *we'll* do something. . . .[9]

I am glad the rebels have been raiding towards Washington and Baltimore. I wouldn't care a fig if they would capture Baltimore, for it has been a nuisance ever since the war began. It would hurt my pride somewhat to have them *capture* Washington, but I wouldn't care if they would invest it and lay siege to it.[10] Then we in the army would see just how much patriotism

9. What Connolly dared not write was, probably, "waiting for McPherson to cross." This is the editor's guess, based on the following passage from Van Horne, *History of the Army of the Cumberland:*

"On the 16th [of July] . . . General Sherman gave orders for the advance toward Atlanta on the following day. McPherson's army had been previously transferred from the extreme right to Roswell; Schofield's was across in front of Phillip's ferry, and Howard's corps on the south side, before Power's ferry. The next morning, General McPherson crossed at Roswell, and moved toward the Augusta railroad, east of Decatur; General Schofield advanced toward Cross Keys, and Palmer's and Hood's corps passed the river on pontoon bridges, at Paice's ferry, covered by Wood's division, which marched down the left bank of the river from Power's ferry, and subsequently rejoined the Fourth Corps, and with it moved toward Buckhead. Garrard's cavalry acted with General McPherson, and Stoneman's and McCook's watched the river and roads below the railroad.

"The movement was a right wheel, with Palmer's corps of the Army of the Cumberland as a pivot." II, 110–11.

10. On July 9 General Jubal A. Early, attempting to relieve the pressure on Lee, threatened Washington. General Lew Wallace interposed a small

there is among the carpet knights at home; then we would see which the people at home love most, their money or their country. If there is not enough manhood in the North to save our country's capital from 40,000 ragged rebels, then let that capital go, and let the pusillanimous North bow its head and take the yoke of its more chivalric Southern conquerors. If this army has been toiling in the field for years, to shield a race of cowards at home, it is time the army knew it, and I therefore rejoice at every prospect of a rebel invasion. The South has been invaded and desolated on every hand, but it still maintains its battle front, and proud, defiant mien.

I would like to see, now, what the North will do if it is invaded. . . . I have been looking out for that mocking bird for you but have not seen one since you wrote me about it. Johnston, in his retreat, appears to have swept along with him, not only his army, but all the white men, white women and mocking birds, leaving us nothing but scorpions, wood ticks and worn out Africans. But I'll not forget your wish, and if I can get one will certainly do so. I see greenbacks are only worth 38 cents on the dollar. Glad I haven't got any, for that is almost on par with confederate money. . . .

Your husband.

Near Atlanta, Ga., July 23, 1864.

Dear wife:

I received yours of the 15th yesterday but hadn't time to read it until yesterday, or rather last night, as we were busy all day getting our troops in position, and reconnoitering to ascertain the exact location of the enemy's lines. We have finally swept over all natural obstacles between Chattanooga and Atlanta. The rivers are all crossed and the mountains all scaled,

Union force which, though defeated, delayed Early long enough for two army corps to come to the rescue of the capital. Early, seeing that an assault had become hopeless, withdrew on July 12.

and nothing now remains between us and the doomed city but the ridges of red clay thrown up by the rebel army. We have crossed hundreds of such ridges between the Cumberland and the Chattahoochee, and the fair presumption is that we can cross those in our front now, but nothing is certain in war, and I shall not, therefore, say that Atlanta is ours until I actually ride through its streets with our victorious columns. As we approach the prize the rebels are becoming more desperate. Johnston has been removed from command, because he pronounced Atlanta untenable, and Hood, who is a reckless fighter, succeeds him.

Hood first manifested his dash and recklessness as a commander of the rebel army, when, on the 20th inst. he massed his whole army and hurled it against what he supposed was our right, but which, unfortunately for him, proved to be about our centre. The attack was a desperate one, but it failed, and the rebel loss was terrible; probably not less than 8000; I believe the Atlanta papers of the 21st admit a loss of about 6000; our loss was between two and three thousand.[11] The attack struck the left of our Division, but we disposed of it in about ten minutes, and didn't have more than twenty men hurt, but we had worked all the night before building strong breastworks, and so were better prepared for the attack than many other Divisions, where the men had slept the night before, and were consequently, caught without fortifications, or but incomplete ones.

This Corps crossed the river on the 17th inst. and the general impression then was that we should be in Atlanta by the 20th, and with almost no fighting, but the night before we started I wrote to Andrew and told him I thought the severe fighting of

11. Jefferson Davis, who had no faith in Joseph E. Johnston and disliked him besides, relieved the wily strategist on July 17 and gave the Confederate command to the "gallant Hood of Texas," whose courage and impetuosity far exceeded his military skill. When Hood attacked the Union forces on July 20 and 22 he suffered a sharp defeat and lost, on the two days, approximately 9,500 men in killed and wounded as opposed to Union casualties of 3,600.

the campaign would take place between the river and the city, and I am now fully convinced of it. The rebels came out and attacked McPherson and Scofield yesterday, and gained some advantage over them, capturing several pieces of artillery, and many prisoners. McPherson was killed.[12]

That is a severe loss, but his place can be filled; should we lose old father Thomas though, it would hurt us equal to the loss of an entire Division. We have been singularly fortunate during the entire campaign; success has crowned almost every movement, and our losses have been light, but we can't expect to get along always without some pretty tough fighting. The rebels have been more vigorous since we crossed the river than they were before, but it is only the vigor of desperation, and the more frequently they assault us, the sooner their army will be destroyed, for they *can't whip* this army; we are like the big boy, "too big to be whipped." They may gain temporary advantage here and there along our line, they may capture a few guns, but they will capture them at the expense of the blood and muscle of their army, and that they cannot replace; so I don't care how often they assault; we are here to *fight* them and *destroy* them, not to *chase* them, and if they have found their "last ditch" all right, Sherman will soon put them in it, and the oftener they attack the sooner he'll have them in it.

From the position of this Division we can't see Atlanta, although it is only about two miles to the city, but the left of our army is much nearer to it, and prisoners say that our shells go into it. The surrounding country is comparatively level, fertile and well cultivated, and the residences are neat and tasteful. All the streams of any considerable size through this country are very muddy looking, the springs are not very numerous, and

12. Major General James B. McPherson, who had commanded the Army of the Tennessee since March 26, 1864. Grant considered McPherson and Sherman as "the men to whom, above all others, I feel indebted for whatever I have had of success."

their water south of the river is not as good as the water north of it. We hold possession of the railroad from Atlanta to Augusta, and have cut the railroad from Atlanta to Montgomery, Ala., thus leaving Atlanta but a single railroad running south easterly to Macon, and thence, by a very circuitous route to Charleston, S. C. Now if we could get possession of the road to Macon it would compel the rebels to evacuate Atlanta, as they would be entirely cut off from all communication, by rail or telegraph, with the rest of the Confederacy. We will probably get that road very soon. The artillery firing is almost incessant, and at this time of night (11 o'clock) the rebel shells from Atlanta are bursting uncomfortably close to where I am writing, so you may guess why this letter is such a scrawl. Just now I hear a heavily loaded train running out of Atlanta on the Macon road; may be the rascals are running away again. This is Saturday night and they always retreat on Saturday nights, but morning will tell. Plague on the shells! They are bursting so close as to make me dodge every time one explodes.

I'm demoralized and can't write any more to-night, so I'll quit and go and hunt for a big tree which will be a better protection than my tent.

Your husband.

Before Atlanta, July 25, 1864.

Dear wife:

It is late bed time, but we suspect an attack, and have been sitting up hoping that if we are attacked it may be before we have gone to bed, for we dislike being hurried out of our blankets in the small hours of the night by the racket of an attacking column. Two deserters, who came into our lines since dark, report that Hardee, with his Corps, and 5000 additional troops, is to attack our right flank to-night. If he does that it will bring us into the fight speedily, but if the old 14th Corps has half a chance, to-morrow's sun will rise upon Hardee a defeated

man. He may make the attack, but I hardly think he will, for the
rebel loss has been so great in such attacks, since we crossed the
river, that they can't afford to lose many more men without
utterly destroying their army. They may attack when and where
they please, whether in front or flank, it makes but little difference, we'll manage some way to punish them severely every
time they undertake it. The musketry is quite sharp along our
lines just now, so come on Mr. Hardee if you think you can
stand it, we will give you a soldierly entertainment at least.

I believe men do become hardened to some extent in the
army. Two years ago I would have had many serious thoughts
over the prospect that presents itself to-night; a threatened
night attack by a whole army corps, would have unfitted me for
writing, driven sleep from my eyelids, and kept me nervously
pacing about during the whole night, but I can't possibly feel
so now. I find myself studying the situation—thinking about the
weak points and the strong points of our line—speculating as to
how and where the enemy will make his first attack—studying
the probabilities as to whether he will make any attack at all,
and finally concluding that they may possibly attack—better
be ready for it anyhow, and they may possibly drive us back
a little way, but they can't whip us, and their loss in the end will
be far greater than ours. I presume that is the way most officers,
who have been any considerable time in the service feel about it
to-night. Questions of personal hazard are of secondary consideration, for individual safety is best secured by securing the
safety of all; and yet I don't think men become callous to danger,
indeed I think it is the reverse, and for myself, I know I took
more and greater risks during my first year of service than I
would take now, for I was verdant then, and took risks without knowing it, possibly for fear some one might say I was
afraid to do this or that. I guess I had better not write any more
to convince you of my moral degeneration, and as my eyelids
begin to feel heavy I'll lay down my pen and venture to my

blankets, and if Mr. Hardee is running around tonight he had better follow my example, that is, not get into *my* blankets but into his own; so hoping that a quiet night may usher in a quiet morning, I'll say good night.

July 27th. Well, here it is, the evening of the 27th, two days later, and still Hardee has not ventured to attack us. I turned in to my blankets on the night I commenced this letter, at about one o'clock in the morning, but was not permitted to have a quiet night, for about half past two an orderly came galloping up to headquarters, and his noise awakened me; I heard him enquire of the guard which was the General's tent, and the guard directed him to it; in a very few minutes the General, in drawers and slippers, came to my tent, lighted my candle with his, and handed me the note from General [Palmer], our Corps Commander, which I enclose.[13] After I had read the note, the General directed me to go to our picket line and collect from the pickets, and from my own observation, all the information I could, in regard to movements within the enemy's lines. So you see how speedily my hopes for a quiet night vanished. As soon as my horse could be saddled I was off for the picket line, where I remained until morning, listening to the rebels moving about in Atlanta, and listening to the extravagant and often contradictory stories of the pickets, as to what they had heard during the night. The result of my observation was that I was able to report that the rebels had been busily engaged all night

13. The note read as follows:

"July 26, 1864.

"General:

"General Hooker reports to Department Headquarters that the enemy have been all night removing artillery and infantry trains to the right. They seem, according to this report, first to move to their right, and then to their left (our right). Show this to General [Baird] and order your pickets to observe closely and report.

Respectfully,
John M. Palmer
Maj. Genl."

in moving troops and trains and artillery, but I could form no idea where they were moving them to. I heard one railroad train come into the city on the Macon railroad and go out again, and but one. General Howard assumed command of McPherson's army today.

There are movements going on today and tonight, in Sherman's peculiar style, the result of which you will undoubtedly read in the daily papers long before you read this. People may rest assured that the rebels will not give up Atlanta until they are compelled to. They withdrew from Knoxville and Chattanooga last year, hoping, subsequently, to crush Rosecran's army, and re-occupy both places.

They came very near doing it at Chickamauga, but they didn't quite, and the result was that they permanently lost two of the very important points of the Confederacy. They will profit by their experience of last year, and not give up this vital point, with the delusive hope of crushing Sherman afterward and re-occupying Atlanta. With the fall of Atlanta two Southern Capitals must fall, Milledgeville and Montgomery. Montgomery was where the Southern Confederacy first flung its banner to the breeze; it was the first capital of the Confederacy, and when Montgomery falls it may be said we have reached the root of the Confederacy.

The first and last Capitals of the Confederacy are trembling in the balance; Petersburg the key to one, Atlanta the key to the other. "Time, the great tomb builder of Nations" is rapidly digging "the last ditch" for Dixie, and History, with busy pen is hurrying up its epitaph. We may be as long before Atlanta as Grant before Petersburg; the loyal hearts of the North may grow sick with waiting for the tidings that Atlanta has fallen; clouds of gloom and despondency may hang over the North; faint hearts at home may falter at the prospect, and begin to whisper the craven words of *compromise,* but notwithstanding all this *Atlanta must fall.* This army has its front to the doomed city, and it will take no step backward; we do not look to croakers and demagogues at home for strength, our reliance is in God and a just cause, and "by that sign we conquer."

We have had terrible fighting since crossing the Chattahoochee; our path from the river to the very gates of the city is paved with soldiers' graves, but oh! how gloriously our brave boys have borne our flag on every field! The path has been a bloody one but a glorious one for this army, and I believe, today, that the veriest coward in our ranks has no fear of the rebel army that crouches within the entrenchments of Atlanta. We can shell the city at our pleasure, and a bright light in that direction tonight, indicates that some of our shells have fallen among inflammable substances.

I am provoked to think that Mr. Greely permitted himself to be wheedled by Geo. N. Sanders and those other rebels at Niagara, and I should think Mr. Lincoln would have had more sense than to have permitted Major Hay, a military officer, to have figured in any way, in that ridiculous correspondence. Permitting his name to appear will redeem the affair from some of its farcical features, and may possibly, in the eyes of the world, elevate the whole affair to the dignity of a serious negotiation. Why should we appear to be in haste to negotiate with treason now? Why send an officer of rank to talk about peace and compromise with a parcel of seedy traitors? [14] The army carries its arguments for rebels in its cartridge boxes and caissons, and if the rebels want peace let them come to our picket lines in front and say so. That's what they must do finally. We

14. The reference is to an abortive attempt of Horace Greeley, the officious editor of the New York *Tribune*, to bring about negotiations for peace between the Federal government and Confederate "commissioners" then at Niagara Falls, Ontario. Lincoln forced the reluctant editor to visit the Confederate representatives and discover for himself that they had neither credentials nor authority. John Hay, one of Lincoln's secretaries, was only an intermediary between the President and Greeley. Hay's title of Major had about as much military significance as that of a present-day Kentucky Colonel.

246 Three Years in the Army of the Cumberland

had a shower today, and it is quite cool tonight; indeed the
nights have been cool for a week past, and I hope they may
continue so during the rest of the season. Sidney Wood is in
hospital at Nashville and his wound is getting along nicely.
Out of stamps again. . . .

Your husband.

Before Atlanta, July 31, 1864.

Dear wife:

It is Sabbath evening, and just one week ago this evening you
were writing me the letter which I received yesterday.

There is one good thing about this campaign, and that is
that our mail has kept up with us in all marches toward the heart
of Georgia, and today the little missives come as promptly to
the soldier in the trenches before Atlanta, as they would if he
were at his own northern home. The value of this prompt trans-
mission of mails cannot be too highly appreciated, and the
tender and humanizing influence of the dear little home letters,
as they are read and re-read by the light of the camp fire is
worth more than all the efforts of army Chaplains and Christian Commission men.

On Thursday, the 28th, we had another heavy engagement
with the enemy, and as usual they were terribly repulsed in
four distinct efforts to break our lines, leaving most of their
dead and many of their wounded in our hands.[15] I was over the
ground next morning, and the dead lay just where they had
fallen, festering and decomposing in the hot July sun. I rode
over a space about 400 yards long by about 75 yards in width,
and in that area scanned the faces of 225 dead rebels, and then
had not seen more than one-third of those who lay there, but
that number satisfied my appetite for blood, and I returned feeling very thankful that I was not a rebel and especially a dead

15. Hood again attempted to break the Union stranglehold, and as before,
suffered heavy losses.

rebel. Colonels, Lieut. Colonels, Majors, Captains, Lieutenants and privates lay mingled together on that field of blood, all reduced to the same rank. One Colonel, one Major and one Captain had been buried before I got there. Poor fellows! They fought manfully, like Americans, and I honor them for their valor, even though they fought for a bad cause. The Captain who had been buried, had fallen nearer to our line than any other rebel, and he had evidently been decently interred by some Masonic brother in blue, for a head board made out of the lid of a cracker box, had been erected at his grave and inscribed with the masonic "square and compass", and his name "Capt. Sharp, 10th Miss., Buried by the 35th N. J. Vols. I know that he will arise again," all written on it with a pencil, and possibly by the hand of the same soldier that killed him a few hours before. Our men buried 642 rebels on that ground that day, and taking the usual proportions of wounded to killed, their loss on the 28th cannot have been less than 3,500 killed and wounded, and we took 400 prisoners, while our loss cannot have been more than 900 killed and wounded, and no prisoners.

The rebel loss in their several attacks on us since we crossed the river, must be fully twenty thousand, while ours has scarcely reached one third that number. I felt satisfied that the rebels would fight to the bitter end for Atlanta, after we should cross the river, but did not expect them to manifest such senseless desperation. Why it was a perfect murder. We slaughter them by the thousands, but Hood continues to hurl his broken, bleeding battalions against our immovable lines, with all the fury of a maniac. Reason seems dethroned, and Despair alone seems to rule the counsels within the walls of Atlanta. Nothing but defeat and utter destruction stares Hood in the face—he has sense enough to see it, and now, brave traitor, as he is, has determined to die fighting, with "harness on his back." Our men would take it as an easy task to repel an assault anywhere on our lines.

In company with Gen. [Baird], I chanced to be where Gen. Sherman was during the fighting of the 28th. When the firing commenced, away off, two miles to our right, we didn't know what it meant; Sherman remarked: "Logan is feeling for them and I guess he has found them." The scattering musketry, and occasional roar of artillery, swelled louder and louder into the full chorus of battle; presently a staff officer from Gen. Howard dashed up to Gen. Sherman and announced that the enemy were making a heavy and determined assault on Logan's corps, which was on the extreme right of the Army of the Tennessee, now commanded by Gen. Howard; "Good" said Sherman, "that's fine" "just what I wanted" "just what I wanted, tell Howard to invite them to attack, it will save us trouble, save us trouble, they'll only beat their own brains out, beat their own brains out." And so, in this confident tone our chieftain talked on gaily, while his boys in blue were reaping the terrible harvest of death. He understood his own strategy, he saw it was working as he had designed, and he was satisfied.

In your letter of a week ago, you congratulated me on our having taken Atlanta. If we have taken it yet I haven't heard of it, and we are in the front line where we will be likely to know it very soon after its capture. I see by the papers that the *correspondents* captured it a week or ten days ago, but the *army* hasn't got that far yet. True, we can look into the streets of the city from the front lines of this Division, but there are several heavy fortifications, filled with huge guns and greybacks, between us and those streets, and they were firing shells, as large as a water bucket, at us yesterday from those very fortifications. One of them struck near our headquarters yesterday and failed to explode; some soldiers dug it up, and on weighing it, found it weighed 65 pounds. I'm just coward enough to dodge all missiles of that size, for I'm sure I couldn't stop its flight if I'd "try my best," and what's the use of a body trying to do what a body knows a body can't do?

A methodist minister, Rev. George W. Pepper, whom I used to hear preach in Chesterville, O., when I was a small boy, called to see me yesterday and took dinner with me. While he was sitting on a chair in my tent and I was lazily lounging on my cot, one of those big shells came screaming along right over my tent, and burst near by; down on the floor of the tent went my reverend friend, as flat as a frog, and I was so irreverent as to laugh immoderately at the ridiculous figure he cut, sprawling on the floor. He raised up, brushed the dirt off his clothes, and looked as long faced as if he was preaching a funeral sermon, and very soon bade me good bye. Several shells came our way during dinner, and he made his pastoral call to these headquarters very brief.

A great many such shells passed over our headquarters yesterday, and we had a great deal of sport laughing at each other for our dodging. Falling flat on the ground or jumping behind a big tree are the prevailing modes of dodging these shells. I completely flattened myself on the ground once yesterday, when I thought, from the sound of the shell, it was coming right for me; our Medical Director, who was sitting near me at the time, also tried to flatten himself, but his pantaloons being very tight, he couldn't get down quick enough, though in his vigorous efforts to get down, he succeeded in rending his unmentionables most fearfully, and furnished the rest of the staff a half hour's laughter. So you see the hours pass lightly with us much of the time, and we levy contributions of merriment from every day as it glides along. . . .

Your husband.

Four miles S. W. of Atlanta, Aug. 6, 1864.

Dear wife:

It is Saturday night, and raining. I am tired and sleepy, for we have been fighting today, yesterday and day before yesterday, and I shall only write a note tonight, to let you know I am safe. We were moved from our former position before Atlanta, around to the extreme right, at this place, on Wednesday, the 3rd inst., driving the enemy after a sharp skirmish, took up position and fortified it, keeping up a continual skirmish during the night; next day we advanced one of our brigades to make a reconnoissance of the enemy's position and works—had heavy musketry and artillery on the part of the rebels—lost a good many men—captured some prisoners, and at night, withdrew the brigade to its original position.

Next day, which was yesterday, we were ordered to advance our whole line, and if found practicable, storm the enemy's works. This meant work. At an early hour yesterday the men were stripped for the assault, and about 10 A. M. the bugles sounded the charge; with a wild yell our men dashed forward through the dense timber, and in an instant the air was filled with the little leaden "messengers of peace"; in a few more minutes the rebel artillery opened along our entire front, but by this time we had captured their entire skirmish line, officers and men, numbering over 200, and as it was evident, from the artillery fire, that the rebels had massed their artillery in our front, the General determined that to advance against their main works would probably result in a repulse, and in the loss of hundreds of men without accomplishing any good, so he ordered the line to halt, and the men fell flat on their faces, to avoid the storm of shells that was howling over them. A message was immediately sent to our Corps Commander informing him of what we had done, and that it was not deemed practicable to assault the main works, and his order was received to hold the ground we had gained, and fortify ourselves.

Our men have dug so much during this campaign that it don't take them long to fortify now, and in about an hour, under a very heavy artillery fire, the men had erected fortifications that afforded excellent protection; other Divisions were then moved forward on a line with us, and there we are still. The enemy made a couple of feeble efforts to drive back our lines today, and annoyed us very much all day with their artillery, but they can't drive us back, and I guess they will behave themselves tomorrow. We will get them out of Atlanta some of these days, but they are holding to it with the greatest tenacity. A difficulty about a question of rank between Gens. [Palmer] and [Schofield] has thus far, resulted in one of them resigning command of his corps.[16] If they had happened to be killed the army would go along just the same. . . .

Your husband.

Four miles S. W. of Atlanta, Aug. 11, 1864.

Dear wife:

There is no mistake about it, "procrastination is the thief of time." I meant as much as could be, to have written you yesterday, but the day was hot, and I was so lazy, that I just lounged in my tent all day, listening to the constant cannonade going on around the doomed city, or dreamily, lazily thinking of home, and wondering what you were doing. Thus the day passed on, until the diminished heat and lengthened shadows, told me that the sun was about setting; I then determined to wait until after supper, and then, with lighted candle and everything ready, spend the evening chatting with you, but after supper came a sick headache, and although I resolutely lit my candle, got out my pen, ink and paper, and seated myself to write, it was all no use, and I had to give it up and retire, for my head ached wretchedly, and I knew if I undertook to write I would get too much headache in the letter. The last letter I have had from you was written July 31st, and on the next Sunday evening I was sitting in my tent here reading it. If I supposed my letters went to you anything like as rapidly as yours come to me, I should

16. General John M. Palmer had refused to take orders from General John M. Schofield, who, Palmer claimed, was his inferior in rank. Palmer submitted his resignation, and it was accepted. Connolly's comment was realistic.

feel better satisfied, but I'm afraid our letters from the army are delayed much longer than is necessary. . . .

I am afraid this political campaign is destined to be a very stormy one, and I shall not be at all surprised to see the flames of Civil war bursting out in many places in the North. Oh well! Let them burst out whensoever and wheresoever they may; if the able bodied men of the North won't "go to the war" they must expect *the war to go to them.* We have been getting reports from deserters, who are coming into our lines rapidly, that Mobile is in our possession, but it is not credited here in the army, although we expect it soon will be in our possession.[17] We expect Atlanta will soon be in our possession too though I haven't much idea how soon, but I feel quite certain that if our Generals hadn't fallen to quarreling among themselves, Atlanta would have been ours now. I'm glad I'm not a General to be quarreling with my companions about questions of rank, like a bunch of children quarreling about their painted toys. We will get Atlanta some way, though, in spite of our family broils, and I am equally certain Grant will, in some way, circumvent Lee, notwithstanding the stampede of his Africans before Petersburg the other day. Negroes *may* make as good soldiers as white men, but I don't believe it and never will.

I had my first mess of green corn yesterday at dinner, and had some more today, but it is scarce here, and indeed vegetables of all kinds are scarce, almost none to be obtained. The result of this scarcity of vegetables is that a great many cases of scurvy have appeared in this army, even among officers. Oh! if I could only be at home a couple of weeks now, wouldn't I luxuriate on green corn, potatoes, peas, beans, tomatoes, &c., &c.? Talk about bread being the "staff of life" it's all humbug. I'd give more for an ear of green corn down here than I would for two loaves of bread.

17. Farragut closed the port in the Battle of Mobile Bay on August 5, 1864, but the city withstood capture until April 12, 1865.

To my surprise I received a letter today from little Frank.[18]
. . . He tells me that he and his ma had been to Mansfield, and
that he bought two books with his own money, and that one of
the books tells about a drummer boy who captured the first
prisoner at the battle of Roanoke. Frank's military ardor is
evidently aroused, as I remember mine was when, as a small
boy, I used to read stories about the Mexican war, and earnestly
wished I was a man, so that I could go to war like the men in
the pictures, wearing a nice blue coat and red pants, flourishing
a great yellow sword over my head, and dashing into the thickest
of the fight on a furious, coal black horse. But I find that the
glowing fancy of youth lent a large amount of "enchantment
to the view," and now, that I have tried the sober reality, I find
it very unenchanting. Frank may find it out some day too, but
he is happy in the enjoyment of his delusion now, and it really
seems a pity that his rose tinted fancies of drummer boys and
war should ever be effaced from his mind. I am glad you
heard from Henry, but I suppose he is not at Macon now, as
that is not a very safe place to keep "Yankee prisoners" just
now. You haven't given me the author of that quotation I wrote
you about last month. You won't forget it will you? It is now
night and I must shut up shop for this time.

Your husband.

Four miles S. W. of Atlanta, Aug. 16, 1864.
Dear wife:
It is just about sunrise, and here I am, up and dressed, and
seated to commence a letter to you. Your letter of 7th inst., I
received yesterday. . . .
I sometimes get mad at the miserable cowardly sneaks at
home, and wish that about 10,000 rebel cavalry would make a
raid through every Northern State, burning, robbing and
destroying everything in their pathway. They did burn Cham-

18. Frank K. Dunn, Mrs. Connolly's young brother.

bersburg, Pa., and I rejoiced. It gave me pleasure to think of the drunken rebel raiders dancing and howling over the ruin they had wrought. I wish they could do the same to fifty other towns in the North; I want to see the ill gotten gains of Northern shoddyites and money mongers go up in smoke.

Evening, August 17th. Just as I wrote the word "smoke" above, breakfast was announced and I was compelled to stop "20 minutes for breakfast," as they say at railroad stations, but after breakfast, the General wanted to examine our front lines and wanted me to go with him, so I had to lay aside this letter, and I have been so busy since that I've had no time to finish it, and I just determined to steal a few minutes from my sleeping time tonight, to finish it.

Rebel cavalry in our rear has commenced cutting our communications, and mails are somewhat irregular. I have received your letter of the 7th, written at Mrs. Woods, and containing the welcome postage stamps. (On referring to the beginning of this letter I see I had already acknowledged the receipt of that letter, but no matter, I'm in a hurry, for I must get to bed so as to be up early, and besides it is somewhat doubtful whether this gets through to you anyhow). Extensive movements of this army commence tomorrow. I read the orders in detail this evening, and though I dare not say more about them, I still may say that *something will be done.* I am acting as Inspector General of the Corps now, and will so continue until the return of Lieut. Col. [Von Shrader], who is the Inspector General, but who is absent and will probably be for two weeks yet. I hope to write you tomorrow night, but if the trains are not running will not write, for letters can't get through.

Your husband.

Four miles S. W. of Atlanta, Aug. 21, 1864.

Dear wife:

It is Sunday afternoon, almost evening, and I will write you anyhow, even though there be but little prospect of my letter

getting through very soon, if at all. I received your letters of the
12th and 15th yesterday, which delighted me, especially the
latter one, written after you had got back home; its improved
tone will enable me to endure my Arabs life down here much
better, from the consciousness that you are in fine spirits at
home. I also received a letter from sister Maggie and one from
a friend at [Charleston], Ill., so you see I was well supplied
with mail matter yesterday, but there had been a great dearth
of mail here for several days previous, owing to the operations
of rebel cavalry in our rear, and our Division postmaster returned from the River about noon today, saying he could
get no mail as the railroad was out again. Thus we are living
down here, rebels all around us, but not enough of them to
disturb our equilibrium in the least, except in so far as their
raiding parties occasionally succeed in stopping our mails.

Our situation before Atlanta is not changed from what it was
when I last wrote you, and I don't think it will be during the
remainder of this month. Orders for operations when I last
wrote you were withdrawn at the last moment. Things were not
ripe. Quite a considerable number of officers are tendering
resignations and asking for leave of absence now. Much as I
would like to get home a few days I will not ask for leave now at
the crisis of the campaign, when every head and heart and hand
is needed right here at the front. We who are already in the
field must do our whole duty now, for it is daily becoming pain-
fully evident that those who are left at home do not intend to
do theirs. They can toss their hats in air and shout hurrahs
when we win victories, but they have no intention of placing
their own persons within the reach of rebel bullets. The columns
of the daily papers I see filled with advertisements of Northern
cowards, offering large sums for substitutes to take their places
in the ranks. Oh! how such men are despised here! They expect to prove their patriotism by lavishly expending the money
they have made by speculating on the misery of their country.
It is really an annoyance to me to think that when I become a

citizen again I will have to associate with such despicable creatures. To use your own language, "how long, oh how long must these things be." The war sentiment among the people of the North appears to be at its lowest ebb; everybody is either scrambling for wealth or for office, and giving only an occasional thought to the soldiers in the field, just about as the Southern planters used to think of their slaves, toiling in the cotton and the cane.

I suppose I wouldn't complain much about it if I were getting a fair share of the wealth in the general scramble, but as I don't think I am I suppose it is only natural that I should complain some. Oh well! there's no use in crying about it; those fellows at home are just raking up the money in convenient little heaps, I'll get home after a while, and they can't watch their heaps so closely but what I'll get some of them. Thank fortune, but little over two months until the Presidential election! A few days more and the agonies of the Chicago Convention will be over.[19] I have but little curiosity to know what it will bring forth. We have been lying here in one place so long that I am beginning to get "fidgetty"; time begins to hang heavily; I have so much time for thinking that I begin to conjure up a great many bright pictures of home, and thoughts of home don't add much to contentment down here, so I hope we'll push on soon, and with this hope I'll start this little courier to run the gauntlet of the rebel raiders, wishing it *bon voyage*.

Your husband.

Jonesboro, Ga., September 3, 1864.

Dear wife:

The long agony is over, and Atlanta is ours![20] This army is frantic with exultation, and the rebel army is scattered over

19. The Democratic National Convention met at Chicago on August 29 and nominated General George B. McClellan as the party candidate for President.

20. Hood evacuated Atlanta on September 1; Sherman's troops marched in the next day.

the country. This Corps eclipsed their glories of Chickamauga
and Mission Ridge, by its charge of day before yesterday. Our
Division, of course, was in it, and we were the first inside the
enemy's works, capturing about 500 prisoners, 4 pieces of artillery and 3 flags, one of the prisoners being a brigadier general.
Our Division Commander had two horses shot under him, his
aide de camp was shot in the arm, the rest of us are safe. I only
have time to let you know I am not hurt. Will write at length
first opportunity. We won't stay here long.

Your husband.

Atlanta, Sunday, September 11, 1864.
Dear wife:

It is a pleasant, breezy afternoon in September, and as I sit
here in my tent, on a beautiful grassy hill in the suburbs of the
fallen city, and watch our National colors floating gaily from
its spires, I feel profoundly thankful that God has permitted me
to pass safely through all the stern struggles of this long campaign, and that mine eyes are permitted to see the old flag floating over still another stronghold of the enemy. I knew we would
triumph; in the darkest hours of this campaign my faith in our
ultimate success was strong; I did not expect the city would
fall into our hands without terrible fighting, but I knew we
could do the fighting, and had no fears of the result.

Our Corps had the honor of giving the grand finishing stroke
to the campaign, on the first day of this month, at Jonesboro,
on the Macon railroad, about 20 miles south of Atlanta, where
we met the enemy, charged his works and carried them with
the bayonet, capturing 8 pieces of artillery, instead of 4 as I
wrote you before, several stands of colors, over 1,000 prisoners,
instead of 500, among them Brig. Gen. Govan, and utterly
routing and scattering the rest of the army confronting us. Oh,
it was a glorious battle! But this Division suffered terribly.
There was no chance for flinching there. Generals, Colonels,
Majors, Captains and privates, all had to go forward together

over that open field, facing and drawing nearer to death at every step we took, our horses crazy, frantic with the howling of shells, the rattling of canister and the whistling of bullets, ourselves delirious with the wild excitement of the moment, and thinking only of getting over those breast works—great volleys of canister shot sweeping through our lines making huge gaps, but the blue coated boys filled the gaps and still rushed forward right into the jaws of death—we left hundreds of bleeding comrades behind us at every step, but not one instant did that line hesitate—it moved steadily forward to the enemy's works—over the works with a shout—over the cannon—over the rebels, and then commenced stern work with the bayonet, but the despairing cries of surrender soon stopped it, the firing ceased, and 1,000 rebels were hurried to the rear as prisoners of war.

The General rode forward with the front line despite our protests and had two horses shot under him during the charge, my tent mate, Capt. [Acheson] [21] was shot in the right arm, why the other five of us escaped is one of the strange things found in a battle, when we were all similarly exposed to the fire. When the cheer of victory went up I recollect finding myself in a tangled lot of soldiers, on my horse, just against the enemy's log breast-works, my hat off, and tears streaming from my eyes, but as happy as a mortal is ever permitted to be. I could have lain down on that blood stained grass, amid the dying and the dead and wept with excess of joy. I have no language to express the rapture one feels in the moment of victory, but I do know that at such a moment one feels as if the joy were worth risking a hundred lives to attain it. Men at home will read of that battle and be glad of our success, but they can never feel as we felt, standing there quivering with excitement, amid the smoke and blood, and fresh horrors and grand trophies of that battle field.

That night, as we lay on the ground without blankets or tents,

21. Captain John W. Acheson, assistant adjutant-general of the division.

we were aroused by sound of distant explosions away off to the North, in the direction of Atlanta, and many were the conjectures as to the cause, but the afternoon brought us the intelligence that the enemy had "evacuated Atlanta last night, blowing up 86 car loads of ammunition, and destroying large amounts of public stores." Then went up more lusty cheers than were ever heard in that part of Georgia before. Atlanta was ours; the object of our campaign was accomplished, and *of course,* we were happy. I expect the newspaper correspondents will tell you all about the various movements by which Hood was deceived, his army divided, and Atlanta won; it would take me too long to do it here, and besides I want to reserve it until I get home, and then I'll tell you all about it, and puzzle your head over military maps, plans, diagrams, &c., until I make quite a soldier of you.

Now I suppose you want to know something about the great "Golden Apple," Atlanta, for the possession of which these two armies have been struggling so long. It is situated on high rolling land; two or three small streams run through the city in irregular courses, breaking the continuity of streets, and giving those parts of the city a very ragged appearance; the population is variously estimated at from 15,000 to 70,000; a good many citizens remain in the city, but the majority of them have gone to other Southern cities to escape from "the vandals." I have noticed some fine residences in the city, but the business buildings, so far as I have observed, are of mediocre quality, not comparable with business buildings in a Northern city of similar size. Atlanta looks more like a new, thriving Western city than any place I have seen in the South.

It has none of that built-up, finished, moss grown, venerable, aristocratic air, so noticeable in Southern cities; and in days of peace, I have no doubt Atlanta throbbed with the pulsations of that kind of enterprise that is converting our Western prairies into gardens, and dotting them with cities that rise up with the magic and suddenness of the coral isles. I notice that many of the buildings in the region of the depot have been struck by our shells, but I have only been in the city once since we returned from Jonesboro, and have only seen a small part of it, so that I do not know the full extent of damage our artillery did. As soon as I can get time I shall explore it thoroughly, and can give you a full report when I get home. I presume everybody at home is so deeply immersed in politics as to scarcely give a thought to the armies in the field. One party seems to want peace. That suits us here. We want peace too, *honorable* peace, won in the full light of day, at the cannon's mouth and the bayonet's point, with our grand old flag flying over us as we negotiate it, instead of cowardly peace purchased at the price of national dishonor. I received your letter of August 30th today. . . .

I don't know how it will be about leaves of absence from here now, but will soon know, and if there is an opportunity I will get a leave, but I think our stay here will be brief, Hood has *some* army left, and we must destroy it, and I want to be "in at the death." You have not yet told me about that poetical quotation I wrote you about. Please don't forget it.

Your husband.

Atlanta, Ga., September 18th, 1864.

Dear wife:

This is a beautiful evening, quiet and starlit; the mellow tones of a flute come floating through the evening air from the camps beyond, up to my tent on the hill top—a flute, played perhaps by some war worn soldier whose heart is softened by the peace and quiet of this Sabbath evening, and his thoughts turned back to the Sabbath evening tryst, in "auld lang syne" with a dear loved one.

Ah! how many hearts are turning northward from this city of camps tonight; how many hearts, hardened by years of toil

and scenes of blood on scores of historic battle fields, are softened by the mellow twilight of this evening, and their owners,
sitting alone, in musing mood, looking at the stars in the Northern skies, and wondering what the dear ones beneath those stars
are doing. And how gratifying it is to those whose hearts are
in this struggle to know that among all these thousands of war
worn men, who are thus thinking of home, there can scarcely
be found a single discontented spirit. We are all in the bright
glow of victory, happy as lovers in their honeymoon, and ready
to follow Sherman and Thomas to the ends of the Confederacy,
for the "God of Israel" is wielding his sword in our behalf and
we know no such word as fail. . . .

Your first letter addressed to me at Atlanta I received today.
You ask me what I think of McClellan's letter of acceptance.[22]
I like it very much for the reason that he don't whine about
peace in it, he talks *war,* he thinks he means war himself—as a
soldier he would not dare think anything else, but the trouble
with him is that he is not Major General McClellan who fought
stubbornly before Richmond, but is "a man of straw" set up by
Wood, Richmond, Seymour, Cox,[23] *et id omne genus,* to enable
them to steal into the Capitol and the Cabinet, and the foreign
missions, patch up a dishonorable peace and pocket the spoils.
He is like a verdant spooney whom old gamesters have in-
veigled into their snares, he is taking a hand with them, he
means no harm by it, he *thinks* he is honest himself and that
they are too; they have convinced him that his chances to win
are good, so spooney keeps in the game only to find himself
plucked by his new found friends, and then thrown aside. I
couldn't vote for McClellan either on a *peace* platform or on a
war platform. A President needs *back bone* these days and

22. McClellan, in accepting the Democratic nomination, promptly repudiated
the peace-at-any-price platform which the convention had adopted.

23. Fernando Wood, Dean Richmond, Horatio Seymour, and Samuel S.
Cox—all either Peace Democrats or, in modern parlance, fellow-travelers of
that faction.

needs no platform. There is but one question at issue in this
country now, that is: "Shall this Nation live or die." All
loyal men must take one side and all disloyal must take the
other. The disloyal ones should be outside our picket lines,
with no more right to vote at the coming election than we
Illinois soldiers have. Lincoln says, unequivocally, that the
Nation shall live, McClellan does not dare to say so, neither
does he dare to say it shall not live. He lacks backbone. His
nerves are not strong enough for this storm. We must have
the man who dares to say: the Nation must live. We can trust
ourselves to no other pilot.

Still I am glad McClellan does not announce himself as a
peace man. I am glad he ignores the Chicago platform, for his
doing so will undoubtedly be favorable to the war sentiment
in the North, will tend to lessen opposition to drafts, and will
show to the people of the South that the people of the North
are not willing to stop the war, because of the cost in men and
money. But a truce to politics. . . . I send you an autographed
letter of Alexander H. Stephens, Vice President of the Confederacy. It was picked up in a house in the city by one of our
staff and given to me. I have ———— thousand dollars salary
due me and not one cent in my pocket. That's a fine condition
for the "head of a family" to find himself in, isn't it? I can
get credit for everything but postage. Send me twenty postage
stamps.

Your husband.

Atlanta, Ga., Sept. 25, 1864.

Dear wife:

Your letter of 15th inst. was received yesterday, and I am
delighted to find it ran the gauntlet of Wheeler's cavalry and
reached me safely. . . .

A few days ago General [Baird] received a note from Gen.
Thomas asking him to forward to him the names of officers

of his command whom he desired to have recommended to the
President for promotion. I knew nothing of it at the time,
but about an hour ago our Asst. Adjt. Genl. showed me
General [Baird's] report which he has just forwarded. In
that report the General says: "I recommend Major [Connolly]
of [the 123rd] Ills. Vols., Asst. Inspector Genl. of this Division,
to be made Lieut. Col. by brevet, for gallant and distinguished
services during the late campaign." I must confess to be vain
enough to feel proud of the commendation contained in those
few lines. It is entirely unsolicited and comes very unexpectedly
at this time. I do not know whether the President will ever give
me the brevet, but it makes no difference to me now—the
consciousness that I have earned it is reward enough for me
—for I entered on my military career with fear and trembling,
having never had the least experience in military affairs, and
didn't know but what my legs were of the "Peace" persuasion,
and would rapidly carry me away from the first shot of a
hostile gun.

I presume ordinary gratitude would compel me to return
thanks to those members of my physical system for *not* carrying
me away.

Wheeler captured and burned a mail for this army yesterday, but I don't think there was anything in it for me, as I
received a letter from you yesterday, which, I presume arrived
in Atlanta the day before. I hope he may not interfere with
any of my letters, but I suspect he has on several occasions.
Sheridan appears to be doing handsomely in the Shenandoah
valley. He is one of our Cumberland Army Generals, and we
are very much gratified at his success. The men in the camps
are cheering continually over the telegrams from Washington,
and no one here doubts either the fact or the propriety of
Lincoln's election. McClellan stock is not quoted at all—none to
be found in this market. I don't know yet anything more about
when I shall get home, but I shall feel the General's pulse a

little on that question this week, provided he appears to be in real good humor, and if there is not some good strong reason against it I think I may get a short leave, but don't expect it too strongly, for I may not get it. It is quite late and I will close, for I must be out with the General at seven o'clock in the morning for a general inspection of our troops, preparatory to a grand review to come off soon.

Your husband.

Atlanta, Ga., Oct. 2, 1864.

Dear wife:

It is Sabbath evening again and I can't help writing you a short letter even though I am pretty certain you will not get it. It has been a week since I last wrote you, but I knew it was no use to write, for no mails have been carried over the road for a week.

The rebel cavalry is hovering about the road all the way from Nashville to the Chattahoochee, and although they are doing very little damage, yet it is not thought prudent to send mails over the road for fear they might be captured. It is not now probable that I will ask for a leave of absence, for a little while at least. I have said nothing about it to the General, but from what I know about the present condition of things, I think it not improbable that something important may occur in a very few days, and it would not surprise me even to receive marching orders tonight yet. You must not think from this that we are in any trouble here; far from it; we have plenty of rations for men and animals, and are ready to march east, west, north or south on 10 hours notice. A great many officers have gone home on leave, and a great many more had leaves in their pockets and were ready to start home, when an order was issued revoking the leaves of all officers who had not yet started, and declaring that no more leaves would be granted on any account until further orders.

I am "old soldier" enough to know what that means without any further explanation. Mrs. General Thomas and Mrs. General [Baird?] started from New York ten days ago to come here, but they have not yet arrived, and General [Baird?] is getting "fidgetty" about his wife, not having heard from her since she started. If she should be captured I would sympathize with him, of course, but can't say I would be very sorry, for while officers and soldiers may get along here very well, it is not a *good* place for their wives. Still these little interruptions may soon be remedied, and things resume their accustomed channel again in a very few days. I have been working hard to get my official business in good shape so that I can be spared a little while, and if things go all right it may not be very long until I can get home, unless I should be captured on the road, but I don't fear capture very much, and they can't keep me if they should capture me, for I know I can escape. The Adjutant of my regiment who, you will recollect, was dismissed the service, was exchanged a few days ago, and came through here on his way to the regiment. I did not see him. It is not improbable that he will be reinstated in the service. I hope it may be done, and have done what I could to effect it while he was a prisoner. It is so extremely uncertain whether you ever get this letter that I will not extend it for some rebel raider to read.

Am out of stamps again. Love to all at home.

Your penniless husband.

Chasing Hood

SHERMAN, having taken Atlanta, conceived the notion of marching across Georgia to Savannah. But for more than two months
his Confederate adversary, John B. Hood, dictated the Union
commander's movements.

Soon after the fall of Atlanta, Jefferson Davis left Richmond
to confer with his western generals. At this conference it was
decided that Hood's army should operate on Sherman's communications with Chattanooga, and then, reinforced by forces
from Arkansas and Louisiana, should sweep north through
Tennessee and Kentucky, mass on the Ohio River, and menace
Ohio or Indiana. Van Horne, historian of the Army of the
Cumberland, remarks: "Critics have been swift to condemn
Hood's advance to the North, and considered as an independent
movement, it is seemingly, at least, open to criticism; but
regarded as a part of a comprehensive plan, it is not apparent
that his army could have been used to better advantage."

At any rate, Hood remained at Lovejoy's Station, twenty
miles south of Atlanta, building up his forces until September
20, when he moved to put the Confederate strategy into effect.
Crossing the Chattahoochee River southwest of Atlanta, Hood
moved northward to throw his troops on the railroad that

connected Chattanooga and Atlanta. For the next several weeks Sherman sent detachment after detachment to find out what Hood was up to, and to thwart his plans if they could. To service of this kind Baird's division was committed until early November.

Anticipating campaigning so active that the army's mail service would be disrupted, Connolly decided to keep a diary instead of writing frequent letters to his wife. The diary entries he would summarize, when he had leisure, in letters. He did succeed in writing occasionally, but for the last three months of 1864 his diary constitutes his principal record of his experiences.

[Diary]

Monday, October 3d [1864].

Struck tents at 1 o'clock P. M. and commenced the march [from Atlanta]. The 1st Brigade in advance conducted by myself; the 2d Brigade following conducted by Genl. Baird. Some misunderstanding having occurred about the road, Genl. Baird sent Capt. Moulton forward to me to have me turn off at a certain road, but the head of column had gone beyond the point for turning, so I kept on—Moulton with me—and saw nothing of the General until next morning. We marched until late at night, through mud and rain, when Lowrie came forward to the head of the column to find out whether we knew where we were going; on discerning that we knew where we were going, he returned to the General and I went ahead with the column. About ten o'clock Capt. Morrison came to find Genl. Baird, but communicated the order to me to Encamp as soon as we could find ground suitable. It was raining and I soon found ground, and the 1st Brigade commenced going into bivouac, but not more than three or four hundred men could be found, the rest had stopped on the road side, discouraged by the mud and darkness, and the two following Brigades halted in the same way, and lay down in the fence corners—the General with them, so Moulton and I, with our orderlies, lay down in an old house that had been stripped of its weatherboards, and without supper, with saddle for pillow and saddle blanket for covering, slept soundly until morning. Este's Brigade had lost its way during the day, but by marching nearly all night, reached the rest of the Division before morning.

Tuesday, October 4th [1864].

Moved at daylight, and crossed Chattahoochee on pontoon bridge short distance above R. R. bridge at 6 A. M., marched around by bye-roads, which Genl. Davis [1] claimed were short cuts, but which like all his short cuts, proved to be very much out of the way, and very bad roads. Bivouacked at 1 P. M. in the position occupied by Davis' Division on the 5th of July during the march against Atlanta. Pitched our tents, got some dinner, and lay down for a good long sleep, but at 3:15 P. M. reached orders to march immediately, and at 3:30 P. M. were on the road. Marched about 4 miles this afternoon. I went ahead to find our place of bivouac, which was pointed out to me by Lt. Col. McClurg,[2] Genl. Davis' Chief of Staff. I put the Division in camp after dark, and got to bed about midnight very tired.

Wednesday, Oct. 5th [1864].

Moved at 8 A. M. without wagons, all trains except ordinance and ambulances sent forward to Marietta by another road to our right. This looked as though we might strike the Enemy before night, but we didn't. Struck Army of the Tennessee, and

1. Brigadier General Jefferson C. Davis, of Indiana, now commanding the 14th Corps.

2. Alexander C. McClurg of Chicago, then chief of staff of the 14th Corps.

followed after 15th A. C. which halted and bivouacked at 4
P. M. when we passed it, and moved on through a crowd of
Army wagons until we reached the military college at Marietta,
when I was ordered to go and select Camp ground west of
Marietta. I did so, and returned and brought the head of the
column to the ground selected, but at that moment an order
came directing us to press forward, all night if necessary, until
we should reach "Jack's House," which is about a mile in rear
of the position we held in June last at the foot of Kenesaw
mountain. This was discouraging news, for the night was very
dark, the roads very muddy, and it was raining quite hard, but
the bugles sounded "forward" and on went the column of tired
and hungry men floundering through the mud. Genl. Baird
directed me to return to Marietta, find Capt. Seely, our Q. M.
and have him send our Head Quarter wagons forward as soon
as he could find them, for we were without a blanket or a bite
to eat except what was in our wagons. Capt. Acheson went
back with me—found Seely, he gave us supper, put up a tent
by the roadside for us, fed our horses, so telling our orderly
to wake us at midnight we lay down to take a nap; when I
wakened it was daylight, the orderly declared that he had called
me at midnight, that I answered him & he thought we were
getting up until he went and looked into the tent and found us
still asleep, he then thought we had concluded to wait till
daylight & let us sleep. French's Division of Stewart's rebel
Corps attacked Allatoona to-day—Genl. Sherman watched the
conflict from the summit of Kenesaw mountain. He signalled
the Commander at Allatoona to hold the place at any sacrifice.

Thursday, Oct. 6th [1864].

The fight at Allatoona is over, and rumor says the rebels
were repulsed with heavy loss—that's first rate. I started at
daylight to overtake the Division, with half a loaf of bread in
my hand. Eating it as I rode along, and Acheson ditto—this

would be considered very undignified by some of the elegant gentlemen who do their soldering in Northern drawing rooms. As we rode along we discussed the question as to what temper we should find the General in, & readily concluded he would be very unamiable after his night in the mud & rain, so we determined to say nothing about our having supper and a tent to sleep in, but would complain as bitterly as any one about the hard night we had passed. We overtook the Division about 3 miles out where it had stuck fast in the mud last night and could get no farther. They were just moving out as we came up; the General and rest of the Staff were wet to the skin and covered with mud; when Acheson and myself commenced our groans over the hard night we had passed they wouldn't believe a word of it, but insisted that we had slept in a tent or house, for we were not wet, and our clothes not muddy, so we had to "plead guilty" to having slept in a tent and eaten supper, and it was taken as a good joke. The roads so bad we didn't reach "Jack's House," which is near Pine Mountain, until 11 o'clock to-day. Went into line on left of 4th Corps. Hood is scared and is trying to get out of our way. Went over to my regiment to-day. Found Capt. Adams in command, Lt. Col. Biggs being temporarily absent at Columbia, Tenn. I think it is in very bad condition. Everything done very loosely. Roads in very bad condition.

Friday, Oct. 7th [1864].

At 5 A. M. received orders for the Division to make a reconnoissance in the direction of Lost Mountain, which was about five miles from our camp. Column moved out at 8 o'clock A. M. without Artillery or wagons. Struck Dallas & Marietta road after a march of about 1½ miles. No enemy encountered until head of column had nearly passed the base of Lost Mountain, which loomed up on right like a huge sugar loaf, its sides covered with scrubby pine, oak and chestnut timber.

Here a few shots were fired by a squad of rebel cavalry, constituting the rear guard of a brigade of rebel cavalry said to be commanded by a Colonel Lowrie. A line of skirmishers was immediately deployed and the rebels driven away. Division advanced to a fork in the road and was deployed in line of battle on either side of the road. Arms were stacked, pickets thrown out, and the General and Staff rode to the summit of "Lost Mountain." The view from the summit was very beautiful. Far to the N. W. was visible the point of Lookout Mountain, overhanging Chattanooga; nearer to us was the range of Allatoona hills, and Allatoona Gap, where the battle of day before yesterday was gallantly fought and gloriously won by Corse; east of us and nearer to us Kenesaw with its dromedary humps loomed up from the plain, and still nearer arose Pine Mountain from the summit of which, last June, the soul of Rev. Bishop General Polk went to its long home. The plains between these mountain points were ridged like a plowed field with Federal and rebel breastworks, and it might shock the humanitarian to have stood there with me on the summit of Lost Mountain, and reflected that every square rod of soil within his view had lapped the blood of a human being and had furnished him a grave.

Our Cavalry were out on a reconnoissance to-day too, and while we were on "Lost Mountain," looking to the west we saw a line of horsemen emerge from the woods—their sabres flashed in the sunlight—artillery and musketry commenced to roar, the line of horsemen swept forward rapidly and were soon hidden from our view but in half an hour the noise ceased, and we knew that our cavalry had driven whatever force of the enemy had been opposing them. Coming down off the mountain the General ordered the column forward, and we advanced about three miles further, when the fact was developed that two rebel Corps (Stewart's and Lee's) had gone before us yesterday on this same road, to Dallas. This settled the question that Hood was running from us. An old man brought us out a little basket of apples to-day, but as they said the rebels had taken everything they had to eat except about a bushel of apples they had hidden away, I disliked to take any, but the old man insisted, so we gobbled up his apples, and rode on merrily leaving the old man and woman alone with their poverty and grief. We marched back to camp, which we reached safely at 6 P. M.

Saturday, Oct. 8th [1864].

I was in my first battle two years ago to-day at Perryville, Ky. Division received marching orders at 2½ P. M. and we were on the road at 3 P. M. After seeing the Division all on the march I started forward to see Genl. Davis and find where he wanted us to encamp. Found him about 4 miles from Ackworth, just at dark, and looked over the ground on which he wanted our Division. Head of column came up about an hour after dark, and I placed the several brigades in camp as they arrived. Genl. Baird came up at the rear of the column. Head quarters at a house occupied by Genl. Howard as his head quarters last June.

A person, calling himself Dr. Bundy, came into our lines to-night, and was brought to our headquarters, says he is Surgeon of the 9th Ills. Mounted Infy., and has just escaped from the rebels. I knew him as soon as I saw him, but I believe he is a spy. I never saw him but once before, that was at Mattoon, Illinois, in the spring of 1862, he was then being taken to Washington under arrest, charged with uttering disloyal sentiments, and with encouraging enlistment for the rebel Army, in Southern Illinois. After questioning him a while, I told him of all this, and he seemed somewhat surprised but he admitted it all, and said that on his trial the charges were not proven and that he was released, and had been in our army about 3 years. We hold him under guard to-night.

Sunday, Oct. 9th [1864].

Moved headquarters a few hundred yards this morning, and pitched our tents. Weather quite cold & windy. Foraging parties sent out to-day. Division remained stationary. Rode out with the General to-day, and went to "Old Durham's" at whose house we had our headquarters several days during the advance on Atlanta.

Monday, Oct. 10th [1864].

Received marching orders at 3½ P. M., Division moved at 5 P. M. It is evident that Hood is still moving northward, for the General directs me to take the head of the column and conduct it to Allatoona. I rode ahead rapidly with a couple of Orderlies (for the purpose of finding the road) the column following leisurely, and about dark reached the main road from Ackworth to Allatoona, which road I found occupied by the troops and trains of the 4th Corps, and Genl. Davis coming up soon after directed me to mass our troops on either side of the road, when they came up, and let them bivouac until the 4th Corps should pass, which I did. Genl. Baird came up with the rear of the column. The road being clear we started again about 10 o'clock, and marched through Allatoona (which consists of about a dozen shabby frame buildings) and through the gap (the scene of Corse's fight) by moonlight. Just after getting through the gap, I saw a light in a house by the road side, and being very thirsty, stopped to get a drink of water; they told me they had no water, but could give me a drink of "persimmon beer," something I had often heard of, but had never seen or tasted. I gladly accepted it, but it was poor stuff— tasted about like vinegar diluted with water, and colorless like water. We crossed the Etowah River, about 2 o'clock in the morning and bivouacked on the flat bottom land on its north bank. I laid down about 3½ o'clock very tired, sleepy and supperless.

Tuesday, Oct. 11th [1864].

This is election day in Ohio. Division moved at 7 A. M. The day quite warm and pleasant. Halted by the road side from 12 to 3 P. M. to allow Ohio Soldiers to vote. Very few Copperhead votes cast at this road side election. Moved forward at 3 o'clock, passed Cass Station, and through Kingston, going into Camp about 1½ miles W. of Kingston, in the direction of Rome. Had a beautiful place for headquarters. Recd. 15 sacks of mail for our Division to-night—the first we have received for a long time. I received 6 letters, and though very tired and sleepy, I laid down on the grass before our rail fire, and read them all without thinking once about sleep. Letters are the only links a soldier has to bind him to civilization, and no one but a soldier knows how highly he prizes them. We were here at Kingston last May marching southward, with the enemy in our front, now we are here again marching northward, and still the enemy is in our front. This has been a funny campaign from Atlanta north, the rebels have been using our breastworks of last Summer, and we have been using theirs.

Wednesday, Oct. 12th [1864].

Received orders at 3 o'clock this morning to move at daylight, but didn't get started until 8 o'clk. Took the road toward Rome, but left it, about 3 miles out from Kingston, and took a bye road which brought us into the Rome and Calhoun road about 8 miles east of Rome. At this point the road runs through as beautiful a valley as I ever saw. The road being blocked by trains, we halted at a house about two hours to-day, to let the wagons get ahead out of our way. Had a fine time gathering chestnuts during this halt. An old negro came to the General and told him that the soldiers had driven his steer into a drove of cattle that were coming, and the men wouldn't let him have him; the General questioned the old African a little about the ownership of the steer and being satisfied that it was the property of his sable friend, made the soldiers turn out the steer, when the drove came up, and the negro was profuse in his thanks to the "Ginral."

We are now in the region of good water again. All the streams north of the Etowah, are peculiarly clear, and the water is excellent. The streams between the Etowah and the Chattahoochee are not so clear, and the water not so good. When we struck the Rome and Calhoun road the General directed me to go forward in the direction of Rome, find Genl. Davis, and get his orders for our camp. I rode ahead to within 3 miles of Rome, and after a good deal of difficulty found Genl. Davis, and his Inspector General indicated the position of our camp. I got the Division in camp about 9 o'clk in the evening. My faithful horse "Henry" that carried me through Middle Tennessee, through Chickamauga and Mission Ridge has been bleeding at the nose all day and I expect the poor brute will die.

Kingston, Ga., Oct. 12, 1864.

Dear wife:

I received seven letters from you at this place last night. We have been following the rebels eight successive days. We reached here last night, got our first mail for three weeks, and start on toward Rome this morning. Have no time to write more. Am well, the army is in fine condition, and before we get through with Mr. Hood he will be put out of business. Since mails have been so much interrupted I have been keeping a diary. Good bye for this time.

Your husband.

[Diary]

Thursday, Oct. 13th [1864].

Marching orders not received until 3½ o'clock this afternoon. Capt. Acheson and myself rode in to Rome to-day. It has evidently been quite a business place. Our Division is entirely out of rations, and we get rations to-day from the stock on hand for the garrison at Rome.

Rations being distributed, the Division marched at 9½ P. M. for Calhoun. While waiting for the distribution of rations the General and Staff stopped at Mr. Hanes near where our tents had been pitched. Capt. Acheson astonished the ladies by playing finely on the piano. Col. Gleason's Band came up in front of the house, and played several pieces very finely. I had been talking with the old gentleman while the band was playing and he was expressing his regrets to me that he was not in a condition to treat us as hospitably as he could have done before the war; suddenly the band commenced playing the "Star Spangled Banner," the old man became silent, tears came into his eyes and rolled down his cheeks, his head bent forward, and his thoughts were evidently busy with the distant past, recalling to him the days when those same patriotic strains stirred the pulses of his young heart; turning to me when the music ceased. "Ah!" said he, "that reminds me of the day when I sailed into the harbor of Stockholm, on the first American Steamer that ever entered that port, with our glorious old Star Spangled banner flying from every mast head; oh, Sir, I felt proud of that flag then, and by G-d I'm proud of it yet, it makes me feel young again to see it." The old man spoke from the botton of his heart, his tears attesting his earnestness.

I bade the old man good by, and mounted for the night march at 9½ o'clock. We marched about seven miles in the direction of Calhoun and bivouacked at 2 A. M. About midnight the

General directed me to go forward, find where we were to stop, and have our tents put up—our wagons being in advance. Had headquarters put up about a mile in advance of the Division, and when the General found out where they were he said they were too far from the troops and swore he wouldn't stay there—but he did.

Friday, Oct. 14th [1864].

Acheson's nigger "Cato" left the saddle on the Captain's horse all night, so Acheson commenced the day by blowing up "Cato." I didn't like to get up this morning; had nothing but a piece of hard cracker and a cup of coffee for breakfast. Crossed the Oothkalaga to-day, and passed through Calhoun. At Calhoun started in advance to find our camp. Met Genl. Davis near Resaca on south bank of Oostanaula; he directed me to encamp the troops on south side of river, which I did about 7 o'clk P. M. and got to bed about ten.

Saturday, Oct. 15th [1864].

Division moved at 6 A. M. across the river. The enemy hold Snake Creek Gap, west of Resaca. We marched north from Resaca, along the R. R. to Tilton, turned west there and marched to the base of Mill Creek Mountain; halted about 2½ hours, awaiting orders; commenced the ascent of Mill Creek Mountain at dark; we had to walk up in single file; the ascent was difficult and I was very tired when I reached the summit. Troops bivouacked on the top; we were supperless, and had no blankets, so we built a fire, lay down and were soon asleep. All this mountain march was useless; the enemy evacuated Snake Creek Gap in the afternoon and we might have gone through that. I guess Stanley, who ordered us over the mountain, took one drink too many to-day. As we marched up the R. R. to-day, we had an opportunity of seeing how

Hood's men destroy R. R.; every tie was burned by them and every rail bent; I suppose they have studied our work in that line, so frequently, they are now nearly as good as ourselves at it.

Sunday, Oct. 16 [1864].

Division moved at 6 A. M. down the west side of the mountain, into Snake Creek Gap, through which we passed and halted an hour for dinner in the valley beyond. I had nothing to eat for myself, but as my horse had been without feed for 24 hours, I rode out into a corn field, and after a half hour search found a few "nubbins" for him. It now became evident that Sherman had scared Hood away from the R. R. for the Army was turned southward once more, and it was also evident that Sherman meant to make him fight if possible, for he ordered that the trains should move on the wagon road and that roads should be cut through the woods alongside, on which the troops could march, which would greatly hasten the march of the column.

This Division being the advance of the Corps, the General ordered me forward with a party of pioneers to select and cut a road through the woods, bridge streams, corduroy swamps &c so as to make a passage for the troops to Villanow, which I did; at Villanow I met General Stanley who directed me to keep right on to Ship's Gap, so I went on road making with my pioneers until I reached Dick's Gap, two miles from Ship's Gap, where I met General Sherman, who called out to me: "Hallo, Major! where do you belong?" "14th Corps, Sir"; "Where's Gen'l. Davis?" "I don't know, Sir"; "Where's the head of your column?" "About a mile back coming on rapidly." "That's first-rate; tell Gen'l. Davis I want him to encamp his Corps right here," and away rode "Tecumseh," to look after some other part of his 60000. When Gen'l. Davis came I delivered Gen'l. Sherman's order, and placed our Division in Camp on the ground which I had examined while waiting for the column to come up. I lost "Flora" to-day. While selecting a picket line this evening, came across a brother Mason in his little cabin; said he was a Union man and begged me to protect him. So I sent a soldier to him for a guard. Wagons not up to-night, therefore no tents or supper. Got a large iron pot, put about peck of sweet potatoes in it, had the orderlies boil them, then General and all sat down around the pot and ate sweet potatoes for supper.

Dicks Gap, Ga., Oct. 16, 1864.

Dear wife:

I am well. We are reduced to parched corn and sweet potatoes, but we are close after the copperheads commanded by Hood, and if the stay at home patriots will follow the copperheads commanded by McClellan in the same manner I shall be content. We may possibly force a fight out of them tomorrow, and if we can succeed in doing so, then good bye Mr. Hood. Have no time to write more. This is written by the light of a burning house with my knee for a desk.

Your husband.

Dicks Gap, Ga., Oct. 17, 1864.

Dear wife:

I wrote you a very hasty scrawl last night to send to Chattanooga by a courier who was already mounted and waiting for my letter. Our wagons reached us today, and as our postmaster is going to Chattanooga for mail I will write you a few words more. We are now within about one day's march of the famous Chickamauga battlefield. We have marched day and night since leaving Atlanta, but the rebels did the same and we have not overtaken them yet, though yesterday morning at daylight a part of our army was on top of the mountain while a rebel corps marched by in the valley, not over a half mile distant, and in full view. We are halting today to let our army concentrate, and to collect our wagons and send them back to

Chattanooga. Sherman has just issued an order the purport of which is that the rebels are now retreating toward Montgomery, Ala., and we are to send back to Chattanooga our wagons, baggage and everything that can in any way impede our march, and we are to start tomorrow morning to pursue them. We are to subsist on the country through which we march, and will pursue until we compel the rebels to fight or until their army breaks up and scatters over the country in small detachments. Atlanta is still in our possession, garrisoned by one corps, and the cars run regularly from there to Resaca, but the road from Resaca as far north as Tunnel Hill is badly destroyed, and it will take two weeks to put it in running order. Still, Sherman is determined to hold Atlanta at all hazards, and I think there will be no difficulty in doing so now, for the rebel army is exhausted and ours is in excellent condition, and the men are clamorous to be led southward again in pursuit of Hood. Sherman is really mad now because he was compelled to march so far north again, and is determined to annihilate Hood and his army, if possible to reach him. The postmaster is just ready to start and I must close.

Your husband.

[Diary]

Monday, Oct. 17th [1864.]

Division stationary to-day. Wagons came up 9 o'clk. Tents put up. Wrote a letter to Bromwell and others to-day, accepting nomination for Prosecuting Attorney; also wrote to Mary, and Sister Ella. Orders received to march to-morrow.

Tuesday, Oct. 18th [1864].

Division moved at 11 A. M., passed through "Dick's" and "Ship's" Gaps, and struck "Old Alabama Road"—fine road

—marched three hours and halted for dinner. Resumed march along west side of Taylor's ridge, and encamped at its base about 10 o'clock. Men straggled very much after dark, and the night was very dark. Head Quarters in Smallwood's Cabin. Old woman gave me pocket full of chestnuts on which I made my supper. Broke my saddle girth to-night while putting Division in camp. Valleys here are beautiful and productive, but are now infested by Gatewood's guerrillas.

Wednesday, Oct. 19th [1864].

Division moved at 8 A. M. toward Summerville. Passed thro' camp of 4th Corps. Met "Jake Conklin"; crossed Chatooga river—very clear stream about 5 rods wide at ford. I encamp Este on south side of stream under orders from Genl. Davis; Lowrie improperly halts other two Brigades on north side of stream; Genl. T. J. Wood Comd'g 4th Corps makes complaint about it; I finally get the Brigades across and encamped. Loyd buys "collards" of woman at white house. Eat some dinner out of the General's basket, and move on after halting two hours, and encamp near Summerville at 4 P. M. Two young ladies, riding mules, bare back, and with rope bridles, come to our Head Quarters and invite some officers to go and stay at their house so as to "perteck" them, but no officers went.

Thursday, Oct. 20th [1864].

Loyd inquired for his collards this morning. Wash, our cook, slept on them last night. Loyd mad, and we laugh him into good humor. Division moved at 9½ o'clk A. M. through Summerville on road to Gaylesville. Summerville is a small town, probably had 400 inhabitants before the war; but it now has a weatherbeaten, damaged appearance. Met Charlie Miller of Mt. Vernon, O., in Summerville; he was a school mate of mine at Chesterville, O.; he is now Captain in 76th O. V. I.

Crossed Raccoon Creek and halted an hour for dinner after marching 7 miles. Resumed march in an hour, and encamped at 9 P. M. 2 miles from Gaylesville, Ala. Line of march to-day has been near to and parallel with Chatooga river.

Friday, Oct. 21st [1864].

At 8 A. M. marching orders received and tents struck. Marching orders countermanded at 9 A. M. and tents pitched again. Visited Gaylesville to-day. It is a poor little town, all on one street, and on the right bank of the Chatooga. Rode out with Capt. Seely A. Q. M. and forded the Chatooga, but couldn't get out on opposite bank. Rode up to Cavalry Train and saw Adjt. Hamlin of my regiment who was exchanged a few weeks since.'He looks hard.

Gaylesville, Ala., Oct. 22, 1864.

Dear wife:

It is ten o'clock at night, and the band of the 79th Pennsylvania is out in front of our headquarters serenading us, but I have just been told: "Have your letter ready in twenty minutes, major, and I'll wait and take it with me." This was told me by the assistant adjutant general of the corps, Col. A. C. McClurg, who is going to Chattanooga at daylight in the morning, and as that is the only opportunity I know of for sending you a letter, I'll embrace it, though I can't write you one thousandth part of what I want. I am very well and in fine spirits as I ever was in my life. I have heard the election news and I'm happy. Ohio, Pennsylvania and Indiana have proven themselves worthy homes of the soldiers they have sent to the field. Thank God for it! He is giving our old flag victories with the ballot as well as with the bullet. Oh, how the election news cheers this army! How proudly our soldiers step as they think of the defeat of Northern traitors! It is second alone to the fall of Richmond.[3] I received news today that everything will go Union in Illinois by tremendous majorities. I received two letters from you today, the latest dated October 9th. I will surely not be home before this campaign ends, and I have no idea when that will occur. We may go to Mobile or Savannah first. A letter from brother Will today informs me he has enlisted in the 180th Ohio Regiment. He is pretty young, but I guess he will make a good soldier.

General Thomas has gone to Nashville. I guess Sherman will turn Hood over to him to look after. We have no regular mail communication now, and I don't know whether any of my late letters reach you, but I write a little every time I have a chance to get a letter started, hoping that in some way it may get through. Peanuts grow in abundance here. They are cultivated like sweet potatoes and the vines look like sweet potato vines. I enclose a couple of leaves from a peanut vine, so you may see what they look like. Time's up and I must close.

Your husband.

[Diary]

Sunday, Oct. 23rd [1864].

Division Stationary. Capt. Moulton and myself started on a foraging expedition with the 18th Ky. Vols. Went in a northwesterly direction through Alpine, on a spur of the Lookout range, and stopped at night at Major Williams' House in Broomtown Valley, about 22 miles from our camp. These valleys are rich, and forage is abundant. We are after wheat, hogs, sheep and cattle. We have 40 wagons and expect to load them all with wheat. Major Williams gives us his best bed and parlor to-night, but notwithstanding that we must have about 300 bushels of his wheat in the morning. He is a fine specimen of the haughty but hospitable Southern planter.

3. Ohio, Pennsylvania, and Indiana held state elections in October. All went Republican in 1864.

Monday, Oct. 24th [1864].

Loaded up 250 bushels of Major Williams' wheat this morning. Started wagons and men off in various directions and in a few hours the wagons came back loaded, and the men with plenty of hogs, cattle and sheep. Mrs. Williams wanted to buy my pocket knife, and I gave it to her. Started for camp about 11 o'clock. Moulton and I rode ahead rapidly, trusting to luck to escape guerrillas, and reached camp safely a little after dark, leaving the foraging party to come on as fast as they could. Result of Expedition—about 1000 bushels wheat, 150 sheep, 50 hogs, 75 cattle and 30 bushel sweet potatoes, besides a large amount of poultry. The valleys of Northwestern Georgia, between Lookout Mountain and Taylor's ridge, are beautiful, well watered, well cultivated and productive.

Tuesday, Oct. 25th [1864].

General Baird started for Nashville this morning on ten days leave, and I accompanied him with the escort. The distance from our camp to Rome is about 25 miles, the road running about parallel with the Coosa River. We passed over the same road to-day that Col. Straight traversed with his ill-fated expedition against Rome in the Spring of 1863. I saw the place where his men stacked arms when he surrendered. I think there was no good reason why he should not have reached and destroyed Rome, at least, before surrendering. Spent the night in Rome at Genl. Corse's Head Quarters, sleeping on a sofa. Genl. Baird got off to Kingston to-night, by rail.

Rome, Ga., Oct. 26, 1864.

Dear wife:

I came here from Gaylesville, Ala., yesterday with General [Baird], and he went on last night, by rail, to Nashville to meet his wife. I shall return today with the escort to Gaylesville, provided the guerillas don't pick us up on the way. I was somewhat in hope the General would let me go on to Nashville with him, and I could then have stolen a few days to run up into Ohio, but he wanted me to be with the division during his absence, so I shall not get home yet a while. He told me I should go the first opportunity; that's rather indefinite as to time, but it is sufficient to ground a hope on.

I thought I might find a paymaster here at Rome so that I could draw my pay and send it as far north as Nashville by the General, but there is no paymaster here. If my next letter to you should be dated at Mobile or Savannah or some other point on the Atlantic or gulf coast, you must not be surprised. Preparations are being rapidly made for one of Sherman's peculiar movements, which will transfer this army far from the scene of its present operations. That movement will not be completed until a month or six weeks from this time, and will not be begun for several days yet. The whole programme may be changed; the movement may not begin at all, but I think it will, and I really wish it was over with, for then I shall be able to get home, but probably not before, and I'm actually becoming a little "homesick" occasionally. The adjutant of my regiment, while a prisoner, saw your brother Henry at Macon, and he says he was well and enjoying himself as much as a prisoner can.

I have 27 miles to ride yet today, and it is now 11 o'clock, so I must close and start on my journey.

Your husband.

[Diary]

Wednesday, Oct. 26th [1864].

Started from Rome, with the Escort at 10 A. M. and reached camp beyond Gaylesville, without incident worthy of note, a little after dark, but very tired for I have been in the saddle almost constantly for the past four days and have ridden at least 120 miles. Found Col. Este at Head Quarters on my return he having assumed command of the Division during Genl. Baird's absence. He has no business to assume command; Hunter is the ranking Colonel, and is entitled to the command, but he don't know it, and if Este can play Division Commander over Hunter for a few days, all right.

Thursday, Oct. 27th [1864].

Division Stationary. Rain last night and to-day. Maj. Lowrie received notice of acceptance of his resignation. Serenade in the evening by Band of 38th Ohio Vols. Evening chilly and clear. Rumors of an important and very extensive movement are circulating about different Head Quarters. Some hint that Sherman has his eye on Mobile, others on Savannah, but if there's anything in it at all, I incline to the opinion that Savannah is the point, for that brings us to what must become our next "objective" viz. Lee's Army, whereas Mobile would take us farther from it than we now are. One thing is certain, there is no use of this Army of 70,000 "gallivanting" up and down through Georgia after Hood and his 40,000 any longer, for its like an elephant chasing a mouse; he wont let us catch him, and unless we can catch him so as to whip him soundly, his 40,000 are worth more to the rebels, than our 70,000 are to us, for it takes less to clothe, feed and pay them. So I believe we *are* going to do *something,* but I hardly dare guess what, yet.

Friday, Oct. 28th [1864].

Division Stationary. Orders received at 3 P. M. to move at daylight tomorrow morning, on the road to Rome. Our Divison is to be in the rear and we are to burn the grist mill in

Gaylesville and the bridge across the Chatooga after we have crossed.

Saturday, Oct. 29th [1864].

Division moved promptly at daylight across the Chatooga; sent a detachment back into town and burnt the mill with a large amount of wheat and flour in it, then burnt the bridge and started toward Rome. Encamped at dark 5 miles from Rome, having marched 20 miles. Placed pickets entirely around the Division to-night. Received mail to-night, and my share was 3 letters from Mary.

Sunday, Oct. 30th [1864].

Division moved at 5:45 A. M. marched 5 miles, and en-camped just across the river from Rome, on the bank of the Oostanaula near its confluence with the Coosa. Went over to Corps Head Quarters and met Maj. Newcomer, Pay Master, who promised to pay me if I would go up to his office in town. So I went up and got my pay in full up to to-morrow night in 7:30 Bonds, less the income tax, which these Pay Masters deduct, and thus save Uncle Sam some trouble in making collection. It is ridiculous to compel officers to pay 5 per cent tax on the salary they receive for services in the field. Those who stay at home and reap golden harvests out of the war should be compelled to pay the taxes.

Capt. Buttrick A. D. C. got back from Nashville this evening. Gave Maj. Lowrie $1,000 to express to Mary from Nashville, this evening. Stinchcomb in my tent this evening, drunk and filthy as usual. I know now why he resigned.

Monday, Oct. 31st [1864].

Division Stationary. I guess we are preparing for a grand raid through Georgia, to strike the coast at Savannah if practicable, and if not, then to strike it wherever we can. It's an extensive contract, but I like it, and hope we may undertake it for I'm sure we can get to the Coast somehow; I'd like very much to go home first, but I see no prospect for that now. Weather pleasant. Troops being paid off.

Tuesday, Nov. 1st [1864].

Division Stationary. Orders received to march for Kingston tomorrow morning at daylight. I understand Rome is to be abandoned by our forces. All the cavalry except Kilpatrick's Division is to go to Nashville. More rumors about a great movement through Georgia. Night dark and rainy.

Wednesday, Nov. 2d [1864].

Division marched at daylight crossing the Oostanaula on pontoon bridge, and passing through Rome. Like the Rome of Romulus and Remus it is situated on a number of hills, whether "seven" or not I can't say, for I didn't count them; the Coosa is its Tiber; why didn't they call it Tiber? I presume the Indian name is considered more euphonious. Since the Federal occupation of this place, it is said the Roman matrons and maidens have forgotten their absent lords, and turned Cyprians. Quite cold and disagreeable to-day; roads sloppy. Went ahead about noon to select camp. Head of column came in sight of Kingston for the third time this summer, about 3 P. M. and I placed it in Camp near our Camp of October 11th, our Head Quarters being almost exactly in the same place they then were. It is said we are to go to Atlanta from here, tearing up the R. R. as we go. I hope its true, there's something to stir the blood in such a bold operation as that.

Thursday, Novr. 3rd [1864].

Division Stationary. Weather wet and disagreeable. Troops being paid off. It is now certain that we are to march to Atlanta destroying the R. R. as we go, burn that city, and then strike boldly through the heart of Georgia to Savannah, if we can get there, and if not, then to any other seaport. This is indeed a hazardous undertaking, but we must "trust to luck"; I wouldn't miss going on this expedition for 6 months pay. I hope I may see Milledgeville. I have wanted to see it ever since I was an urchin stumbling thro' my Geography in Newark. Doct. Sloat, Surgeon 14th Ohio Vols., tried to sell me his horse this evening; told him I'd think about it until to-morrow evening.

Friday, Novr. 4th [1864].

Division Stationary. Windy, cold, unpleasant. Genl. Sherman orders estimates for clothing to be made out immediately. Bought Doct. Sloats gray horse "Frank" for $150. Cheap enough I think.

Saturday, Novr. 5th [1864].

Division Stationary. Bright, sunshiny day. Great many officers asking for leaves, and tendering resignations. They are appalled at the idea of a winter campaign through Georgia; their timid souls are shrinking before the possible difficulties and dangers of the march; the idea of cutting loose from the North, and marching to the coast is too much for their nerves, and they are making every exertion to avoid it. Their conduct is disgusting, and they ought to be dishonorably mustered out of the service. If we succeed it will be glorious; if we fail it will be no more than Napoleon and his grand army did in the Russian campaign. I, for one, shall go, let our fortune be what it may.

Kingston, Ga., Nov. 5, 1864.

Dear wife:

For many days I have been waiting, watching and hoping for a quiet hour to devote to you, but have waited and hoped in vain, and am now compelled to write you with men standing around talking to me every few minutes about business, inquiring about papers, &c., but I dare not defer writing any longer, for today may be the last opportunity I shall have of writing you for perhaps two months, and I am sure, from reading your letter of the 23rd ult. you couldn't stand that at all. By some surprising freak of the mails your letter of the 27th ult. reached me yesterday, but I'm sure I need not tell you I was very glad to get it. If I could get your letters as regularly and frequently as I did during the summer, I could endure it much better without a leave of absence, but as it is now I come pretty near having the blues sometimes. I cheer myself with the reflection that this must soon come to a close. . . .

My horse died a few days ago, and I was compelled to buy another, which I did yesterday, for $150. I couldn't find a respectable horse for any less price, but I declare I didn't like to pay that much for a horse to wear out in the service. He is a dark dapple grey, 6 years old, and paces fast under the saddle; I think he is a fine horse and that I shall like him very much. He was brought into the army from Cincinnati by the Col. McCook who was killed in an ambulance by guerillas about a year ago. Matters in this army are in such an unsettled condition that I can't tell anything about when I shall be able to get home. From your speaking of snow I judge winter has begun in Ohio, although it is quite warm and pleasant here. . . .

I can't speak with certainty as to what this army is to do, but it appears that the 14th, 15th, 17th and 20th Corps are to meet at Atlanta within a few days, and starting from there, under the immediate command of General Sherman, march either to Mobile on the Gulf coast or Savannah on the Atlantic coast. If we march on Mobile we will take Macon *enroute,* and if we go to Savannah we will take Milledgeville, the capital of Georgia. The march will be made as rapidly as possible, and as

the distance to either point is only about 300 miles, it is calcu-
lated we can make the march in from three to four weeks, particularly as there is no rebel force in our way should we go to
either place. When we start, Atlanta, and all the line of railroad from there to Chattanooga will be abandoned, and for the
three or four weeks we may be occupied in the trip we will be
entirely cut off from communication with the North, so that
I suppose it will be at least two months from the time we start
from Atlanta, before any letters we write can reach the North.
All this programme may be changed, and we may not go at
all, but I have reason to think we will, and am expecting orders
to move to Atlanta every day. I am quite certain we will start
there within the next two days. My regiment has returned to
Nashville to be remounted, so it will not be with us in our grand
march through the Confederacy. Thomas will remain in Tennessee to operate against Hood, so we will not see him again
for a long time; I regret that very much, but I presume the
service demands it and we must submit. I learn that brother Will
is assigned to the 25th Ohio. . . .

Your husband.

[Diary]

Sunday, Novr. 6th [1864].

Division Stationary. Weather cold and unpleasant. Genl.
Baird returned from Nashville and resumed command of Division. Acheson and Buttrick quit the General's mess and came
into ours this evening.

Monday, Novr. 7th [1864].

Division Stationary. Weather dark and cloudy. Captain Biddle, Ordnance officer, ordered to Atlanta to procure arms and
equipments for the unarmed recruits we may have with us when

we reach Atlanta. Pretty rough initiation for these recruits, this Georgia march will be!

Tuesday, Novr. 8th [1864].

Division Stationary. This is election day. I think Lincoln will be re-elected to-day, though we who are in the army know very little about the undercurrents of politics in the North, and we may all be surprised by finding McClellan elected.

There are comparatively few McClellan men in the army. In one brigade of our Division consisting of the 17th, 31st, 89th and 92d Ohio, 82d Ind. and 23d Missouri, the vote polled to-day stood Lincoln 1229, McClellan 101. Everything as quiet and orderly as usual in camp, the election creating no outward excitement.

Wednesday, Novr. 9th [1864].

Division Stationary. Rained quite heavily this evening. 74th Indiana Vols. sent out to-night to try and catch some guerrillas who captured and murdered some of their comrades to-day.

Kingston, Ga., Nov. 9, 1864.

Dear wife:

I suppose this is my last chance for writing until we reach some coast either at Mobile or Savannah, so I will take advantage of it. The weather is fine, the army in excellent spirits, and I am really anxious for the campaign to begin. After the triumph which I am sure the Union cause met with at the ballot box yesterday, it will be glorious to ride clear through the Confederacy. There is to me something romantic in the conception of this campaign, and I am really charmed with it. Nothing in military history compares with it except the invasion of Mexico by Cortez, the Spaniard, who, landing on its hostile shore, burned his ships, destroyed all his means of retreat, and then turning to his army, told them they must rely on God and their own right arms; that they must conquer or die.

So with Sherman: he goes to Atlanta, destroys the city and all railroad and telegraphic communication with the North, and then tells his army it must march either eastward or southward to the coast, or must perish. Won't that be a glorious day, when we reach the coast after having carried our flag in triumph from the Ohio to the Ocean?

Yesterday was election day; many soldiers voted here, but we Illinoisans are disfranchised. From the returns I have seen this morning I think Jeff Davis would have received as many votes in these camps as McClellan did. . . .

I shall write you again just as soon as I have an opportunity of sending a letter North, but I don't expect to have such opportunity for from four to six weeks, and it will then probably take the letter two weeks to reach you, so that after you receive this you may not expect to receive another for six and possibly eight weeks.

That is a long time I know, but military necessity compels it. It will be harder on you than on me, I am sure, for I will be moving daily amid new scenes, seeing new faces, new cities, towns and villages, and will have something of interest to occupy every moment of time, but you will be surrounded by the same persons, amid the same scenes, without anything to break the monotony of your daily round except the renewed anxieties, caused by the lurid reports of newspapers, predicting disasters for our army, all of which will be without foundation, so I am afraid before the six or eight weeks have passed you will be far more uncomfortable than I will be.

Rest assured we will come out all right; there will be no fighting in this campaign if it can be avoided without running away. We are to march as rapidly as possible day after day, until we reach the coast, destroying all railroads, telegraph lines, mills, manufactories, &c., &c., capturing such towns and cities as we

can, without besieging fortified places. So you see, while the
campaign will be a long one, it will not be a hard one, and at its
close I think there will be a chance for a good long leave of absence. If we should remain tomorrow I will write you again.
Address me as usual. The letters will get to me some way, if the
Johnnies don't gobble them.

Your husband.

[Diary]

Thursday, Novr. 10th [1864].

Division Stationary. Weather rather cold. 74th Ind. Vols. returned from their guerilla hunt, bringing in the Captain of the
band, and some suspicious citizens. I telegraphed to Charleston
to-day asking Tirrill to inform me, by telegraph, of the result
of my race for Prosecutor. By the suggestion of Genl. Davis,
I directed him to send his despatch to me at Atlanta, as he tells
me we will be there before the despatch can reach the North
and a return despatch get back; this being the case I suppose
I shall hear nothing about my election until we reach the Southern coast. The telegraph tells us to-day that Lincoln has carried
everything except Kentucky. Well, Kentucky, i. e., the "leading
families" has always been as disloyal as South Carolina.

Friday, Nov. 11th [1864].

Division Stationary. At noon to-day received orders to march
to-morrow morning at 6½ o'clock; so, I suppose, begins our
part of the great campaign through Georgia. We can't exactly
see our way through now, but I guess it will all come out right.
What a flutter this marching order is creating amongst our weak
knee'd brethren in shoulder straps; up to the last moment they
are tendering resignations and clamoring for leaves on account
of sick families, sick wives, &c., but all their applications meet
with a flat, stern refusal. Thank fortune I have no sick family,

my wife is well, and I know she wouldn't have me shrink from this expedition, at this time, on any consideration. Trains are constantly running from Atlanta to Chattanooga loaded with cannon, so I suppose the fortifications of that city will be dismantled and the city destroyed. The 20th corps is there now; and the 15th and 17th Corps somewhere near there; the 4th Corps has gone to Chattanooga to join Gen. Thomas, so Sherman's Army, for the Georgia Campaign, will consist of the 14th, 15th, 17th and 20th Corps and 2 Brigades of Cavalry under Kilpatrick.

Kingston, Ga., Nov. 11, 1864.

Dear wife:

When I wrote you on the 9th inst., we had orders to march next day, and I then supposed that by this time we would be in Atlanta at least, but the orders for marching have been suspended from day to day until now; everything is ready though now, and we start tomorrow morning sure, so after you receive *this,* you cannot expect to hear from me again for the next six or eight weeks.

A great many officers are resigning to avoid the coming campaign, and a great many others are trying to resign but cannot. They are being laughed at by the whole army here, and by their present conduct they are losing such soldierly reputation as they have made. I can't see why they are so much afraid of this campaign, for I regard it as one of the easiest campaigns I have engaged in.

Perhaps they have been away so long that their wives are urging them to come home, and the great boobies are consequently backing out and trooping off home as fast as they can get away. I am glad my wife is too patriotic and has too much good sense to do anything of that kind. They will all be sorry for going home before they have been there a single month, while we will have no regrets of that kind to disturb us. I want to ride my fine grey Frank—entirely through the Confederacy and let him drink out of the Atlantic—if he wants to—I shall then be content. If there should be any possibility of sending a letter back to you after we reach Atlanta, I shall do so, though I don't expect there will be, for railroad and telegraph lines will be finally broken when we start from here.

Weather quite pleasant and quite unlike the wintry weather I suppose you are having in Ohio. I am writing this in my tent without any fire and am warm enough. I have the "Atlantic" and "Harpers Monthly" for November, so I shall have some civilized entertainment, even in the heart of "Dixie." For fear my letter might miss the last mail I must close and send it off. We may all be disappointed about the campaign, it may be shorter than any of us expect, and for your sake I hope it may be.

Your husband.

[Diary]

Saturday, Novr. 12th [1864].

Division moved through Kingston toward Cartersville at 8 A. M. Weather pleasant. As we were marching through Cass Station, we could see the one solitary church spire of Cassville, the rest of the village having been burned yesterday by our soldiers, on account of its being a guerrilla haunt. Cassville is or *was* about ¾ of a mile N. E. of the road from Kingston to Cartersville, and is said to have been a very pretty *little* village. We reached Cartersville at 3 P. M. and on riding into the town with the General, found Genl. Sherman sitting on the hotel porch sending his last telegraphic message to the North. When the message was finished I saw the wire broken, and thus we were left "away down South in Dixie", without any means of communicating with friends at home. I knew the last train passed us this morning on its way from Atlanta to Chattanooga, and when I saw the wire severed—the "last link broken"—I must say I was forced for a few minutes to think about our isolated situation, and ask myself, in a variety of ways, the question, "What has Fate in store for us?" But in a few minutes we turned our backs on Cartersville, and the Division moved forward across the Etowah River, on the same bridge we crossed going northward on the 10th ult., and encamped at the ruins of the "Iron Works" near Allatoona. General Morgan's Division encamps to-night on the north side of the Etowah, and General Carlin's between the river and our camp. We commence destroying the R. R. to-morrow morning. Morgan to commence at the Etowah River. During the day, orders were received to march to-morrow, at daylight, and commence the destruction of the R. R. at Allatoona Creek, destroying it from there to a point one mile beyond Acworth.

Sunday, Novr. 13th [1864].

Division marched at daylight. Very cold this morning. Passed through Allatoona at 8 A. M. After getting through the town we found that Corse's Division of the 15th Corps, on its way from Rome to Atlanta, was blocking up the road ahead of us, and we would be compelled to halt, probably two hours; this was very annoying, as we were anxious to get forward and begin our work on the R. R. soon as possible, so that we might get it completed and get into camp before dark. The General was out of humor. I, however, remembered a bye-road which I had been on on our march north, and suggested to him that we could take that road, and reach the point for beginning our work without being interrupted by Corse's Division. At first he wouldn't listen to it—told me I didn't know the road &c but I quietly insisted that I *did* know the road, and after some time, prevailed on him to go with me and look at it. After going on this bye-road about a mile and making inquiries of some of the sallow, poverty-stricken, snuff-dipping women of the neighborhood the General became satisfied I was right and sent back an orderly to direct the head of the column to move forward.

We reached our point on the R. R. without further trouble, destroyed our allotted portion of the Road—our soldiers burned the village of Acworth *without orders,* and we went into camp at "Big Shanty" about dark. Acworth has been a thriving R. R. village, but to-night it is a heap of ruins. I was the only one of the General's staff in the town when the fires first began, and I tried to prevent the burning, but while I watched one house to keep it from being fired, another some where else would take fire; so I concluded to give it up. I succeeded in saving a few houses, occupied by "war widows" and their families, but all the rest of the town went up in smoke. It is evident that our soldiers are determined to burn, plunder and destroy everything in their way on this march. Well, that shows that they are not *afraid* of the South at any rate, and that each individual soldier is determined to strike with all his might against the rebellion, whether we ever get through or not. If we are to continue our devastation as we began to-day I don't want to be captured on this trip, for I expect every man of us the rebels capture will get a "stout rope and a short shrift."

Monday, Novr. 14th [1864].

Division marched promptly at daybreak. The General had us in the saddle while all the stars were still shining. This was a beautiful morning, bright and cold. Marched through line after line of entrenchments, built both by ourselves and the rebels last summer, and as we neared the spur of "Kenesaw" over which the Marietta road runs, I couldn't help regarding that mountain with some of the same shy respect which I entertained for it last June, when we lay burrowing in rifle-pits at its foot, and its summit was crowned with rebel artillery, which so often at mid-day and at midnight thundered away at us, and encircled the mountain with wreaths of fire and smoke. But "Kenesaw" was quiet to-day, and as our troops emerged from the woods to the open plain at its foot, and beheld our own flag, flying where they had so long and anxiously watched the rebel flag, cheer after cheer rang out.

Just before crossing the spur of the mountain Capt. Acheson's horse got into a quick sand hole and instantly sunk almost entirely under with the Capt. on his back. He and his horse were extricated with great difficulty. The General was mad, and I laughed until my sides ached. I guess the General was mad at me for laughing too, but I couldn't help it; covered with mud, and struggling in the mud hole with his horse he looked so ridiculous I should have laughed if he had never got out.

When we reached Marietta we found that all the business part of the town was burned by Kilpatrick's Cavalry last night. Marietta was a very pretty town and its private residences are still beautiful. Halted to let the troops get dinner about 4 miles out from Marietta. Rode ahead with the General and General Davis across the Chattahoochee. The General then directed me to go on a couple of miles further toward Atlanta and select a camp ground. I did so, and when the trains came up to me placed them in park; had Division and Brigade Head Quarters put up on the ground I had selected, but it was now after dark and no troops came. I rode back to the river to find out what was the matter and there found the General very much out of humor for he didn't know where the troops were. Finally the head of the column came up, the men very much fatigued; the leading Brigade had taken the wrong road and marched to Turner's Ferry, the other Brigade of course following, and then had to march back to where we now found them; so we just let them march across the river and encamp anywhere they could. I got to bed about midnight. Moulton and Acheson were with the column, and of course they feel to some extent responsible for the blunder, although they were not in the least to blame. We are having sport with them about their hunting for new roads, and taking the Division along as an escort.

Tuesday, Nov. 15th [1864].

Division moved at daylight toward Atlanta. The General directed me to go ahead to the city—to ascertain the streets on which we were to march through the city, so as to leave it on the McDonough road, and to select a camp ground east of and convenient to the city. I reached the city, accompanied by Capt. Acheson about 9 A. M. and found every street so crowded with troops and wagons that it was almost impossible to get along on horseback. I then tried to find our Corps Commander, Genl. Davis, to report to him that the head of the column would soon be up, and get orders from him what to do, as it was evidently impossible for our troops to get through the city for many hours; failing to find Genl. Davis, I went directly to Gen. Sherman's and was directed by his Aide-de-camp, Capt. Dayton, to apply to Maj. Gen. Slocum for orders; after half-an-[hour] search for Gen. Slocum, I found him in the street on foot, trying to crowd his way back to his Head Quarters. I reported to him, and he told me that we should halt and mass the troops on arriving at the edge of the city, and that the troops and trains would be out of our way so that we could get through the city sometime during the afternoon. He also told me that our Corps would march out of the city on Decatur Street.

With this information I rode back to where our column was to enter the city and there met the General, to whom I communicated it. Directing me to select the ground and mass the Brigades as they came up, he rode into the city, telling me I would find him at the Head Quarters of Col. Beckwith, Chf. Commissary, Mil. Div. Miss. at which place I soon joined him. About 1 o'clk P. M. our Division moved through the city, and encamped about ½ mile east. I managed to get the General to consent to having Head Qrs. in a *house* to-night—something *very* unusual. The 20th Corps marched out some distance toward Stone Mountain to-day; the 15th and 17th Corps (Right Wing) marched out toward McDonough, and Kilpatrick's Cavalry toward Jonesboro on the extreme right of everything. About dark to-night our orders came to march at daylight toward Decatur. General Sherman goes with this Corps (14th).

Our Commissaries have been busily engaged all day in loading rations, and our Quarter Masters in issuing clothing and shoes to the troops. Up to about 3 P. M. this issuing was carried on with something like a show of regularity, but about that time fires began to break out in various portions of the city, and it soon became evident that these fires were but the beginning of a general conflagration which would sweep over the entire city and blot it out of existence; so Quartermasters and Commissaries ceased trying to issue clothing or load rations, they told the soldiers to go in and take what they wanted before it burned up. The soldiers found many barrels of whisky and of course they drank of it until they were drunk; then new fires began to spring up, all sorts of discordant noises rent the air, drunken soldiers on foot and on horseback raced up and down the streets while the buildings on either side were solid sheets of flame, they gathered in crowds before the finest structures and sang "Rally around the Flag" while the flames enwrapped these costly edifices, and shouted and danced and sang again while pillar and roof and dome sank into one common ruin. The night, for miles around was bright as midday; the city of Atlanta was one mass of flame, and the morrow must find it a mass of ruins. Well, the soldiers fought for it, and the soldiers won it, now let the soldiers enjoy it; and so I suppose Gen. Sherman thinks, for he is somewhere near by, now, looking on at all this, and saying not one word to prevent it. All the pictures and verbal descriptions of hell I have ever seen never gave me half so vivid an idea of it, as did this flame wrapped city to-night. Gate City of the South, farewell!

The March to the Sea

Hood had hoped, by his campaign north of Atlanta, to force Sherman to retreat from that city. In this design he had not succeeded, but he had perplexed the Union commander and had confined him to the vicinity of Atlanta for several weeks.

By mid-October Sherman concluded that Hood would soon withdraw from Georgia and strike north through Tennessee and Kentucky. With this contingency in mind, Sherman had already sent Thomas, with 35,000 men, to Nashville. Properly reinforced, as he would be, Thomas could deal with Hood. Sherman could then embark on his cherished adventure: a march across Georgia to Savannah, living off the country and desolating it as he went.

Sherman's force for the march to the sea consisted of 60,000 infantry, 5,500 cavalry, and one piece of artillery for every thousand men. All were picked troops, battle-tested and hardened by long campaigning. They were organized into right and left wings, the former, under General O. O. Howard, consisting of the Fifteenth and Seventeenth Corps; the latter, under General H. W. Slocum, of the Fourteenth and Twentieth Corps.

In the last days of October and the first two weeks of November, Sherman made his preparations. Supplies were accumulated: forty days' rations of beef, sugar, and coffee; twenty days' rations of bread; a double allowance of salt for forty days; ammunition enough for any possibility. There was little feed for horses; that, and most of the food for the troops, would come from the country through which the army would pass.

The campaign began on November 11. On that day General Corse, in obedience to orders, destroyed the foundries, shops, and military supplies in Rome, Georgia. On the twelfth the telegraph wires extending northward from Kingston were cut and the several corps ordered to Atlanta. Three days later the Fifteenth, Seventeenth, and Twentieth Corps moved out on their respective lines of march. The Fourteenth, which included Connolly's division, followed the next day.

On the march Connolly continued his voluminous diary, writing only one letter before the capture of Savannah.

[Diary]

Wednesday, Novr. 16th [1864].

The eventful day has come; we turn our backs upon Atlanta, and our faces seaward. How many prayers for our success went up from our Northern homes this morning. We must succeed. Not a man in this army doubts it. We'll march straight through and shake the rebellious old State from center to circumference. Division marched at 9 A. M., all our bands playing, flags flying and men cheering. We marched to-day over the ground where the bloody battle of July 22d [was fought] and where the brave McPherson fell. That field is studded with the graves of our gallant comrades, and none lie there more thickly than the men of Illinois.

We passed through Decatur about noon; it has an old, weatherbeaten, unpainted appearance. The Court House, a brick structure, plastered outside, stands in a square in the

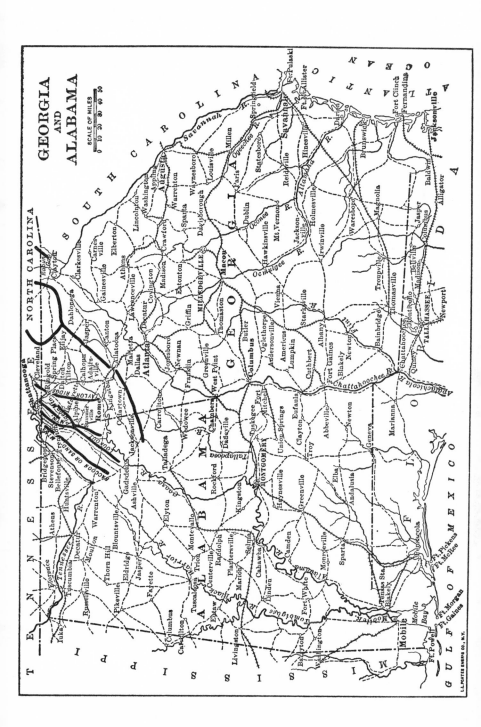

GEORGIA AND ALABAMA

center of the town. The other buildings are nearly all frame, and very antique in style. Encamped on "Snapfinger Creek." Passed through very nice country to-day; open, level, and well cultivated. We left Stone Mountain several miles to our left. It is said to be a mountain of solid stone, devoid of a particle of herbage, and used to be considered one of the great natural curiosities of this continent. Head Quarters, to-night, being near a house, I went in after supper, to see what the natives looked like. There was the old man, the old woman, four marriageable but unmarried daughters and one married daughter whose husband, as she told me, had been "taken off in the conscript more'n a year ago, and she didn't know where the dickens he was." Supposing that they all used snuff (a safe presumption amongst the country people in the South) I asked the *ladies* how they managed to get snuff now, but they all denied using it; I however, took out my paper of fine cut tobacco and it was but a few moments until each one of them had a quid of it in her mouth "just to see what it tasted like"; they pronounced it "fust rate," "most as good as snuff." I discovered that they supposed we were out from Atlanta on a foraging expedition and thought we would return in a few days; they had no idea that we intended to keep right on. These people owned 100 acres of land there, but no negroes, and the girls had never been in a school house.

Thursday, Nov. 17th [1864].

Division marched at daylight. Passed through Lithonia, on the R. R., at 9 A. M. where I noticed Gen. Sherman standing on the R. R. track giving directions as to how he wanted the track torn up and destroyed. Several buildings were burning as we passed through. We arrived at Conyers at noon, and as our Division had four miles of R. R. to destroy before moving any further, Capt. Acheson, who plays the piano finely, and myself started out to walk around through the town and find a piano, so that we could have some music while our soldiers were destroying the track. Meeting a little girl on the street who told us where there was a piano, we went to the house and on knocking at the door a grey headed, meek, ministerial looking old rebel opened the door and asked what we wanted. I had agreed to do the talking so I told him "we wanted" to destroy the R. R. first, and asked him what he thought of it. The old gent looked wise and said nothing; I then asked him if he had a piano in the house; the old man looked worried and replied that his daughter had one. All right, said I, that's just what we want, we want some music; the old man said he didn't think his daughter could play, and looked incredulous when we pushed by him into the room, and the Captain sat down at the piano; but the Captain's fingers soon made the keys dance to the air of the Star Spangled Banner, and the old man sat there astonished at the thought that a rough, vulgar, brutal Yankee should be able to play so skillfully. Then the Captain played "Dixie" in excellent style; this made the old man talkative, brought in the daughter and some other young ladies, and we soon had them playing for us, while the Captain and I sat back and quietly enjoyed the discomfiture of the old man, and laughed at the efforts of the rebel damsels to appear composed. Finally, to cap the climax, we induced these Southern ladies to sing us the "Confederate Toast," which they told us was their favorite song, and one verse of it I remember, viz:

> "Here's to old Butler and his crew,
>   Drink it down!
> Here's to old Butler and his crew,
>   Drink it down!
> Here's to old Butler and his crew,
>   May the devil get his due,
> Drink it down! Drink it down! Drink it down!"

We left them, though, notwithstanding their elegant and patriotic songs—they, no doubt, hoping we might be shot before night. Our troops having finished their work on the R. R. we moved forward 4 miles, and encamped on Mr. Zachry's plantation having marched 15 miles today, and utterly destroyed 4 miles of R. R. Old Zachry has a son who is a Colonel in the rebel army in Virginia, and the negroes, i. e. his own negroes tell us tonight that the old sinner has a federal flag hid away in his house which his son captured and sent home from Virginia a year ago. We have searched the house all over for it, but can't find it yet, and the old man and old woman deny having it, but one of their house servants told me most positively tonight that it *is* in the house, and that they know where it is. If we don't get it before we leave tomorrow morning the old fellow's house will surely be burnt, for the soldiers have all heard of it. They *did* burn the old fellow's cotton gin, filled with cotton, tonight. Passed through fine country today. Conyers is a village of about 500 inhabitants, and Lithonia about 300, both stations on the R. R.; a good many negroes came into camp with us tonight; they are of all shades and sizes; and are apparently happy if they can be permitted to go along with us.

Friday, Nov. 18th [1864].

After striking tents this morning I took old Zachry out one side, and with an air of great concern, and in the greatest confidence told him that unless he produced that flag, the soldiers were determined to burn his house as soon as General Baird got out of sight. The old sinner was alarmed and asked me to leave him a guard until the soldiers all passed, at the same time protesting that he knew nothing about the flag. I, of course, told him that we never left guards, and parted from him, expressing deep sympathy, for I assured him that the soldiers would in all probability burn his house. In less than ten minutes the old rascal brought the flag out and delivered it up. I don't know whether his house was burned or not. I know he owns about 40 niggers less tonight than he did last night.

We crossed "Yellow River" about noon, and commenced destroying R. R. just after crossing. We destroyed about 4 miles. Yellow River, where we crossed, is quite a deep clear stream, about 6 rods wide and with high bluff banks. I stopped at a dwelling on the east side of the river, which the occupants (Merriwether's) dignified with the name of "Airy Mount." Had quite a discussion here with a strong minded elderly woman, on Abolition and Amalgamation; the old lady forced it on me, and as there were three or four very light colored mulatto children running around the house, they furnished me an admirable weapon to use against the old lady's remark that the Northern people were Amalgamationists. She didn't explain to my entire satisfaction how her slaves came to be so much whiter than African Slaves are usually supposed to be.

Marched on through Covington and encamped a short distance east of it. Covington is a place of some pretension, and on the whole is rather a pretty place. The houses are very neat, built in modern Southern style, and painted white. The good people of Covington only heard of our advance yesterday so they are all at home, not having had time to run away. The "leading citizens" were affable when we entered the place, and everybody invited officers to stay all night at their house. I was in the Court Room and Masonic Lodge, the door of which was open.

Saturday, Nov. 19th. [1864].

Division moved at daybreak and crossed the Ulcofauhatchee River. This stream is not very deep, rapid, without any well defined banks, the water spreading out and making a swamp on either side of the stream for a considerable distance. The name of this stream is pronounced by the inhabitants "Alcovy." Land in its vicinity looks very poor; the ears of corn only grow about 6 inches long, and the stalks are very light. An old man told us today that some of his land averaged 6 bushels of corn to the acre and some of it "don't average anything." There are no wealthy planters in the immediate vicinity of the "Ulcofauhatchee" along our line of march. The farms are all in hundred acre lots, but their owners call them "Plantations"; the citizens look at our troops as they pass, with the utmost astonishment; they have no idea where we are going, and the negroes stare at us with open eyes and mouths, but generally, before the whole column has passed they pack up their bundles and march along, going, they know not whither, but apparently satisfied they are going somewhere toward freedom; but these wretched creatures, or a majority of them, don't know what freedom is. Ask them where they are going as they trudge along with their bundles on their heads, and the almost invariable reply is: "Don't know Massa; gwine along wid you all."

Our men are foraging on the country with the greatest liberality. Foraging parties start out in the morning; they go where they please, seize wagons, mules, horses, and harness; make the negroes of the plantation hitch up, load the wagons with sweet potatoes, flour, meal, hogs, sheep, chickens, turkeys, barrels of molasses, and in fact everything good to eat, and sometimes considerable that's good to drink. Our men are living as well as they could at home and are in excellent health.

Rain falling all the forenoon, roads heavy and marching difficult. Passed through Sand Town today about 2 o'clock. It is a little weather beaten village of about 250 or 300 inhabitants. The citizens were not much expecting us, but they heard of our approach day before yesterday and have spent the time since in carrying off and hiding in the swamp their valuables, but the negroes told the soldiers of these hiding places and most of these hidden valuables found their way into our camp to-night. Went into camp at dark. We have neither seen nor heard of any armed rebels yet, and we march along with as much unconcern as if we were marching through Ohio. We are beginning to talk about Milledgeville, and speculate on the probabilities of a battle there. There can't be much of a battle there though, for we have troops enough to eat up all the army Georgia's capital can muster.

Sunday, Nov. 20th [1864].

Division moved at daylight, and at 9 A. M. passed through "Shady Dale." I have known for the past 3 days that our line of march led through "Shady Dale," and judging from the name I had fancied to myself that Shady Dale was probably a nice, clean, quiet, aristocratic country town, situated in some romantic, shaded valley, and as we started this morning I retouched my mental picture of "Shady Dale," so that I might have it entirely finished to my taste before seeing the place itself, and then have the satisfaction of determining whether "there's anything in a name" by comparing my ideal "Shady Dale" with the real "Shady Dale."

I am now satisfied that "there is something in a name," but it was proven to me this morning in a manner that totally surprised me. As we rode along we came to a beautiful plantation, and by the roadside was a cluster of about 50 whitewashed negro houses, and in the midst of them an old fashioned frame house with porch all around it and dormor windows. The negro houses were filled with nice cleanly looking negroes of all ages and sizes, and as the head of our column came up with band playing, such a nest of negroes I never saw before; they poured out of those cabins to the road side in such numbers as to lead one to suppose they had been packed away inside like mackerel in a barrel. The music of the bands started the young niggers at dancing, and they capered around like little imps; the old ones stood with uncovered heads, hands raised, mouths open and eyes turned up; the young negresses stood bowing and curtseying, trying to bow to every soldier that passed; while each negro in his or her own style kept uttering ejaculations of wonder such as "Lawd, jest look at em"; "whar'd dey cum from"; "looks like de whole wuld was comin" &c, &c. Each one expressing his wonder in some original and quaint style. I sat on my horse and listened to and watched them, while I laughed at their comicalities until tears rolled down my cheeks. There is as much difference between the negroes we see in the North and the plantation negroes of the South, as there is between a cultivated gentleman and a clown in the circus ring.

Presently I asked a venerable old African patriarch where "Shady Dale" was, and he told me: "Dis is it massa"; why, said I, is it called "Shady Dale?" "Cos" said he grinning, "deres so many of us black uns here." Whereupon I laughed too, and rode on, satisfied that there *is* something in a name, when a plantation can figure on the maps as "Shady Dale," on account of the number of "Shades" living there.

This plantation is owned by a man named "Whitfield," and it is the finest one I ever saw, but by the time our column has all passed Mr. Whitfield won't have a sweet potato, a pig, chicken, turkey, horse, mule, cow, and scarcely a nigger left. The negroes on all these plantations tell us their masters have given them no meat to eat during the past two years, and as a consequence the negroes have been in the habit of prowling about the country at night, foraging, as they call it; that is stealing chickens, hogs, &c, and killing them in the swamps. They raise turnips extensively through Georgia so far as we have been, and every turnip patch we pass is thoroughly stripped by the soldiers and negroes, who, by the way, make excellent foragers. Our stock of negroes is increasing rapidly; many of them travel on horseback now; they furnish their own, i. e., their masters, horses, saddles and bridles, so they are no expense to Uncle Sam; a great many of our privates are getting negro servants for themselves; the negro walks along beside the soldier, with his knapsack and cooking utensils strapped upon his back, thus relieving the soldier of his load, and helping him along. What soldier *wouldn't* be an abolitionist under such circumstances. We have marched through beautiful country today. Halted one hour for dinner. We made 18 miles today, and encamped 6 miles from Eatonton, and 27 from Milledgeville.

Monday, Novr. 21st [1864].

Division moved at daylight. Crossed "Murder Creek" at noon, and went into camp 4 miles beyond, having marched only 9 miles today, and being, tonight within 18 miles of Milledgeville. Rain falling heavily all day. Roads in a horrible condition. Things have not looked promising today. What would become of us if this weather should continue two weeks? We couldn't march; would be compelled to halt here in the midst of a hostile country, and thus let the enemy have time to recover from his surprise and concentrate against us. Well, let the worst come, we'll get to the capital of Georgia anyhow, and my long desire to see it will at length be gratified.

We are all wet through and covered with mud, and our horses jaded, but our supper of coffee, fried chickens, sweet potatoes, &c, and a good sleep will bring us out all right in the morning, and if our horses give out, the stable of some wealthy Georgian must furnish us a remount. Citizens everywhere look paralyzed and as if stricken dumb as we pass them. Columns of smoke by day, and "pillars of fire" by night, for miles and miles on our right and left indicate to us daily and nightly the route and location of the other columns of our army. Every "Gin House" we pass is burned; every stack of fodder we can't carry along is burned; every barn filled with grain is destroyed; in fact everything that can be of any use to the rebels is either carried off by our foragers or set on fire and burned.

Tuesday, Nov. 22d [1864].

Division moved at daylight, crossing Cedar Creek at 9 A. M., passing through the camp of Morgan's Division, and taking the advance for Milledgeville. Rather cold today. I spent most of the day in advance of the column searching for roads to the capital and picking up such items of information as I could get from negroes and white citizens in regard to the enemy, but I have not been able to ascertain that there are any rebel soldiers in the city. The negroes and others say that all the soldiers that were in Milledgeville have gone to Macon, under command of General Howell Cobb. We are encamped tonight on a plantation belonging to "General Cobb," and the 23d Missouri has received permission to burn all the rails and buildings on the plantation tonight. General Sherman has his tents pitched in the dooryard of the overseer's house on this plantation tonight.

About 3 P. M. while the column was halted I rode ahead in the direction of Milledgeville, in company with General Baird, Colonel Poe, chief topographical engineer on General Sherman's staff, and Captain Buttrick of our staff. After we had ridden about a mile ahead of the column, admiring the beautiful country and speculating on the probability of taking Milledgeville without fighting, we suddenly discovered a mounted man in the middle of the road coming toward us. He was then about one-half a mile from us and just on the crest of a little hill in the road. He discovered us at the same time we did him and we halted at the same time. Glasses were out in a minute and we discovered that his uniform was gray. Ah, ha! This, then, is the outer picket watching our approach to the capital. This settles the question; we'll have to fight for Milledgeville. The solitary horseman in rebel uniform turned his horse toward the city and disappeared behind the crest of the hill.

There were some negro houses by the roadside about half way between where we were and where the gray clad horseman appeared. The negroes were out in the road looking at us. We were very anxious to get as far down the road as the negro houses, but didn't think it safe. In a few moments two gray clad horsemen appeared on the hill. They looked at us—were counting us evidently; they turned their horses around uneasily. Presently another horseman appeared, then another and another, until at least twenty were in sight on the crest of the hill. They were evidently too strong for us, even if we had been well armed, which we were not. But they were at least half a mile from us and our column was only about a mile from us—the road behind us was good, we were well mounted and we felt that if they *did* make a dash at us we could run the mile back to our troops before they could overtake us. But what if one of our horses should stumble and fall in the chase? Oh, well! Let the rider jump over a fence and run as fast as he can somewhere, anywhere, to gain a few minutes time.

But look! The gray clad horsemen are starting forward and now they are waving a white handkerchief. It must be a deputation of citizens coming out to surrender the capital to us. So the General thought; so we all thought. The General directed Colonel Poe to go forward and meet the party and see what they wanted and who they were. Forward dashed Poe, and there we sat watching the scene with intense anxiety. Can it be possible that we are to meet with such good fortune as to receive the formal surrender of Georgia's capital? Poe meets the horsemen, they halt a few moments, then Poe turns, and they all come on to where the General, Captain Buttrick and myself are waiting in the road. We ask each other what this means. Can there be treachery here? Do they mean to deceive us with a white flag and capture us all? They approach within 200 yards and we plainly see their rebel uniforms. Shall we run or stand? Moments are precious. They come steadily on. The General looks pale. I *feel* pale and nervous, but the General stands, and therefore I *must*. They reach us, rein up their horses and the gray clad officer riding at the head of the party salutes the General and announces himself and party as Kilpatrick's scouts just from Milledgeville; they say they rode through the city, and that there is not a rebel soldier there. Hurrah! Milledgeville is ours, and our sensations are now quite different from what they were ten minutes ago.

The scouts go on to report to General Sherman and we ride on to the negro houses ahead, which the negroes tell us belong to "Ginral Cobb." In the dooryard of the overseer's house stand three large new iron kettles for boiling sorghum. Poe picked up an axe and with a few blows shivered one of them into atoms. Buttrick took the axe and shivered the second one. I then took the axe and paid my respects to "Ginral Cobb" by shattering the third one. The General sent back and ordered the troops forward and placed them in camp on the arch rebel's plantation. General Sherman coming up in about an hour, placed his headquarters in the yard where we broke the sorghum kettles. About dark this evening, it is said, the old negro who is the commissary of the plantation told some of General Sherman's staff officers that he wanted to see the great General, just to see how he looked. He was taken to the door of Sherman's tent, and the old man took off his hat, looked at the General a few moments, then bowing respectfully turned and walked off, saying to himself as he walked off shaking his head: "He's got the Linkum head, the Linkum head, he's got the Linkum head." We are only ten miles from Milledgeville tonight.

Wednesday, Nov. 23d [1864].

Division moved at daylight. A bright, beautiful day; roads excellent and surrounding country magnificent. We reached the capital at about 9 A. M., but our troops didn't get up until noon on account of the 20th Corps, which came in from Eatonton, entering the city on the same road with us and in advance of us, as they struck the road first. Our troops encamped just outside the city limits on the west side. Our headquarters in the city in a dwelling house of some runaway citizen. General Davis' headquarters in the city near the Governor's mansion. General Sherman's in the mansion and General

Slocum's at the Milledgeville Hotel, opposite the capitol square.

Here I am, finally, at Milledgeville. My boyish desire is gratified, and I find that my boyish fancy in regard to the appearance of the city was quite correct. The dwellings are scattered and surrounded by large and tastefully decorated grounds. As one rides along its sandy streets, even at this season of the year, the faint perfume from every variety of tree and shrub, bud, blossom and flower fills the air with delicious fragrance. The exterior of the residences bespeak refinement within, and everything about the city serves to impress one with the idea that he is in an old, aristocratic city, where the worth of a man is computed in dollars and cents. The streets are regularly laid out and the capitol stands on a slight elevation rather east of the center of the city and overlooking the Oconee River. It is built of reddish looking sandstone and is a large square building, with rather a superabundance of fancy cornice outside. It has entrances on the north, south, east and west, each having a broad flight of stone steps. The offices and State library are on the first floor, the legislative halls on the second floor, and also the committee rooms. Each chamber has life size oil paintings of the prominent old men of Georgia hung around its walls in plain gilt frames. I should have thought "Oglethorpe" [1] would have appeared in this State picture gallery, but he does not. General Jackson does, though, tricked out in a line officer's coat with a general's epaulettes on his shoulders, a line officer's sash around his waist, and a sort of cross between a Turkish scimeter and an artillery sabre by his side.

Our soldiers and even some officers have been plundering the State library today and carrying off law and miscellaneous works in armfuls. It is a downright shame. Public libraries should be sacredly respected by all belligerents, and I am sure General Sherman will, some day, regret that he permitted this

1. James Edward Oglethorpe, English soldier and philanthropist, who founded the colony of Georgia in 1733.

library to be destroyed and plundered. I could get a thousand dollars worth of valuable law books there if I would just go and take them, but I wouldn't touch them. I should feel ashamed of myself every time I saw one of them in my book case at home. I don't object to stealing horses, mules, niggers and all such *little things,* but I will not engage in plundering and destroying public libraries. Let them alone, to enlarge and increase for the benefit of the loyal generations that are to people this country long after we shall have fought our last battle and gone into our eternal camp. The State penitentiary was burned last night. There are but few business buildings here, and the population never could have been more than ten thousand. I shall devote myself to looking around town tomorrow, as I understand we will not march in the morning.

Thursday, Nov. 24th [1864].

A bright, beautiful morning, and as I slept in a house last night and on a *real bed* like "white folks," I slept rather late. A Mrs. Doct. Jarrett told me today of a sister of Mrs. Ficklin's of Charleston, Ills., who is at Scottsboro, four miles south of here, but that being outside of our picket line, I didn't go to see her. I am rather sorry I didn't go now, but it's too late to regret it; we march in the morning. I should have gone out to see "Oglethorpe University" today, but I got into the State library this morning and became so much interested in the musty old records of the Colony of Georgia that I found there, that I used up nearly the whole day in reading them, and had no time to visit the university, which is about two miles southwest of the city. I am surprised to see that all the churches of the city are built right around the capitol in the same enclosure with it, and look more like public offices than they do like churches; indeed, I thought they were the offices of the State officials yesterday. The streets and most of the sidewalks are unpaved, but the soil is so sandy that I suppose they never become muddy. The names of all the streets are marked at each corner on neatly painted little signboards, attached to the buildings or fences. The houses are nearly all frame, except the business houses; they are of brick, and I don't think there is a building in the city over two stories high, except the "Milledgeville Hotel," which is three. Very few of the citizens show themselves on the streets, but the negroes are all out, draped in their gayest outfit, and looking as happy as clams at high water.

All the troops except our division marched through the city today and crossed the Oconee. We march in the morning. I presume the citizens think that the whole of Sherman's army has gone through here. They don't know that there are 35,000 more Yankee vandals about 25 miles south of here, marching on parallel roads with us. As our division alone occupies the city tonight, I have entire charge of the picket line surrounding it. I'll try and preserve "Joe Brown's" [2] capital from invasion by rebels until tomorrow morning anyhow, and after that we'll leave it for "Joe" to take care of himself. When we established our headquarters here yesterday I unrolled the flag we took from old Zachry on the 18th inst., made a staff for it, and raised it in front of our headquarters, where it is still flying. Little did the old sinner think, when he first received this trophy from his rebel son, that Yankee hands would ever unfurl it in triumph over the capital of his State.

Friday, Nov. 25th [1864].

Division moved at daylight, the first and second brigades crossing the Oconee, while the 3d Brigade remained in the city to gather up all stragglers and prepare the State magazine to be blown up. About 9 o'clock everything being in readiness, and the citizens having been warned to keep out of the way, a soldier of the 18th Kentucky applied the torch and in an instant

2. Joseph Emerson Brown, Georgia's war governor.

the State magazine was blown into the air with a terrific explosion. Our last troops then crossed the river and the kindling being all ready, our escort set fire to the bridge. In ten minutes it was burned down and the broad Oconee rolled between us and Milledgeville, with no means of crossing it; but our men were all across and, of course, it's no business of ours whether anybody else gets across or not. The Oconee at this point is a muddy looking, rapid stream, about 350 yards wide, with low, sandy, crumbling banks, which are overflown at nearly every freshet. Milledgeville, when viewed from the east bank of the river, presents a very shabby, rickety appearance, as only the eastern edge of the city can be seen, and that appears to be the quarter in which the niggers and poor white trash are collected.

The bridge across the river was a toll bridge, and the toll keeper, a fat, dirty, lazy looking citizen who made himself known to me as a Mason, lives at the east end of the bridge. He stood there looking at us with a woeful countenance as he beheld us fire the bridge. "Othello's occupation" was "gone"; yea, verily, it went up in smoke. He assured me he had "allers bin for the Union, and wus yit." He told me he was born on the Oconee and had never lived more than five miles away from it in his life. After seeing the bridge tumble into the river we bade farewell to Milledgeville and encamped fifteen miles nearer the Atlantic tonight. The 20th Corps is now on our right and Kilpatrick's cavalry on our left. I understand tonight that Kilpatrick has left all his wagons with our corps and the 20th and is off for a raid to cut the railroad between Savannah and Augusta and release our prisoners at Millen, as it is supposed there are 20,000 of them there.

Crossed Buffalo and Bluff Creeks today (both small) and encamped on "Giles' farm" on the east bank of Bluff Crk. Passed through very poor "piney woods" all day. Grasshoppers couldn't live in these "piney woods." The pine trees grow so thickly in them that a man can scarcely walk through them. They grow tall, straight and without limbs for from 30 to 60 feet from the ground, and the ground is covered with a thick matting of the dead pine leaves that have fallen, so that when walking through these "piney woods" your feet feel as if treading on a carpet well stuffed with straw underneath. Citizens say that strangers traveling through these woods will get lost as readily as on a prairie if they go far from the road, and I can readily believe it, for we passed over many miles today in which every tree and spot looked exactly like every other tree and spot. Notwithstanding the extreme barrenness of these "piney woods," we now and then passed a miserable looking little cabin today, about which we generally found two or three sickly, sallow women and from five to fifteen children, all looking like persons I have read of called "dirt eaters"; I guess these *are* dirt eaters, and I think they must live on it, for I don't see place for anything except children to grow in these "woods."

We are now going toward the Ogeechee, and citizens tell us we will find very poor country all the way from the Oconee to the Ogeechee. Our foragers came into camp tonight pretty well loaded, and I can't imagine where they found so much stuff through this country. I suppose the negroes assisted them. Where can all the rebels be? Here we are riding rough shod over Georgia and nobody dares to fire a shot at us. We burn their houses, barns, fences, cotton and everything else, yet none of the Southern braves show themselves to punish us for our vandalism. Perhaps they are preparing a trap to catch us all, but I don't think we will go into their trap, if we can find any way to go around it. We don't care where we come out; would a little rather come out at Savannah, but if we can't do that we'll go somewhere else. Georgia is an excellent state for foraging. We are living finely, and the whole army would have no objection to marching around through the State for the next six months. Indeed, the whole trip thus far has been a holiday excursion, but a very expensive one to the rebels.

Saturday, Nov. 26th [1864].

Division moved at daylight. Confound this moving at daylight. It's the only thing about this trip that's unpleasant. I am seriously opposed to rising so early in the morning. We marched through the same wretched looking "piney woods" again today; passed through Sandersville and encamped at the junction of the "Fenn's Bridge" and "Louisville" roads, about three-fourths of a mile northeast of the town. Wheeler and some of his rebel cavalry were in the town when the head of the 14th Corps reached here, but they were driven out without even halting our column; the men marched right into town loading and firing as they advanced; bands playing, flags flying, and Mr. Wheeler and his rebels, of course, running almost without returning a shot. So nicely timed was the marching of the two corps (14th and 20th) on widely separated roads that almost at the same moment the heads of the two columns entered the town, ours from the west and the 20th from the southwest.

This cavalry in Sandersville today is the first show of opposition the left wing of the grand army has yet met with, but they were brushed out of our way as readily as if they had been only green flies. Still, it behooves us to move cautiously now and to be every moment on the alert, for this opposition may be greater tomorrow and may continue to increase from day to day, now that they have ascertained the roads on which our columns are moving. We understand that the right wing, 15th and 17th Corps, under Howard, have reached the Ogeechee some thirty miles south of here and are unable to cross, the rebels being in force and strongly posted on the opposite bank. We will reach the Ogeechee tomorrow, and if *we* find the rebels on the opposite bank, too, in force, it may give the whole army considerable trouble to get across. Indeed, we don't know but that the rebels are in strong force on the other side of the Ogeechee and intend to make that river their line of defense. It is said to be a difficult river to cross, and even if we don't find the rebels there tomorrow we may expect to find all the bridges burned and the roads blockaded, so that our advance must necessarily be very slow. Wheeler's cavalry are said to have orders to burn all bridges in our front and destroy all forage and provisions in the country.

The rebel papers we get hold of from Augusta also call on all the citizens to turn out and fall timber across the roads— destroy their forage and provisions, and do everything possible to harass us and retard our march. Let them do it if they dare. We'll burn every house, barn, church, and everything else we come to; we'll leave their families houseless and without food; their towns will *all* be destroyed, and nothing but the most complete desolation will be found in our track. This army will not be trifled with by citizens. If citizens raise their hands against us to retard our march or play the guerrilla against us, neither youth nor age, nor sex will be respected. Everything must be destroyed. This is the feeling that has settled down over the army in its bivouac tonight. We have gone so far now in our triumphal march that we will not be balked. It is a question of life or death with us, and all considerations of mercy and humanity must bow before the inexorable demands of self preservation. We are nearing the coast, threatening both Augusta and Savannah. The rebels are quite certain we are first going to Augusta, *but we are not,* and that erroneous opinion may relieve us of a large amount of the opposition we would otherwise encounter. Still, it is safe to presume that every step we advance will bring us more opposition. We'll get through, though; they *can't* stop us now, but I would like to be able to see about ten days into the future—the next ten days will be the crisis with us.

Sandersville is rather a neat, quiet, thrifty looking county seat of about 500 population. The court house is a rather stylish brick building, plastered outside, and of a kind of yellowish color, with a dome on top. It stands in the middle of a public square in the center of town, and in the same square, without any enclosure, stands a very nice white marble monument to ex-Governor Jared Irwin of Georgia, who, according to the inscription on the monument, entered the Army of the Revolution as a private and was a General at its close.

Kilpatrick's cavalry not yet heard from. As the rebel cavalry is immediately in our front, they must be between us and Kilpatrick; but I guess he'll turn up all safe some of these days, yet I don't believe he'll find any of our prisoners at Millen if he gets there. The rebels now have had notice enough of our advance and will, of course, remove to some place of greater safety. Orders received to-night for our division to march at daylight on the Fenn's Bridge road to Louisville, followed by Morgan's Division, while Carlin's Division, with all its trains, moves on the direct road to Louisville, so it is intended that we will be on the extreme left of the army and cover the trains that move with Carlin. I expect we'll have some fighting tomorrow and probably find Fenn's Bridge across the Ogeechee burned.

Sunday, Novr. 27th [1864].

Division moved at daylight. Oh! these moves at daylight; I *must* groan over them, they interfere so much with my comfort and inclination; but they can't be "cured," and so must be "endured"; never mind, when I get home, I'll have full satisfaction, by sleeping just as late as I please in the morning, and if Mary undertakes to order me to march at daylight I'll place her under arrest.

As we neared the "Ogeechee" we found the country growing better; more land cultivated, soil more productive, and plantations larger. Persimmons grow by the roadside in abundance; our orderlies gather them in their handkerchiefs as they ride along, and bring up to us, so that we just ride along and eat persimmons, until we are almost tired of them. They are much finer than I ever supposed they were; tasting very much like excellent figs; I have eaten persimmons in Illinois, but they are very little like the persimmons of this part of Georgia.

It appears rather strange to me, coming, as I do, from a country where the hay crop is an important one to find that no hay at all is raised in this country. I haven't seen a particle of hay in this State. The only "long forage" they have here for animals is "blades" as they call it, which consists of corn leaves, stripped from the stalk while green, and carefully cured in the sun like hay, then tied up in bundles as hay or wheat in the North, and either stacked in the field or stored away in barns for winter feed. Horses and cattle like these "blades" very much, but I don't think there is very much nutriment in them.

We have found the road today, all the way as far as the "Ogeechee" filled with cavalry tracks going eastward, but, about ten rods west of the river we found that they had turned off on side roads to the right and left. We approached "Fenn's Bridge" cautiously, deploying two regiments and moving them forward in line, with a strong line of skirmishers in front of them. Being as full of curiosity as a woman, and being anxious to get the first sight of the rebels, I rode along with the skirmish line, watching every tree and stump, listening very intently, and moving as quietly as a cat in the sandy road, expecting every moment to hear the crack of a rifle from some concealed rebel; at such a moment the excitement is so intense that all thoughts of personal safety are forgotten, the senses of sight and hearing are extraordinarily acute, but they take no notice of anything passing, being intent alone on discovering the enemy before he discovers you; we moved up until we could hear the sound of the rushing water—no other sound could be heard; if at this moment my horse had neighed I should have been startled as if from a dream, but "Frank" was quiet, and moved steadily with his ears erect as if he too were looking for the graybacks; a little turn in the road brings us in sight of "Fenn's Bridge," a long frame structure spanning the "Ogeechee"—not a plank disturbed, and not a rebel in sight; Col. Este commanding our third brigade is with me; we hesitate a moment to assure ourselves that we are not mistaken then at once and with a shout put spurs to our horses, dash ahead of the line of skirmishers, cross the bridge the first ones, and send our orderly back on a gallop to the General to inform him that "Fenn's Bridge" is all right and we are across the "Ogeechee."

This is a most important success, and we can scarcely credit our senses; we find ourselves on the east bank of the "Ogeechee," and so important a bridge undestroyed and undefended by the rebels, but it is all explained by the female toll collector of this bridge, who lives just at the east end of it, and who informs us that a large rebel force crossed the bridge this morning, going westward toward us, but that they tuned off to the south just after crossing the river, telling her that they were going down to burn the bridge on the main road between Sandersville and Louisville, and intended to come back here *tonight* and burn this bridge, but we saved them that trouble by crossing all our troops over, and then burning it ourselves. The Lord was "on our side" this time, surely, for if that rebel brigade had burned the bridge this morning when they were here, we would have been compelled to build one before we could cross, and we could not have built one at all if there had been a regiment of rebels on the east bank to oppose us, and at any rate we couldn't have crossed before tomorrow afternoon. Our passage here insures the passage of the whole army across the river for we can just sweep down the east bank and clear the way for those who are trying to cross lower down.

After crossing we halted an hour for dinner, at the same time sending a regiment (38th Ohio) about 3 miles out on the main road to Augusta to burn a bridge there over "Rocky Comfort" Creek. After halting the hour, we started toward Louisville and encamped on "Wilkinson's Plantation" within 6 miles of it. Since crossing the Ogeechee the country looks better, and the roads are beautiful; weather warm as summer in the North; the roads look red, the sand being of a reddish cast, and reminded me of the roads in New Jersey. I had a chase after a rebel cavalryman today on the Augusta road, but he jumped off his mule and ran into the woods; some of our men got the mule, but the cavalryman escaped.

Monday, Nov. 28th [1864].

Division marched a little before daylight—worse and worse. Reached "Rocky Comfort Creek," just in the edge of Louisville at 8 A. M. and the bridge being burnt, we had to lay down pontoons and make a bridge, which was completed at 3 P. M. at which time we commenced crossing. We marched through Louisville and encamped one mile east of it about 5 o'clock P. M. We understood last night, from negroes, that there was something of a rebel force in Louisville so we expected to meet with opposition in crossing "Rocky Comfort" which is a swift clear stream, spreading out on either side into a swamp, and the creek proper, as well as the swamp is filled with cypress trees and "Cypress Knees," the latter being the name for the young cypress trees; these "Cypress Knees" grow up out of the water, are very broad at the base and taper to a point; the water in the swamps through this cypress country has a dark tint, something like water pools in which large quantities of dead leaves have lain for a long time. The people call this

"Bay Water," and say that its peculiar color is given it by the roots of a tree called the "Bay Tree," which somewhat resembles our northern "Dog Wood."

We are now in the country where the "Spanish Moss" begins to show itself, and General Baird tells us that we will find it still more abundant as we approach the coast. It is a parasite like the mistletoe, has a dark grayish appearance, and hangs in ringlets from the limbs, draping the trees completely, and giving them a gloomy, funereal appearance; the General says that this moss is gathered, scalded with hot water, then dried and whipped, when all this outside coating of gray flies away in dust, leaving the black, glossy curly moss used by upholsterers.

I reached the "Rocky Comfort Creek" this morning in company with a sergeant and 4 men of Kilpatrick's cavalry, a little after daylight, and at least an hour before the Division came; when I reached the creek the fire was just fairly started on the bridge, but I was probably 20 minutes too late and couldn't save it. I could have reached it in time, but as we found the road barricaded about every mile by fences built across it, we had to approach very cautiously for fear of an ambuscade; and in this way we lost time. It was more risk than I ought to have taken for I was 4 miles ahead of the Division, with only 5 men with me, but it's all over now, and I'm not captured so it's all right. One doesn't think of these risks until they are passed. Louisville was the early capital of Georgia, is a somewhat old fashioned looking town, and has or had about 1,000 inhabitants.

Tuesday, Novr. 29th [1864].

Division stationary. Weather warm and pleasant. Our headquarters are in the edge of a beautiful grove of pines. This grove was formerly cultivated land, and the marks of the furrows are as distinct now as if the land had been plowed

two years ago. Yet there are many pines growing on it now
that are a foot in diameter, and in most places the pines
grow so thickly as to render it almost impossible to ride
through them.

This is the kind of land that is called "Old Fields" in the
South, and when this country was in possession of the Indians
these "Old Fields" were frequently selected as places of rendezvous for war parties or for conferences amongst different
tribes, and the "Fields" were known amongst them by their
distinctive names, as our cities, towns and villages are now
known to us. Citizens tell me that in about 20 years, a cleared
field, if left uncultivated, will grow up into a forest of pines, but
some of these "Old Fields" I think have not been cultivated
for double that period.

"Broom Sedge" grows spontaneously here. It is a coarse,
tall, wild grass, containing scarcely any nutriment. It looks
somewhat like the "Cheat" of our Northern wheat fields.
Farmers here never cut it, and at this season of the year, a field
covered with it has the appearance of a field of rusty, weather
beaten oats. It is very dry now, and along the line of our march
every one of these Sedge fields is fired by the soldiers "just to
see the fire run." The "Crackers" as the poor whites are
called, and the negroes make a sort of broom out of this
sedge. Louisville, near where we are now encamped was made
the Capital of Georgia by the Constitution of the State, May
16th, 1795, and continued such until 1804, when Milledgeville
became the capital. It is now simply the county seat of Jefferson
county, the court house being built of the materials which
formerly composed the state house. It was here that the papers
connected with the celebrated "Yazoo Acts" were publicly
burnt.[3] Major John Berrien, father of Hon. John M. Berrien
of Georgia, lived and died in this county.

3. The Yazoo Act, passed by the legislature of Georgia in 1795, granted
the major part of the present states of Alabama and Mississippi to farm land

I was awakened this morning before daylight, by somebody in my tent calling to me; it proved to be one of Kilpatrick's staff officers, and he was very much excited. He told me in broken sentences that they had been fighting day and night for the past three days; that Wheeler's cavalry was all around them with a vastly superior force; that they were out of ammunition, and men and horses were utterly worn out; that Kilpatrick didn't know where our infantry was but had started him off at midnight last night to try and make his way to some infantry column and beg for support or they would all be lost. I have seen enough of Kilpatrick's Cavalry to know that their stories of hard fighting are cut after Baron Munchausen's style, but I also knew that Kilpatrick left us at the "Oconee" to make a raid toward "Augusta" and Millen" and that he might possibly be seriously involved; this appeared more probable too on account of none of our infantry columns meeting with any serious opposition, so we couldn't tell but that the whole force of the enemy was closing around Kilpatrick. I jumped up immediately, went to the General's tent without dressing, told him the story, he called up the officer and talked with him a few minutes, then ordered one of our brigades to march immediately (without breakfast) to the relief of Kilpatrick.

The brigade was in motion before sunrise, and after marching about five miles they began to hear sounds of skirmishing ahead; selecting a good position they immediately formed a line, and in about ten minutes Kilpatrick's jaded cavalry hove in sight, skirmishing with Wheeler and retiring before him; but when they saw the line of blue coated infantry drawn up in line across the road, and extending off into the woods on either side, they knew that they were saved, and sent up such shouts as never before were heard in these "Piney Woods" which our

---

companies. The act, the passage of which was secured by bribery, was rescinded by a new legislature the following year and burned in a solemn ceremony.

infantry responded to with right good will. Mr. Wheeler, taking
the hint, from this shouting, prudently refrained from pursuing
any farther, and quietly withdrew; while Kilpatrick moved in
near our camp and went into camp. He reports that he has
been near to Waynesboro, has burned a R. R. bridge on the
road between Waynesboro and Augusta; has destroyed two
or three miles of R. R. between Waynesboro and Millen, but
didn't reach the prison pen at Millen as Wheeler, with some
Georgia militia got after him; he says however, that our
prisoners are all removed from Millen; that there is plenty of
forage in the country ahead of us, but that Wheeler's men will
destroy it all, and fall timber in the roads ahead of us. If they
do this they will seriously annoy us, but as the enemy are still
under the impression that Sherman first intends to take Augusta,
before moving on Savannah, they may do most of their timber-
chopping on the roads leading to Augusta, leaving the roads to
Savannah comparatively clear.

A lot of refugee negroes who are encamped near our headquarters got up a regular "Plantation Dance" tonight, and some
of us went over and watched the performance which was highly
amusing. The dress, general appearance, action, laughter, music
and dancing of the genuine plantation negro is far more
grotesque and mirth-provoking than the broadest caricatures
of "Christy's Minstrels." They require neither fiddle nor banjo
to make music for their ordinary plantation dances, and the
dancers need no prompter, but kick, and caper and shuffle in
the most complicated and grotesque manner their respective
fancies can invent, while all who are not actually engaged as
dancers stand in a ring around the dancers, clapping their hands,
stamping their feet, swinging their bodies, and singing as
loud and as fast and furious as they can, a sort of barbaric
chant, unlike anything I ever heard from the lips of white
mortals; I observed, however, that there is a tone of melancholy
(I know of no other mode of describing it) pervading all their

rude music, which was plainly discernible even when the mirth of the dancers and singers had apparently reached its highest pitch. There is more fact than fiction in the saying that a "Soldier's life is always gay," for here we are in the midst of a hostile country, engaged in a campaign which probably the whole world, at this moment, is predicting will end in our complete destruction, and yet I have spent the evening laughing at the oddities of these negroes until my head and sides are aching.

Wednesday, Novr. 30th [1864].

Division stationary. I have been doing the duty of Adjutant General yesterday and today, on account of Capt. "A" being ———. A report came in by some frightened cavalry man that the enemy were advancing on us in force this afternoon, and I rode out around our picket line to see that everything was in readiness to give them a proper reception, but they didn't come. These cavalry men are a positive nuisance; they won't fight, and whenever they are around they are always in the way of those who will fight. Our infantry have a very poor opinion of the fighting qualities of our cavalry, and very justly so, I think. We have orders to march tomorrow morning. All the business portion of Louisville is burned.

Thursday, Decr. 1st [1864].

Division moved at 10 A. M.

The General pointed out to me on the map, this morning, our line of march for the next few days, and I find that our Division, together with Kilpatrick's cavalry is to form a flying column, to be detached from the main army, and strike ahead boldly toward Augusta, fighting Wheeler, and everything else that comes in our way, stubbornly, driving them before us, and demonstrating in such a way as to confirm the impression that

the army is advancing on Augusta. All our surplus trains
have been sent with the other two Divisions of the Corps, and
all Kilpatrick's wagons have been sent there too, and they are
to move by the most direct road to the line of R. R. from
Millen to Augusta while we cover them on the left, and raid
around through the country without any incumbrance except
the rebel opposition we may meet with. We are now in the most
"ticklish" position of any Division in the army. We are striking
off boldly toward Augusta, possibly to be sacrificed for the
purpose of saving the rest of the army, who knows?

Well, if such is the case I suppose we can stand it, but I
would prefer having somebody else make the sacrifice; for I
really never had any desire to be captured, and I am particularly
unwilling to be captured on *this* campaign. Sherman don't know
what is at Augusta, or between here and there; neither do we
know. A rebel army of 50,000 men may be on us before daylight tomorrow morning, for all we know, but I suppose that
is just the reason Sherman has sent us off this way, and it
will probably all turn out right. The whole campaign is an
experiment—nothing more; but all the great campaigns of the
world were nothing more during their progress, and if this
campaign succeeds it will be a successful military experiment,
that's all; but it will certainly be entitled to a distinguished
position in the military history of the world. We are rapidly
approaching the crisis. We have lived well and had fine times
thus far. Everything has turned out as well as it possibly
could, but the Lord only knows what's ahead of us. It is
possible that we have already passed the dead point of danger,
or we may not have reached it yet. It is this state of un-
certainty that is more annoying than anything else.

The enemy has been in our front all day today and the cavalry
has been continually skirmishing with them. Our troops have
marched today with some of the cavalry on the road in front
of us, some more on the road in our rear, and the rest moving

through the woods and fields on either side of the road; but
it has been evident all day that in case we meet with a large
force and serious opposition our cavalry won't help us much,
for they act as if they thought the infantry was along for the
purpose of doing all the fighting. So if we meet a force larger
than our division can drive we shall be in a bad fix, for I know
the cavalry will only be in our way. Confound the cavalry.
They're good for nothing but to run down horses and steal
chickens. I'd rather have one good regiment of infantry than
the whole of Kilpatrick's cavalry.

We have marched through a tolerably fair country today,
more oak land and less pine, but we saw no fine plantations.
The roads are dry and sandy; the sand is loose and deep,
making it rather hard walking, but it is much better than the
hard, smooth limestone turnpikes and dirt roads we used to
travel on in Kentucky and Tennessee. Hard roads affect men
traveling on them as the paved streets of cities do horses;
they stiffen them and wear them out, but these soft sandy roads
do not. We are encamped tonight just east of Buckhead Creek.
It was supposed when we started from Louisville that the
rebels would be found on the east bank of this creek to resist
our crossing, just as we had expected to find them at the
Ogeechee. We were all surprised, though, when we reached
the creek to find it a very small, insignificant stream, with solid
banks and hard, sandy bottom. We had expected to find it a
deep, swampy, difficult stream, with precipitous banks, and
affording the rebels excellent opportunity for defending its
passage.

The disappointment was a very agreeable one, but we learn
that we have just crossed the headwaters and that the stream
is as we supposed, farther to the south where the rest of the
army has to cross it, but the rebels will not, of course, make any
serious resistance to the crossing of the rest of the army, now
that *we* are on the east side of it; and as they have known

since 10 o'clock this morning that there was a column moving on this road, and yet made no serious opposition to our crossing. I am inclined to the opinion that we will find no considerable rebel force *on* this road, unless we go clear to Augusta.

The fact is our army is spread out into so many columns, marching in so many different directions, threatening so many different points, and careering over the country in such *apparent* disorder, yet really *good order,* that the rebels can't really make up their minds *where* we are going or *what* we intend to do, and fearing that we might catch them in some trap, are just digging dirt and hiding behind breastworks at Augusta and Savannah. That would be an excellent joke if it were true, but we are not "out of the woods" yet, and I won't crow.

Now that we are across the Ulcofauhatchee, the Yellow, the Oconee, the Ogeechee, the Rocky Comfort and the Buckhead, I can see that a rebel force of 20,000 men could have prevented us from crossing any of these streams for a long time, or perhaps entirely, and have compelled us to turn our course toward Mobile. Our headquarters tonight are on the south side of the road and near to it; the camp of the 2d Brigade is crowding up on us too much and the General is grumbling about it. He is evidently very much out of humor. It arises, I think, from the possible difficulties and dangers of our isolated position. I have placed 300 men on picket tonight, completely encircling our camp and that of the cavalry. If our camp should be surprised here, up *I* would go, for there is nobody here to charge with negligence in regard to the pickets but myself. Kilpatrick's headquarters are down the road a short distance from us in a house, he having no tents.

Friday, Decr. 2d [1864].

Division moved at daybreak, and the cavalry also, in the same order as yesterday. Commenced skirmishing with the enemy before we had gone a mile. It became evident, very

soon after starting this morning, that the rebel force in our
front was largely increased above what it was yesterday, and
on learning from negroes that Rocky Creek was about eight
miles ahead from our camp of last night, we supposed that it
was the intention of the rebels to resist in force our passage of
that creek. This idea spread rapidly through the cavalry and
they distinctly showed signs of nervousness, but as there had
been nothing seen in our front but rebel *cavalry,* our infantry
trudged along in the highest spirits, for our men well knew
they could easily whip all the rebel cavalry Wheeler ever
commanded. The General, however, and some of the rest of
us didn't feel so confident about the result, for although nothing but rebel cavalry had thus far been seen, still we knew there
might be a strong force of infantry and artillery on the east
side of this creek and Wheeler might be falling back before
us, without making much resistance, for the purpose of luring
us on until we should suddenly find ourselves confronting a
superior force; hence our movement was slow and extremely
cautious, the ground ahead being well reconnoitred by our
advance parties and skirmishers.

The cavalry party in the advance came within sight of the
creek at 10 A. M., and word came back from them that the
enemy was holding the east bank of the creek in force. The
division was immediately formed in line of battle, one regiment
deployed in front as skirmishers, the cavalry disposed so as
to cover our flanks and protect our few wagons, and when
everything was in readiness the bugle sounded the forward for
our skirmish regiment; the line of blue moved steadily forward,
out of the woods, into the open fields that lie along the west
bank of the creek, the bright sun glittering on their burnished
arms and a Sabbath like stillness pervading the scene. It
looked beautiful, but I held my breath in suspense to catch
the sound of the first shot. I expected it to be an artillery shot
that would come crashing amongst us, tearing off heads and

legs and arms from we couldn't tell who. Crack! goes a rifle
shot from behind the neat white church on the left of the
road and just on the bank of the creek. Our skirmishers don't
stop to reply to it. Their foe is unseen. But with a yell like
an Indian war whoop every one of them dashes forward at
the top of his speed, without regard to order; each one anxious,
alone, to be first at the church from whence that shot was fired.
In almost less time than it takes to tell it our skirmishers were
swarming around the church and scattered behind trees up and
down the west bank of the creek, and nobody on our side hurt,
but the rebels were on the *east* side, and we couldn't tell in
what force. The General, however, was determined to push
ahead, if possible, so the division was moved up to the creek
in line of battle, and a regiment (the 74th Indiana) selected to
cross the creek and attack the enemy on the opposite side.

While these movements were going on, I was sitting on the
bank of the creek behind a large cypress stump, with General
Baird and General Kilpatrick and a citizen, a young man
(about 25) whom some of Kilpatrick's scouts had brought in
about an hour before. While talking to him and asking him
about the roads, &c., the rebels on the opposite side opened
quite a sharp fire of musketry and the bullets rattled around
our old stump and barked the trees around us quite lively.
Just as soon as our citizen friend ascertained that they were
bullets he threw himself flat on the ground with his face downward and commenced shouting in a piteous tone: "Oh, take
me away, take me away; I can't stand this," &c., &c., which was
excellent fun for all of us, and Kilpatrick after laughing at him
a while, made him sit up, and frightened him still worse by
assuring him that he would hang him if he lay down again.
The fellow sat up, but curled himself into the smallest possible
space, assuring us that he "wasn't used to such doins, and
couldn't stand it like 'you all.' "

As soon as the 74th got on the east side of the creek the

rebels "lit out," as the men say. A couple of regiments of our cavalry crossed immediately and had a running skirmish with them for about two miles, which resulted in the death of two rebels, the wounding of three or four more and the capture of one, a Texan, with a wound through the arm. He told us that everybody *knew* we were going to Augusta, and that nobody supposed they could muster enough force to prevent us. He also told us that there was no rebel infantry outside of Augusta, and that Wheeler's cavalry was scattered all over the country; Wheeler not knowing what to do or where to go, for he found Yankees on every road in the State.

We halted at the cross roads one mile east of the creek, and after the men got dinner, turned and marched southward to our camp on Grisem's plantation. The cross roads spoken of are within six miles of Waynesboro, and we would have reached there by keeping straight ahead. Kilpatrick wanted the General to go straight on to Waynesboro, but that would be taking us still farther away from the other columns and the General chose the prudent course by turning southward so as to draw nearer to the rest of the army. If we get any communication from the rest of our corps tomorrow we *may* turn toward Augusta again.

Contrabands are still swarming to us in immense numbers. The General is a nephew of Gerritt Smith's and is quite an abolitionist. He delights in talking with these contrabands when we halt by the roadside and in extracting information concerning their "masters and mistresses" from them. He picked up quite an original character today who calls himself "Jerry." Jerry is a lively, rollicking, fun loving fellow, with a good deal of shrewdness; about 20 years old and rather a good looking boy. Jerry got an old horse, made a rope bridle, mounted bareback and rode alongside the General all the afternoon, talking to him continually. As we rode along Jerry was silent a few minutes, then he suddenly burst into a loud laugh, shook himself all over, and turning to the General remarked: "Golly, I wish ole massa could see me now, ridin' wid de Ginrals."

After getting into camp tonight "Jerry" entertained us for two or three hours with his oddities. He told us about an old preacher in this neighborhood named Kilpatrick (Gen. Kilpatrick's headquarters are at his house tonight) and said he knew Old Kilpatrick's sermon, he had heard him preach it so often, so we got "Jerry" to preach Old Kilpatrick's sermon. I only remember part of it: "O Lord! suffer our ene*mees to Chaste* after us no longer, but turn *dem* gently round, O, Lord, for we's got *notin* but our rights and our property, *an* if our ene*mees chaste* after us any longer we won't have *notin* for our *chillen*. Bend *dar* hard hearts *an probate* necks, O, Lord, *an* suffer *dem* to *Chaste* after us no longer, but turn *dem* gently round." Jerry would roll up his eyes, and deliver this, and much more, in true ministerial style, until we almost split our sides with laughter.

We asked "Jerry" how many "Yankees" he thought he had seen today, and he replied about "five hundred thousand." I have noticed that it is almost universal amongst the negroes in this country, when they first see our column come along on the road to exclaim: "Good Lord! looks like de whole wold was comin." Headquarters on the right of the road, in the edge of an old field—tents facing the west.

Saturday, Dec. 3rd [1864].

Division moved at sunrise. Still continuing our course in a Southwesterly direction. About 9 A. M. we reached "Rosemary Creek," a small, clear stream, about one rod in width where it crosses the road, and found it necessary to build a foot bridge over it for the troops. While engaged in building the bridge Lt. Col. McClurg, Gen. Davis' Chief of Staff, came up to us with information of the rest of the Corps, and with orders for us to proceed to the Waynesboro & Augusta R. R. at Thomas' station; Kilpatrick's cavalry to accompany us. So we let the foot bridge go, turned and marched back about three miles, then took the best roads we could find to Thomas station.

We crossed the head waters of Rosemary Creek about noon, and halted near a church, on the south bank for the men to get dinner. During this halt the General and myself narrowly escaped capture. It was only 5 miles to Thomas station, and as Kilpatrick with his cavalry had gone ahead, telling the General he would go on to Thomas station and go into camp, the General concluded he would ride on ahead to Thomas station himself; so, asking me to ride with him, and leaving orders for the troops to move forward after they had rested two hours, we started off, unarmed, except with swords, and without any escort, supposing of course the road was clear. We passed cross roads about 2 miles from where our Division was, and rode on, busily engaged in conversation, until we were within about 1¼ miles of the station when I noticed the road, and to my surprise discovered that there had been no cavalry along that road; it startled me, and I immediately called the General's attention to it, and he was as much surprised as I was, for not a horse track was to be seen, and the peril of our situation was immediately realized—either Kilpatrick had missed the road, or *we* had, and it made no difference to us which, for we were 4 miles away from any of our troops, without arms, and with cross roads half way between us and the troops, on which a party of rebels might come and cut us off entirely from help.

Says the General: "Major, this is a bad piece of business." "It is indeed, sir," I replied, "but let's run for it, and maybe we can reach the cross roads before any rebels do." "Agreed" said he, "we'll try it," and in a second we were off at the best pace of our horses. In a few minutes, the cross roads were in sight, and the road was clear; reaching the cross roads we checked our horses, and looking up the road to our right which led to Waynesboro, about half a mile distant, I saw a party of rebel cavalry, coming toward the cross roads at a full run, chasing after a couple of our foragers, who, mounted on mules had ventured out there in search of provisions and plunder. The General saw them coming too, and started at a round gallop to where we had left the troops. I saw by the gait they were traveling that I could outrun them with "Frank" very easily, so I remained and began shouting to our two foragers who were being pursued, in order to encourage them; the rebels seeing me, and hearing me shouting checked up— I saw that *brass* would save the foragers, so I yelled "forward" as loud as I could, and spurred my horse forward as if to chase them—the dodge succeeded; one of them fired his pistol, and they all (about twenty) turned tail and ran like whiteheads, the foragers firing after them as they ran.

When the foragers came up to me I *expect* I swore at them a little, for venturing out in that way, and then rode on back to the troops, where I found the General, and we had many a hearty laugh this afternoon and evening over our John Gilpin ride. It's a good joke now, but it would have been a serious affair for us if we had reached the cross roads three minutes later than we did; it might have furnished me a chapter on prison life, for my diary. "All's well that ends well" though, and "a miss is as good as a mile."

The Division reached "Thomas station" about 4 P. M. and was stretched along the R. R. for about a mile and a half to tear up the track, and now, ten o'clock at night, the men have about 2 miles of the track torn up, the ties piled up and burning all along that 2 miles, and the bars of iron laying across the piles of burning ties heating so that the men can twist them and render them useless. This place consists of a water tank, and an overseer's house, surrounded by about 20 whitewashed negro houses, it takes its name from the name of the owner of this plantation. It is eight miles from here to Waynesboro by R. R. and about 33 to Augusta. The rest of our Corps is about 10 miles south of us, tonight, on the R. R. at Lumpkins station, and Gen. Sherman is at Millen.

Five days ago this place was to us *"terra incognita"*; we sat around our camp fires and talked about this R. R. just as we would have talked of China; we thought we *might* get here, but we also thought very strongly that we *might not* get here; yet now we find ourselves here, and are almost inclined to wonder why we ever doubted our ability to get here. Five days ago we were imagining all sorts of dangers and opposition that might beset us in our progress to this R. R. but now we look back over the past few days and find a rich fund of amusement in talking about the feeble opposition of Wheeler and his fugitive cavaliers.

I wonder what the next five days will bring to us? Long continued success is apt to make men over-confident and careless. I hope it may not be so with us. Our getting possession of this road cuts R. R. communication between Savannah and Augusta, except around by way of Charleston. The rebels up the track toward Waynesboro can see the burning ties and will know, of course, that we are destroying the R. R. so I presume the Augusta people, after their long suspense, will breathe free tonight, for they will receive dispatches from Wheeler saying that he has driven off the Yankees and compelled them to turn toward Savannah.

But they are mistaken if they think that, for we have received orders from Gen. Sherman tonight that will again make the hearts of the Augustans quake tomorrow, for Kilpatrick and ourselves are to move up the R. R. tomorrow and drive Wheeler across Briar Creek, 5 miles north of Waynesboro, for the purpose of keeping up the idea that we are moving on Augusta.

The soil here is nothing but poor pale looking sand; it is

good for raising melons though, and peanuts. Indeed I have
forgotten in this diary, to notice the peanut crop of Georgia,
and I ought not omit so important an item as that, for peanuts
are a luxury to northern urchins, and many a time, while a
lad, munching away at my "cents worth of peanuts," have I
wondered where they grew, and how they grew, and wished
I could see them growing. The ground for planting them is
prepared and marked out like corn ground, only the hills are
but about two feet apart; two peanuts are dropped in a hill
and covered lightly with a hoe; in about 6 weeks the sprouts
from each hill have grown up in a thick bunch, not unlike a
bunch of young boxwood; when in this condition a hoe full
of dirt is placed on top of the center of each bunch, bending the
young shoots down and causing them to spread out in every
direction and lie flat on the ground, the shoots then run
along the ground like sweet potato vines (for which I have
frequently mistaken them) and the nuts grow *in the ground*
at intervals along the vine, just as melons do, except that the
melons grow above the ground.

The crop is gathered after frost in the fall by pulling up
the vines and picking off the nuts. All the negroes raise little
patches of them for themselves, and many planters raise from
5 to 100 acres of them for the market. I think the average
crop is from 30 to 50 bushels per acre. The negroes, and most
of the whites too, call them "Gookas," "Gooka Peas," "Gron-
nuts," i. e. (Ground nuts) "Hog Peas," "Hog nuts," "Ground
Peas" and "Pea Nuts," the latter name not being very generally
used.

Sunday, Dec. 4th [1864].

The rebels bothered us last night, but we paid them for it
today. About midnight last night they got a piece of artillery
on the R. R. track and fired down the track at our camp
fires. I believe they killed one cavalry man. Of course, the

General and all his staff had to get up, had our horses saddled, and as I was the only one about headquarters that knew how to get to our pickets up the R. R., I had to act as guide through the woods in the dark. It was very dark and after we had gone some distance, and everything had become quiet again, the General declared that we had already gone too far, that we were already *outside* of our pickets, and that if they followed my lead we would all be captured. The experience of yesterday had made him very cautious, but after some parleying I convinced him I was right and we went ahead to our pickets. But as the fuss was all over, and we could see nothing, we returned, getting to bed again, in bad humor, about 2 this morning.

Kilpatrick drew up his whole division of cavalry in the open fields this morning at 7 o'clock, ready to commence operations for driving the rebels up the R. R. to Waynesboro and through that place. So many cavalry in line in an open plain make a beautiful sight. But it's all *show;* there's not much *fight* in them, though Kilpatrick's men have behaved very handsomely today. They did *all* the fighting and whipped Wheeler soundly, killing, wounding and capturing about 300 of his men, and losing only about 50 themselves. But then Kilpatrick's men had the *moral support* of two of our brigades that were formed in line right behind them and kept moving forward as they moved, so that our cavalry all the time knew that there was no chance of their being whipped. This has been a regular field day, and we have had "lots of fun" chasing Wheeler and his cavalry. Kilpatrick is full of fun and frolic and he was in excellent spirits all day, for Wheeler and he were classmates at West Point, and he was elated at the idea of whipping his classmate. A cavalry fight is just about as much fun as a fox hunt; but, of course, in the midst of the fun somebody is getting hurt all the time. But it is by no means the serious work that infantry fighting is. Wheeler himself had to run at an inglo-

346   *Three Years in the Army of the Cumberland*

riously rapid rate through the streets of Waynesboro today.
That must have been very humiliating to this proud cavalier.
We entered Waynesboro about noon and pushed on after the
flying rebels to Briar Creek, 22 miles from Augusta. I presume
the Augustans were frightened again today when they heard we
were coming so close to their city.

Waynesboro is the county seat of Burke County, the county
having been so named in 1777 in honor of Edmund Burke, the
British champion of American independence. Waynesboro was
incorporated in 1812 and I should think contained about 1,000
inhabitants. In 1850 this county contained a free white population of little over 5,000, while it contained a slave population of
over 10,000. An engagement took place in this county in 1779
between the British and Americans, in which the old flag came
out victorious just as it did today. The soil in this county is said
to be very productive. Cotton and corn are the staples. Since
crossing the Oconee we have seen scarcely any stone. The
wealthiest planters we have seen thus far through the State have
not spent much money in building fine houses. We left one of our
brigades, with our wagons, at Thomas Station this morning,
and after we had pushed Wheeler across Briar Creek the General ordered that brigade to take the trains and march direct
to Alexander. We left Waynesboro at 3 P. M. and taking the
Savannah road met our other brigade and wagons at Alexander
about dark, but we had to march until 8 o'clock this evening in
order to get a camping place near water.

We left Kilpatrick in Waynesboro, with part of his force at
Briar Creek. He will withdraw from there and follow us some
time tonight, so that Wheeler will not know until after daylight
tomorrow but that we intend to push right on toward Augusta.

We heard from the rest of our corps tonight and from the
extreme right of the army. General Sherman with the right
wing is probably within 20 miles of Savannah tonight. Our

withdrawal from Waynesboro and march to this place this afternoon closes all demonstrations against Augusta. We have kept
up the delusion of an attack on that place as long as we can, and
with the sunlight of tomorrow the true design of our campaign
will break upon the bewildered minds of the rebels. It is over a
hundred miles tonight between the two extremes of our army,
and tomorrow morning we commence closing up as rapidly as
possible. The road we are encamped on tonight leads straight to
Savannah. I heard tonight that General Davis turned back a lot
of contrabands at Buckhead Creek, and I don't doubt it, for he
is a copperhead.

The village of Alexander has but two or three houses in it.

Monday, Decr. 5th [1864].

Division moved at sunrise and marched via "Sardis Church"
to "Jacksonboro," a distance of about 19 miles. Our pickets were
fired on a little before daylight this morning, so we expected to
be annoyed by parties of rebel cavalry or guerillas during the
day, but were not troubled by them. Wheeler must have been
chagrined this morning on discovering that instead of being in
our front, as he supposed himself, he is in our rear, and far in
our rear, too—so far that it will now be impossible for him to
get in our front until we are battering away at Savannah. Most
of our march today has been through the "piney woods" country,
and the few women and children we have seen look utterly
ignorant and stupid. Very few negroes are owned in the section
through which we have passed today. Our line of march now is
parallel to the Savannah River and so near to it that no column
of rebels will dare to march between us and that river, hence all
reinforcements for Savannah must go down on the north side of
the river. Jacksonboro looks, on the map, as though it might
be quite a village, but on reaching it we find it to consist of a
single two-story frame farm house, with the usual log outbuild-

ings. It was formerly a county seat, but before Jacksonboro had time to grow any the seat of justice was removed to Sylvania, and Jacksonboro remains in *statu quo.*

Our troops are encamped tonight on Beaver Dam Creek. We should have moved three or four miles farther, but it was 4 o'clock when we reached here and we found the bridge across the creek burned and so much timber felled across the ford and road that it will take about two or three hours to remove it, so the General concluded to encamp here and clear out the obstructions tonight. The rest of the corps is near us tonight on a road perpendicular to the road we have been traveling. Kilpatrick's headquarters are at *the house of* Jacksonboro tonight and our headquarters are in tents in the dooryard. Kilpatrick came out in his bare head and shirt sleeves to the fire in front of our tents this evening and regaled us with an ancedotal history of his student days at West Point. He told us many anecdotes of our General McCook and the rebel, General Wheeler. He says McCook at West Point was a lazy, pompous ass and Wheeler a great sloven.

Kilpatrick is the most vain, conceited, egotistical little popinjay I ever saw. He has one redeeming quality—he rarely drinks spirituous liquors, and *never* to excess. He is a very ungraceful rider, looking more like a monkey than a man on horseback.

Went to bed feeling quite unwell.

Tuesday, Dec. 6th [1864].

Division moved across "Beaver Dam" Creek at 8 A. M., marched about 12 miles and went into camp at "Black Creek" about dark.

Country very poor and sandy, and abounding in swamps. It would appear, from the reports brought in by the cavalry scouts, that the enemy are expecting us to cross the Savannah River somewhere near where we are now, and march against Charleston. They find rebels on the opposite side at all the fords and ferries to prevent our crossing. They are perfectly safe so long as they stay there, for we don't intend to cross the river *now*. South Carolina is reserved for a future day; Sherman intends to finish Georgia, before beginning on South Carolina.

The country being so poor here the men don't find a very large supply of provisions, but they are still finding *enough,* and if it gets no worse we will get along very well.

At intervals during the day we heard heavy cannonading, apparently very distant, and in the direction of the coast; the conjectures as to its whereabouts have been various, but everybody inclines to the opinion that it *may* be the bombardment of Charleston. It seems strange to think that we are within hearing of our guns in Charleston Harbor, and if it is really true that we heard them today I have no longer any fears about the ultimate success of our campaign.

It is certain that those guns were not fired by any part of this army, and it is equally certain that they were fired either *at* or *by* Federal troops eastward of us; in either case it is an assurance to us that some of our forces on the seaboard are cooperating with us. I wish I could know just what is going on there; this blind, groping of our way through the swamps and forests of Georgia, knowing nothing of what our friends are doing to help us, or what our enemies are doing to oppose us, is the greatest annoyance of this campaign, but thank fortune, we are not relying upon our friends for assistance, and as to our enemies we dared them to do their utmost when we severed our communication with the north and started from Atlanta, and we will not fear them now.

Wednesday, Dec. 7th [1864].

Division moved at daylight, Kilpatrick's cavalry being in our rear, and the other two divisions of our corps in advance. Our march was very much impeded, all day, by the slow movement of the troops in advance of us, and on reaching the very deep and difficult ravine of Mill Creek, it was evident that we could not get over it until some time after dark, so the General determined to go into camp without attempting the crossing tonight. Just about dark, the cavalry in our rear came rushing past us pell-mell, and the sounds of musketry informed us that the rebels in *some* force were following our rear closely so our headquarters were taken down again, preparations for supper suspended, wagons reloaded, and the troops disposed in proper order to resist an attack; our lines were opened and Kilpatrick's frightened cavalry permitted to come through and take shelter behind us; about this time came orders that we must cross Mill Creek and move on to the vicinity of "Sister's Ferry" some 7 miles beyond, if it should take us all night. This was hard, for we were all tired and hungry, but there was no time for rest, so about 9 o'clock we got started out again, and after marching all night we reached "Sister's Ferry" at 4 o'clock next morning. I think this was the hardest night march I ever made.

Just before the troops began to cross the "Mill Creek" ravine, word came to the General that the enemy was in our front just on the opposite side of the ravine, and I went ahead to see about it; collecting about ten men who were straggling on ahead I made them load their guns, and took them with me as I cautiously groped my way through the dark ravine, but I found no enemy on the opposite side and sent word back to the General accordingly; I was exceedingly sleepy, and laid down on a brush pile by the road side where I slept an hour, until the General came up with the rear brigade, when we all started ahead; I slept on my horse as we rode along, and at every halt I dismounted and laid down beside my horse to snatch a little sleep, being afraid, all the time, that by some unfortunate mischance, the column might move on and leave me.

During all the march of this day and night we passed through a low, level sandy country, timbered with "Pine" and "Jack Oak."

We passed, today, the house of Doct. Longstreet, a relative of the rebel General Longstreet; there was nothing about it to attract attention except the fact of its owner being a "Longstreet."

For many days past the "Spanish moss" has been found in great abundance. It gives the forest an exceedingly gloomy (funereal, best describes it) appearance. "Sister's Ferry" is on the Savannah River, and the wagon road at this point is within about two hundred yards of the river. On some of the maps it is called "Two Sisters' Ferry," and it is said the name originated from the fact of two sisters belonging to some of the German families that first settled this neighborhood having been drowned here while attempting to cross the river in a canoe. At "Sister's Ferry" the bank on the Georgia side is high while that on the Carolina side is low and swampy. Morgan's Division of this corps, which is in the advance on this road, finds the road blockaded and some slight show of an enemy in front; this may detain us somewhat but Savannah must surely be ours now, for we are within 35 miles of it, and I am sure nothing can save it.

We heard the distant cannonade again to-day and all night

"Nearer, clearer, deadlier than before."

I have heard it suggested to-day that it may be Foster [4] of the Dept. of the South making a demonstration in our favor, by a land attack on some point on the coast. Wouldn't it be a "bore" to have "Foster" attack Savannah now and take it before we get there? He won't do it though. Those eastern fellows never do anything clever, and, as we used to say up in Tennessee over

4. John Gray Foster, commanding the Department of the South, was attempting at this time to cut the routes by which the Confederates might escape from Savannah to the north. The firing which Connolly heard was undoubtedly an engagement between the Federal General John P. Hatch, ordered by Foster to break the Charleston and Savannah Railroad, and General G. W. Smith, commanding the Georgia militia. Hatch was repulsed.

a year and a half ago, "we'll have to go over there and do their work for them yet."

During the night the General and staff rode along at the head of our rear brigade, so as to be near at hand in case the enemy should attack our rear; at one time the column halted about an hour, and we couldn't imagine what caused the long halt, so we rode along, picking our way amongst the tired, sleeping men as they laid along the road, and on reaching the head of the column found Col. Este, the commander of our leading brigade, and all his staff, lying down in the road asleep. The Colonel explained by saying that he was halting to let the wagon train ahead get out of his way, but the fact was that there was no wagon train within 3 miles of him, but he had halted for a rest, and falling asleep, overslept himself.

Thursday, Dec. 8th [1864].

Division moved forward again at 7 o'clock, everybody tired, sleepy and worn out. I tumbled down on the ground by a burning stump at the road side about 5 o'clock this morning, slept until 6 o'clock, got a tin cup full of coffee for breakfast, gave my horse some corn, and by half past six was on the road for the day. I don't think I could stand *this* kind of soldiering *more* than a month or two without *some* rest. After marching about 3 miles, and crossing a small creek, which, I believe is nameless on the maps, we were compelled to halt, Carlin's and Morgan's Divisions which were in front of us being detained by the destruction of the "Ebenezer Creek" bridge. Early in the afternoon the cavalry which was in our rear, being pressed by a superior force of the enemy (*as they said*), passed through our Division; we formed line of battle facing to the rear, and the Cavalry took position on our right, between us and the river; the enemy continued during the day to threaten an attack, and thus kept us on the alert all day, which was very annoying as we were all very sleepy. At 12½ midnight we withdrew in the utmost silence, not

a bugle being sounded nor a loud command being given, and resumed our march, crossing Ebenezer Creek and encamping just
south of it at 6 A. M.

This night's work was harder than that of last night, and I
never was so utterly exhausted and worn out as I was when the
sun rose the morning after crossing Ebenezer Creek. The crossing of Ebenezer Creek was a very delicate undertaking, for the
enemy was just in our rear, undoubtedly listening for every
sound that would indicate a movement on our part, and to cross
the creek we had to pass through at least a mile of the most
gloomy, dismal cypress swamp I ever saw, on a narrow causeway, just wide enough for a wagon to drive along; if the enemy
had discovered our movement and had planted a piece of artillery
in the road to rake that causeway while we were on it they could
have killed or wounded three-fourths of the men in the division,
and we should have been utterly helpless to defend against it.
We were fully aware of the danger of our undertaking though,
and every possible precaution was taken to preserve silence. If
there was no other road to approach Savannah except by this
one over Ebenezer Creek, five thousand rebels could defend the
city against the world. I don't believe they thought we would
be foolish enough to *try* to cross here. Rebel gunboats in the
Savannah threw shells over into our road to-day, but did no
harm so far as I can learn.

The plot really begins to thicken; rebel gunboats begin to oppose us, and the heavy cannonading we have heard for two or
three days past has been more distinct and very rapid all day.
Where can it be? Not a soul in *this* army knows though; not
Sherman himself; but *who* it is or *where* it is makes but little
difference to us, for it assures us that there is an active Yankee
force somewhere near us, and that is enough to encourage any
of us who may be faint-hearted. There is no longer any doubt
that we shall immediately invest Savannah, but the provision
question is beginning to be a serious one with us, however it

may be with the right of the army, for we are squeezed in amongst swamps, rivers and sand hills, where, even in most flourishing times the inhabitants must have had hard work to live, and in a very few days we will eat up everything within our reach, so that some steps must be taken to supply the army with means of subsistence before we can think of entering upon a protracted siege; still, may be I am "reckoning without my host"—we are not yet besieging Savannah—we are not yet within sight of its spires—we know not what miles of "Ebenezers" and of breastworks and what thousands of grey clad soldiers may yet be found to oppose, retard, harass our march, and possibly prevent us ever reaching within sight of the city; the army that took Atlanta though, must not fail before Savannah.

When the head of the column reached the "Ebenezer Causeway" I went ahead with one of Genl. Davis' aids who had come back to point out our ground for camping, and as I reached the bridge, I found there Major Lee, Provost Marshal of the Corps, engaged, by Genl. Davis' order, in turning off the road, into the swamp all the fugitive negroes that came along. When we should cross I knew it was the intention that the bridge should be burned, and I inquired if the negroes were not to be permitted to cross; I was told that Genl. Davis had ordered that they should not. This *I* knew, and Genl. Davis knew must result in all these negroes being recaptured or perhaps brutally shot down by the rebel cavalry to-morrow morning. The idea of five or six hundred black women, children and old men being thus returned to slavery by such an infernal copperhead as Jeff. C. Davis was entirely too much for my Democracy; I suppose loss of sleep, and fatigue made me somewhat out of humor too, and I told his staff officers what I thought of such an inhuman, barbarous proceeding in language which may possibly result in a reprimand from his serene Highness, for I know his toadies will repeat it to him, but I don't care a fig; I am determined to expose this act of his publicly, and if he undertakes to vent his spleen on me for it, I have the *same rights that he himself exercised in his affair with Nelson.* I expect this will cost me my Brevet as Lieut. Colonel, but let it go, I wouldn't barter my convictions of right, nor seal my mouth for any promotion.

The creek "Ebenezer" received its name from the first settlers, who were refugees from religious persecution in the village of "Berchtolsgaden," Germany. The first company consisted of 42 men with their families, in all 78 persons. They arrived at Charleston S. C. in March 1734, where they met Oglethorpe who conducted them to Georgia, landing them first at Savannah.

History says: "they expressed a desire to be removed to some distance from the sea, where the scenery was diversified with hill and dale and they might be supplied with springs of water."

Knowing this to be their desire, Oglethorpe, who appears to have been nothing but a shrewd old land speculator, led these poor Dutchmen away up amongst these dismal swamps, and settled them here on Ebenezer Creek, where nothing but alligators ever ought to live.

These religionists were called Salzburgers and it is said their first act after selecting the site of their new settlement was to erect a stone which they found lying near by, and called it "Ebenezer" ("Stone of help," I believe, for it is said they felt that the Lord had helped them in selecting so beautiful a location). They must have been very easily satisfied, to be content with such a place as this; if I were compelled to live here I should feel as if the Lord were punishing me for my iniquity.

Friday, Decr. 9th [1864].

Division marching again at 11 A. M. I drank a cup of coffee and ate a piece of corn bread about 7½ o'clock this morning, and then lay down to snatch a little sleep, for I was almost sick for want of it, and it was so with the General and all the rest of the staff, but we only had about two hours sleep until we were com-

pelled to march. The first thing I shall do after Savannah is captured, will be to take a nap about 48 hours long; so much loss of
sleep, and night marching begins to make me *feel old*. If any one
at home thinks an officer in the Army has fine times, no hard
work, and plenty of pay, I wish they could have my experience
of the past six months; I rather think they would "see it" in a
different light. It is a perfect dog's life, and I am almost surprised at myself sometimes, for not quitting it; but that would
never do; the young man, who in these eventful times is found at
home, is but a drone in the hive.

We marched 6 miles to-day, taking a by-road to the right of
the main Savannah Road, thus going around the heads of
Lockner's and Kogler's Creeks, and encamping in Piney Woods,
near the junction of our by-road with the main road. These
Piney Woods where we are encamped have once been cultivated
probably by the pious, persecuted Salzburgers whom Oglethorpe
swindled; but the trees are giants and moss grown as if the
storms of centuries had beaten on them; looking at them, so completely overhung with the long streamers of dingy grey "Spanish
Moss" one can almost fancy they were thus adorned for some
fairy festival long ago, all traces of which have now disappeared
except the soft yielding carpet of pine leaves, and the faded
drapery overhead. In White's "Historical Collections of Georgia," I find the names of the original German settlers of this
section of Georgia and I also find that the same names exist
here yet, and the same families, or rather descendants from them,
are the proprietors of the lands. Slaves are not very plenty
amongst them, but this I think arises from the fact that slave
labor cannot be made profitable on this very poor soil. These
people through here were not original Secessionists and are now
in favor of a reconstruction of the Union on *any* terms. They do
not, however, represent the *Chivalry* of the South, nor do they
claim to, I believe. This County, "Effingham," is almost entirely
settled and owned by them. The principal export of the county
has always been lumber, but one enterprising Yankee up in

Maine would export as much lumber from his own farm as they do from the whole county.

We are encamped within 18 miles of the city to-night, and no sounds of fighting in front yet. We hear that Hardee with 17000 troops is in the city to defend it. P'shaw! our corps alone whipped that many *veterans* under Hardee's management at Jonesboro last September, and if *he* is the only Savior the rebels have for their city they may say "good-by Savannah."

The rebel gunboats in the river did some more shelling to-day, but they couldn't so much as frighten a mule. The distant cannonade was heard again about due east of us to-day. It must be in the vicinity of Charleston. I suppose the people in the North know where it is from the newspapers, but we who are within hearing of the guns do not.

Foster *was* to make an attempt to cut the R. R. between Savannah and Charleston about Christmas, and that may be what is going on. A negro who came in from South Carolina today says that there was a battle over near that R. R. a few days ago and that he heard the white folks say the Yankees had been whipped, so I shouldn't wonder if Foster had tried to strike that Road and failed; all these eastern fellows appear to fail in everything they undertake.[5]

We hear, to-night, that the right wing of the army is within 4 miles of the city, and has met no formidable opposition yet; the rebels must have a very short line of defence, but it must be very close to the city, and the result will be, if they fight stubbornly, that the entire city will be destroyed by our artillery. I saw one city (Atlanta) destroyed, and that was enough for me. I want Savannah to fall, but not in ruins.

Saturday, Dec. 10th [1864].

Division moved at 9 A. M. marched 6 miles and went into camp within 12 miles of the doomed city, in a strip of low piney woods lying between the road and the rice plantations along

5. See note 4, p. 351.

the River. About noon to-day our Second Brigade, commanded by Col. Gleason 87th Ind. Vols. was sent off to the left for the purpose of striking the Charleston and Savannah R. R. and if possible destroying the R. R. bridge across the river. They succeeded in destroying about 2 miles of the road but they found the bridge held by the rebels, and as the only means of approaching the bridge was by a trussle work about a mile in length across a swamp it was deemed impracticable to attempt to reach it. The artillery firing in the direction of the city has been very heavy all day, and I should think the tug of war was just about opening. From present appearances it would seem that our division is to be used to cover the rear, and protect the trains of the left wing of the army. The R. R. to Charleston being now destroyed, Savannah is entirely isolated from the rest of the Confederacy, and its fall is now only a question of time, unless we should find it impossible to procure subsistence. A fleet of transports loaded with rations for us is probably in the offing before Savannah now, but the question is how are we to communicate with that fleet, and how get the rations landed? Our first fighting must be for something to eat. The R. R. from Charleston to Savannah is cut, but there is one good wagon road running from Savannah to Charleston on the north side of the river, and unless we can throw our lines across the river so as to get possession of that road the garrison of the city can escape by that road.

Sunday, Dec. 11th [1864].

We sent a regiment (2d Minnesota) over to the R. R. again this morning to make another attempt to destroy the R. R. bridge. The General went over too, and myself. We could get only a short distance out on the trussle work though, for the rebels had a locomotive on the track at the South end of the bridge, with a platform car in front of it, on which was mounted a heavy piece of artillery. As soon as our working party commenced work at the trussle the rebels opened on us and we all had to hide behind sand piles and logs, for their shells came tearing right down along the R. R. and burst right where we had been at work, we being unable to reply to their fire or silence it, for we had no artillery with us. We succeeded however in burning a considerable portion of the trussle. I saw a regular canebrake near the trussle to-day and some very large magnolia trees, over two feet in diameter. I have not seen a rice plantation yet—they are further down the river—neither have I seen a palmetto tree.

Division moved out after dinner, marched three miles, crossing St. Augustine Creek, and encamping immediately south of it, alongside the R. R. and within 9 miles of the city. While we were at the R. R. this morning, some rebel cavalry came down the road on which the Division lay, and fired a few shots at our pickets, but they soon withdrew. The firing toward the city has been heavy and continuous today; I think the rebels must have some heavy guns there.

Monday, Dec. 12th [1864].

Division stationary. Mine eyes have beheld the spires of the city!

This forenoon Capt. Biddle [6] and myself rode down to the river, visited the rice plantations, and rice mills, saw a rebel steamboat, captured by our foragers yesterday, saw the spires of Savannah, saw the sacred soil of South Carolina, saw and talked with the real genuine plantation nigger, and indeed were surfeited with sights to us entirely new. There is as much difference between niggers on rice plantations and "up-country" ones, as there is between negroes and baboons.

Many of those I saw to-day were scarcely a single remove from brutes, and they speak a broken sort of English that I can scarcely understand.

6. Captain William B. Biddle, Eighty-seventh Indiana Volunteers, ordnance officer of Baird's division.

On one plantation I saw about 150 niggers principally women and children, and nearly every one of them sick, not a mouthful for them to eat on the whole plantation, except the rice which was stacked up, in the straw, in huge ricks that look like large wheat ricks. The stubble on a rice field looks very much like the stubble on a wheat field or oats field, but the straw is much more tender, and never becomes harsh and brittle like wheat stubble.

Rice plantations must be on low ground, so that they can be flooded with water; ditches are cut through them, dividing the fields into squares or rectangles about 40 yards by 80, all these ditches communicating with one main ditch or canal which opens into the river. The land is plowed in March I believe, and the rice sown with drills, like wheat, then the gates of the main canal are opened and water permitted to flow into the ditches until the whole field is covered with water about a foot deep; the rice sprouts under the water, and in about two weeks the water is drawn off, then the "hands" have to wade into this muddy field, sinking into the mud over knee deep, and pulling out the weeds, when the weeds are pulled out the field has been dried by the hot sun, and the negroes hoe the rice, then the field is flooded again nearly two feet deep; this is done to make the rice *stretch,* i. e., to make it grow up tall; it stretches up out of the water, and the head forms above the water, looking like the head on oat straw, but much larger; when the grain is full the water is drawn off again; in a few days of hot southern sun the rice field changes from a pale green to a deep, rich yellow, and the negroes with sickles cut the crop, bind it in sheaves like oats, "shock" it, and as soon as convenient *carry* it off the field to the high ground where they rick it as a northern Dutch farmer ricks his wheat.

This is the mode of rice culture, as I have gleaned it from the filthy, ignorant wretches who have almost worn out their lives at it; my description may be inaccurate, probably is, in some of the details, but in the main is, I believe, correct. Negroes employed on rice plantations live but a few years, and I suppose from this fact, the idea has become prevalent that white men could not stand it to labor on southern plantations. If they would take any decent care of their negroes on rice plantations, they would live as long as on any other plantations, but the proprietors of rice plantations live in cities or in Europe. Everything is done by overseers, and the negroes are treated with just the same brutality as our army mules; profits are large, and if a nigger dies it makes but little difference, another can easily be bought. Orders received to move early next morning. After returning from my visit to the rice plantations I gave the General a description of what I saw, and he went down himself this afternoon.

Tuesday, Dec. 13th [1864].

Division moved at sunrise, taking the road to Savannah until reaching the *Six mile post,* when we took a by road to the right, crossing the C. & S. R. R. and moving in a southwesterly direction through "Piney Woods" we crossed "Pipe Maker's Creek"—the Macon R. R.—and the Louisville Road, taking position on the Macon R. R. and Louisville Road, facing to the rear, so as to cover the rear of the left wing of the army. Our Head Quarters to-night are between four and five miles from the city, directly on the Louisville Road. Considerable artillery and musketry firing on the lines in front of the city during the day.

Just as we struck the Louisville road this morning we met Lieut. Col. Ewing, Inspr. Gen., and other officers of Genl. Sherman's Staff, who told us they were on their way to see the attack on Fort McAllister at the mouth of the Ogeechee. All day we were engaged in discussing the probability of the success of the attack on Fort McAllister, but it is over, and McAllister is ours—captured by Hazen's Division of the 15th Corps—so I suppose Sherman will have communication with the fleet to-night, and with daylight in the morning the news of our success will be on its way with all the speed of steam to electrify the millions of the north who are awaiting news from us with breathless interest. We all breathe freer to-night than we have for three months past. Our work of course is not done, Savannah is not yet ours, but the capture of Mc-Allister settles the provision question, and there is now *no* doubt about the fall of the City. Our men are now living almost entirely on rice; we have no meat and no crackers, but little coffee and very little sugar; the whole rice crop of this year is on the plantations though, and I guess we can worry along on rice until some means are devised for getting rations from the fleet. It is not known yet amongst the camps that Fort McAllister has fallen, but the men are living contentedly on the rice which they get in the straw and clean for themselves, for they know that rations will be plenty as soon as Sherman can provide them.

Our horses and mules are living on rice straw, and the Lord only knows how the ten or twelve thousand fugitive negroes within our lines are living, but they appear to be cheerful and happy, grinning and bowing to everybody; they are encamped —all around—everywhere—in squads of ten to a hundred; their little fires form a complete circle around our Head Quarters at night; I believe they have taken a fancy to our Head Quarters, for they come to us with all their little complaints; get all the waste victuals from our mess, and make their little camps as close to us as they dare; indeed the General lets them camp closer to our Head Quarters than he would like to have the soldiers; they appear to shun Davis' Head Quarters though—they find no sympathy there—I think Davis is a copperhead because of that Kentucky Indictment pending against him for the murder of Nelson; he don't know but that he may, some day, be tried for that offense before a jury of Kentucky copperheads, and he is anxious to propitiate them.[7]

Wednesday, Dec. 14th [1864].

Division stationary. Order received from Genl. Sherman announcing the fall of Fort McAllister. Our loss in the assault only 91 killed and wounded. Copies of order sent to brigades and regiments, and the men have been cheering and yelling like Indians all day. Everybody feeling jolly—bands all playing, batteries all firing, flags all flying, and everybody voting everybody else in this army a hero. The enemy rather quiet, they fired but little during the day.

In the midst of all our joy though we must *eat,* so we sent out a large detail this morning with wagons, and they came in this evening loaded with rice in sheaf, so our men and horses will have something to eat for a few days longer.

Finding I would probably have an opportunity of sending a letter North to-day, I wrote just a line to Mary to let her know I am still alive and able to eat rice—had neither time nor opportunity to write more.

7. The allusion is to an episode which Davis never outlived. "Brooding over a severe rebuke received some days before from Gen. William Nelson, his commanding officer, he sought out Nelson (Sept. 29, 1862) in the lobby of a Louisville hotel with the evident purpose of forcing a quarrel upon him. After high words, Davis crumpled up a card and threw it in Nelson's face, and Nelson retaliated with a slap. Davis then left him, but returning a few minutes later with a revolver shot him as he passed through the hall, inflicting a mortal wound. Partly on account of his military abilities, but more, it is surmised, because of the exertion of strong political influence—especially through his friend, Gov. Oliver P. Morton, who accompanied him when he quarreled with Nelson—Davis went wholly unpunished and after a short time was restored to duty." Thomas M. Spaulding in *Dictionary of American Biography.*

Thursday, Dec. 15th [1864].

Division stationary. Weather continues warm and pleasant as mid summer. Capt. Buttrick and myself went to Fort McAllister this morning and returned this evening very tired, having ridden about 40 miles to-day. We rode along the lines of the entire army, and I obtained a good idea of our position in front of the city. If we have to assault the enemy's works we will have a great deal of trouble there are so many swamps and bayous between us and the enemy's lines. On our way to McAllister this morning we met Genl. Sherman coming back from his first visit to the fleet; his orderlies riding behind him were carrying huge bundles of late New York papers. I saw the well known head lines of the "Herald" and "Tribune" as they passed me, and I was almost tempted to ask Mr. Sherman if he couldn't spare me one. I saw my first Palmetto tree to-day; it was about fifty feet high, which, I am told, is unusually high for them. The stalk looked like that of a huge overgrown cabbage stalk.

I also saw a rice field containing probably 400 acres, with the rice shocks scattered over it as thickly as they stand on our best wheat fields in the North. We couldn't get to the Fort, as it is on the opposite side of the Ogeechee from us, but we viewed it from the top of a rice mill, where Genls. Sherman and Howard stood while the assault was going on. We saw our monitors and fleet of transports in Ossabau Sound, and two of our monitors that were engaged in slowly shelling a rebel battery on the side toward the city. I am no hero-worshipper, I think, but what I have seen to-day, convinces me that General Sherman is a leader, of genius equal to that of Napoleon *in the field,* if not in the cabinet.

None but an unusually bold man would have undertaken this campaign, and none but a man of genius could have succeeded as he has. We consider the campaign finished; Sherman says Savannah is virtually his, and everybody feels so; true there are some rebels in there, under the command of Hardee, but we can easily work them out and ourselves in, now. On our way to-day we crossed the Gulf R. R.

Before Savannah, Ga., Dec. 15, 1864.

Dear wife:

It is eleven o'clock at night. I have ridden 35 miles since 9 o'clock this morning and am almost tired out, but the mail boat comes up Ossabaw Sound tonight, and starts back for New York tomorrow morning at daylight, so I must write you a hasty note tonight, tired as I am, that you may know that I am all right, and, as I wrote you from Kingston, have actually ridden my fine grey clear through the Confederacy and let him drink *on the shore* of the Atlantic. Savannah is not yet ours, but we can see its steeples, and it must be ours soon. We have no rations, but are gathering rice and sorghum from the surrounding plantations, and we can live on that until we take the city, or at least until we get rations from the fleet.

At length I have seen "the South" with its negroes, its swamps, its cotton and rice plantations, and its extremes of wealth and poverty, and oh! I have so much to tell you about it that, I think, when I commence to write you a *letter* I shall never know when to stop. We will not move tomorrow and I expect to devote the entire day to you, so you must not call this a letter, but regard it simply as a telegram. I saw Fort McAllister today, with our flag flying over it, and our gunboats and transports swarming up the stream. Shall write tomorrow and give you particulars. My health is and has been excellent. Tell the people at home to have no fears for Sherman or his army; we are able to take care of ourselves and to take Savannah too. Address your next to me at Savannah.

Your husband.

[Diary]

Friday, Dec. 16th [1864].

Division stationary. Weather still quite warm. Heavy artillery firing after dark. A large train was sent from our corps to-day to King's bridge on the "Ogeechee" up to which point large vessels from the fleet, can sail. This train is to bring our mails; we are all more hungry for letters now than for anything else. I suppose, of course, I will get a good supply of letters; if I should be disappointed and get none—can't think of it. The distant cannonading which we heard some days ago proves to have been an attempt by Foster to cut the Charleston and Savannah R. R. near "Coosawhatchie" in which he signally failed. Foster is an old granny anyhow.

Saturday, Dec. 17th [1864].

Division stationary; weather warm and pleasant; this is a very easy sort of seige for us; we are rather short of the necessaries of life, and I am on my last paper of fine cut, but things are progressing as well as we could wish, and if we have good luck we will soon have an abundance of everything.

Sherman sent in a flag of truce to-day, and demanded the surrender of the city; Hardee asked 24 hours to deliberate; he should remember what is said of woman "If she hesitates she is lost." Our mail came to-day; I received letters from Mary (2), Ella (1), Willie(1), Tirril(1), the latter informing me that I received 960 majority in Coles County for Circuit Attorney.

That is certainly a very fine vote to receive at one's own home, and I am abundantly satisfied even though I am beaten in the Circuit. This is the first time I ever was a candidate before *the people,* and I congratulate myself on the fact that this time I asked no man for his vote.

Heavy artillery firing on our right from 4 to 5 o'clock this afternoon.

From Willie's letter, I find he is at Hilton Head, S. C.; I must go up and see him *as soon as we get the city.*

Sunday, Dec. 18th [1864].

This has been the most quiet day we have had, since we have come within sight of Savannah. Probably Hardee went to church this morning. A flag of truce from him, to-day, brought a reply to the summons to surrender. He refuses. "Barkis" ain't "willin' ", this time. Orders received this evening for the army to hold itself in readiness to make an assault on the enemy's entire line; this means business. Sherman having served a "notice to quit" on Hardee, and Hardee refusing to quit, Sherman brings an action of ejectment against the gentleman; I'm on the docket for Sherman; case to be tried by "wager of battle"—any gentleman wishing to take my place in this trial can have it.

I wrote out a rough draft of a letter to-day relative to Genl. Davis' treatment of the negroes at Ebenezer Creek. I want the matter to get before the military committee of the Senate; it may give them some light in regard to the propriety of confirming him as a Brevet Major General. I am not certain yet who I had better send it to.

Monday, Dec. 19th [1864].

Another quiet day; preparations going forward for an assault on the enemy's lines; the fugitive negroes were collected to-day throughout this wing of the army, and marched off to King's Bridge on the Ogeechee, from whence they will be shipped to Hilton Head, S. C. It was a strange spectacle to see those negroes of all ages, sizes, and both sexes, with their bundles on their heads and in their hands trudging along, they knew not whither, but willing to blindly follow the direction given to them by our officers. At least 5 thousand of them must have marched by our Head Quarters.

All our surplus mules and horses were sent off to-day too. The decks are being cleared for action, and if it must come, I care not how soon.

Tuesday, Dec. 20th [1864].

Another quiet day; but the bustle of preparation for the assault can be seen on all hands, and everybody feels confident of the result. Weather warm and pleasant; it is well for us that we are here in winter for we couldn't live here a month in the heat of summer.

Wednesday, Dec. 21st [1864].

With the first streak of dawn our pickets—the fingers of our army—felt their way amongst the tangled vines, and gloomy swamps on the left of our line until they found themselves within full view of the deserted works of the enemy. Almost with electric speed the word ran around the entire lines of our army: "Savannah is evacuated," and in less time than it takes to tell it, the heaviest sleepers in the army, as well as the lightest, were out, some dressed, and some *en deshabille,* shouting and hurrahing from the bottom of their lungs. This was indeed a joyful morning. Savannah is ours. Our long campaign is ended. If the world predicted our failure, the world must acknowledge itself mistaken. I am glad I was permitted to have a part in this campaign. Geary's Division of the 20th Corps marched in and took peaceable possession of the city this morning. Savannah is a beautiful city—the finest I have seen in the South. The rebels left all their heavy artillery, and considerable field artillery—they didn't dare to remove it, lest we should discover them, and make an attack. They left the city on a pontoon bridge, and took the only road left them, toward Charleston.

Here my Diary must end.

Thank God that I am yet alive, and permitted thus to end it.

These notes are for myself and my wife, alone.

If strangers read them they must pardon whatever of egotism appears in them, for I have endeavored to note here, incidents connected with myself, knowing very well that no one else will do it.

I must also apologize to *myself* for the exceeding carelessness of the composition of these notes. In them I find I have terribly mangled the "King's English." My excuse is that they were written in camp—on the march—or anywhere I might chance to take a notion to make a minute of anything.

Savannah, Dec. 27, 1864.

Dear wife:

I have written you twice since we have been here but have received nothing from you. May be you have not from me either.

Are you busy celebrating the Union triumphs of November and December, so that you can't find time to pen a few words to your roving husband, who, like the "Wandering Jew," ever hears the command "march" ringing in his ears? Were it not for the continual round of exciting scenes through which we have passed and are still in the midst of, I should be as homesick a creature as you ever saw; but amid all this whirl and buzz and rattle, this flying of flags, beating of drums, storming of forts, fighting of battles and capturing of cities, one scarcely has time to think of anything but the "pomp and circumstance of glorious war," but I keep eyes and ears open as I go along, and *sometime,* in our quiet northern home, I can sit down with you and tell you what I see and hear in these eventful days.

I wrote you from Kingston, you will recollect, that I thought this would be one of the most glorious campaigns of the war, and now that I have gone through it I still think so, and shall always be proud of the fact that I was in Sherman's army on its march through Georgia, and at the capture of Savannah. General Sherman reviewed our Corps in the streets of the city today, and it was a magnificent spectacle. As I sat on my horse and watched the bronzed veterans as they marched by with proud firm tread, their tattered flags fluttering in the Atlantic breeze, and brass bands filling the city with inspiring music, I could scarcely refrain from shedding tears of joy.

It was indeed glorious to see our gallant boys march so proudly through the streets of this Southern city which they conquered. The 17th Corps will be reviewed in the city tomorrow and the 20th Corps next day. General Sherman appears proud of his army and is determined that the citizens of Savannah shall see it all in its best trim, and I think it will have a wholesome effect on them. I am writing you a detailed history of our march through Georgia, that is I am writing it out from loose sheets I kept in diary form as we marched from day to day, but I am interrupted so much that I get along but slowly, and I thought I would write you a short letter tonight, by way of parenthesis, so that you might not have to wait so long to hear from me. I think we will not find mail communication as good along the coast here as it was in Tennessee and Northern Georgia. I understand that troops along the coast have heretofore received mails only once in 6 or 8 days, but I can see no reason for that, and now that so large an army is here I'm sure it will be changed so as to give us mails more frequently. . . .

General [Baird] told me day before yesterday, to apply for leave of absence and that he would see that I got it, but General Sherman issued an order yesterday prohibiting all leaves of absence at present, and Brigadiers, Colonels, Majors and everybody else are turned away now with a refusal, so I must try and content myself with waiting just as everybody else must. I would grumble about it if it would do any good but I know it won't. I am in excellent health, and if it were not for being a long way from home I would be content.

It certainly cannot be long though until some officers can be spared, who have been longest from home, and just as soon as any leaves are granted I am very certain to get one on applying. I shall go to Hilton Head, S. C., tomorrow morning, with Col. Swayne of the 43rd Ohio. We go by water, and I understand it takes a steamer about 5 hours to make the trip. I am going up to see brother Will whose regiment is there. Will get back day after tomorrow. A mail came to the city tonight and I feel pretty certain it brought me one of your good letters. Am writing in my tent without a fire and it is warm enough; indeed we have had almost nothing but summer weather thus far. We have a rumor here today that Jeff Davis is dead. If that is so, God has been good to him.

We here regard the war as almost over; one good drubbing for Mr. Lee, then it's done, and he'll get that before long. Either Grant or Sherman or both together will do it. Love to all at home. The New Year will dawn before you read this, and that year will take me home, while no other year will ever get me so far away from you for so long a time again.

Your husband.

Savannah, January 10, 1865.

Dear wife:

We all went to the theatre last night to hear the famous "Doesticks" in his lecture on "Pluck." [8]

On the 7th the General received a printed invitation for himself and staff to attend the lecture on the evening of Monday,

8. Mortimer Thomson, a humorist known as "Q. K. Philander Doesticks, P. B." A staff reporter for the New York *Tribune* at this time, Thomson was also a popular lecturer.

January 9th accompanied by a complimentary ticket for himself and staff. Of course we all went and enjoyed the quiet humor of "Doesticks" very much. The house was full of officers, all dead heads, and although he has had more profitable audiences yet I am sure he never had a more appreciative or enthusiastic one. . . .

Your husband.

Savannah, January 18, 1865.

Dear wife:

I have received yours of January 6th, and that is the second letter I have had from you since reaching this city.

I have no idea whether you get my letters or not; I hope you do though, for I know too well what it is to be waiting and watching and hoping for letters, while days and weeks roll away without bringing any tidings from home.

I have been quite busy nearly all the time since we reached this city, and it has been impossible to work at copying my diary as rapidly as I wished, but I have it copied from October 1st, at Atlanta, to November 28th, at Louisville, Ga., *en route* for Savannah. The diary was written on loose sheets every night when we bivouacked, and is so full of abbreviations that you would not understand, if I sent you these loose sheets, that I am transcribing it in plain English. If I were at home to rehearse the events of this remarkable campaign, I could spend a day in describing the many interesting incidents of each day of our march, but it is impossible for me, within the limits of a diary to do any more than allude to such items of the day as occurred to me at night when I undertook to hastily write, and of course many things are omitted. If it gets home to you safely it will give some idea of how easy, comfortable and jolly our long march was. It is three o'clock in the afternoon now, and the mail closes at four, and at daylight tomorrow we march, so you see my time for writing is very limited, and

I have a deal of official business to do between now and day-light tomorrow.

We received news today that "Fort Fisher," that Butler *didn't* take, was taken day before yesterday by a Division of troops under General Terry. That's most glorious! it completely seals up the port of Wilmington; stops blockade running there, and must lead to the fall of Wilmington itself. We have pos-session of the railroad for two thirds of the distance between here and Charleston, and before long your loyal heart will be cheered by the glad tidings that our old flag is flying over Fort Sumter again. We move northward tomorrow; Columbia is, I suppose, our first objective point, and Richmond next. I expect to see our flag flying over the rebel capital by the time Mr. Lincoln's second inauguration takes place.

Our Division commander has been promoted to Brevet Major General, and as you will see by the enclosed document, he has a second time recommended me for promotion to Brevet Lieut. Col. This, like the former one at Atlanta, was unexpected and unsought, but I am only a Volunteer, and probably nothing will come of it.

I also enclose a copy of a letter which I wrote to the Member of Congress elect from my district in Illinois, in regard to the manner in which General [Davis] treated fugitive negroes during our late campaign. I also gave General [Baird] a copy of the letter, and he sent it to New York, and he told me a few days ago that the substance of it has been published in the New York Tribune.

He also told me that the substance of the letter was sent to Stanton, Secretary of War, and that a few days ago, when Stanton came down here, he brought it with him and called on General [Davis] to answer the statements of the letter in writing. My name is not connected with it here, and I don't want it to be, unless the matter comes before the military committee of the Senate, and then I don't care, for I know all the officers whose names I have mentioned will corroborate my statements of fact.

I sent you a map of the State of Georgia by express, yesterday, on which I have traced the route of our Corps from Ringgold to Savannah. The 15th and 17th Corps marched on roads parallel with our Corps and the 20th, but South of us. The heavy red line shows the course of this Corps from Ringgold to Savannah, while the very crooked, narrow red line shows our course from Atlanta, northward and returning, as far as Kingston, Ga., in our chase after Hood. I hope it may reach you safely. There are a great many things I want to write about but am compelled to write "on a trot" so as to get my letter in the mail. . . .

Your husband.

Savannah, January 19, 1865.
Dear wife:

"It's an ill wind that blows nobody good" isn't it? I wrote you yesterday that we would march this morning at daylight, but we couldn't get our rations and forage, consequently didn't march, and as another consequence you get this letter, which, otherwise would not have been written. When I wrote you yesterday in regard to my diary, I believe I forgot to tell you that I have the loose sheets of the rest our trip from Nov. 28th to January 1st, which I will write out in the same manner, as soon as I can, and send you by mail as soon as I find a safe place to send from.

This is a dark, gloomy, rainy day, and I am very glad we are not marching. Our headquarters are in the city. My office is in a fine brick building on "Oglethorpe Square," and Captain ———, aide de camp, and myself have private rooms in another fine residence on the same square. We have gas light, coal fires, sofas, fine beds, bath room with hot and cold water, and all such luxuries; so it won't do for us to remain here long or we shall be completely spoiled for soldiering. Our beds should be at the roots of the cypress trees of Carolina instead of the luxurious couches of Savannah. Soldiers may *be* gentlemen but they can't *live* like gentlemen and do soldier's duty.

I shall leave Savannah very favorably impressed with it as a city. I have been most courteously treated by all its citizens with whom I have come in contact, and I hope that its beautiful squares, its elegant mansions, and its delightful streets may never hear any but peaceful sounds. Our whole army has fallen in love with this city and we all leave it with regret.

Citizens say it has been more quiet and peaceful in the city since our advent than it has been for the last three years; but notwithstanding our attachment for Savannah, we must go for there are rebel flags flying and rebel guns firing between us and our Nation's capital and we must cut our way through to where our banner waves over our war worn comrades on the James; there are fond hearts waiting for us to the northward too; our dearest loves are there, so we start to march toward them tomorrow with high hopes that the God of battles will lead us to victory, and to the dear loves of our Northern homes. Ever since I left you I've been marching from you, but tomorrow I start to march toward you, and the very idea elates me, in common with the 50,000 other wanderers of this army.

My health is excellent and I don't care how soon we get over into South Carolina, for I want to see the long deferred chastisement begin. If we don't purify South Carolina it will be because we *can't get a light*. I must stop for the mail boy is in the office waiting for this.

Your husband.

Through the Carolinas

BEFORE the capture of Savannah, Grant had agreed that Sherman should move northward and unite his forces with the Army of the Potomac. Transport by sea was considered, but abandoned in favor of an overland march through the Carolinas, which would prevent the scattered remnants of defeated Confederate armies from uniting and overawe the people of those states as the march from Atlanta to Savannah had shaken the morale of the Georgians.

Sherman was ready to move by mid-January, 1865, but rain, swollen rivers, and flooded lowlands delayed his departure. The Fourteenth Corps, with Baird's division and Connolly, did not leave Savannah until January 26, and then it was forced to remain at Sister's Ferry on the south bank of the Savannah River for over a week. But the march, once started, continued without serious hindrance until Goldsboro, North Carolina, was reached on March 21. On that date, and in the vicinity of that city, Connolly wrote the last of the letters to his wife that are still available.

Sisters Ferry, Ga., January 28, 1865.

Dear wife:

I have just learned that a gunboat will start down the river to Savannah in a couple of hours, and I write you in the hope that I can send my letter as far as Savannah by that boat. This is a ferry across the Savannah River, 35 miles up the river from Savannah. We are on the Georgia side of the river yet, but will cross to the South Carolina side as soon as we can get the river pontooned. The water is very high though now, spreading out over the country for a distance of nearly three miles, on the South Carolina shore, and it will be impossible for us to lay pontoons that distance, so there is a probability of our remaining here until the water falls, so we can pontoon it.

Our mails are very irregular, and I don't know whether you get more than one out of every ten letters I write. I don't know why it is so, but I know it is a matter about which everybody in this army is complaining, and I presume our friends at home are complaining just as much. It is almost enough to give a body the blues to be compelled to exist among these sand hills of the Savannah and be deprived of the letters we so anxiously look for. Still "it is better and wiser always to hope than once to despair," even though a fellow is cast away among the barren sand hills of Georgia. If you only get the map I sent you by express and the part of my diary I sent you by mail I shall feel satisfied, for I labored industriously to get them in proper shape and I think they will interest you. I shall begin copying the balance of my diary tomorrow and shall finish it as soon as I can. How does it appear to you?

It certainly seems to me that six months more must finish the war. We are moving toward Richmond now as fast as we can. Lee must soon feel our pressure, and it is utterly impossible for him to withstand both our army and Grant's; hence, it seems to me Richmond must soon be in our possession, and with Richmond must fall the Confederacy. Well, I don't care how soon it may come, for I am daily becoming more anxious to get home, and am really tired of this vagabond life.

I was called away from my letter at this point and now it is dark, the gunboat gone and my letter here unfinished. Sorry I didn't get it off, but I can finish it now at my leisure. I think it would be best for neither of us to sign our names to our letters; then if the letter falls into the hands of strangers they can't amuse themselves at our expense. I have often thought of this when I have been amusing myself over captured letters, but have always forgotten to mention it when writing you. . . .

When I do get home you will find your husband grown exceedingly awkward in all the usages of polite society, and I do not say this in jest, but in sober earnest, for I feel it. Two years and a half of campaigning in the field wears off very much of the polish of civil life and is apt to make one regard those little niceties of civil life as mere frivolities, unworthy a man's attention.

I used to like to have a nice necktie, neatly tied; now I never wear one. I used to wear a neat fitting boot; now I am content with a boot two or three sizes too large. Once I didn't feel dressed unless my boots were blacked; now I am content if they are covered with mud. I used to wear clothes that fitted me; now I *don't* wear clothes that fit me. I used to be particular about my victuals and bed; now I am content with whatever I can get. Now, don't you think I shall need a great deal of polishing up to make myself presentable? . . .

Oh, how I am wasting my time! I ought to be at home in my office, instead of wandering around through the swamps and sand hills of Georgia. In after years, the time I am spending now will cause me many a regret, I know; not because of the purpose for which they are spent, but because of the manner in which they are spent. But perhaps a few years of close application to my books and business will enable me to make up for much of the time I am now losing. If I could only study in camp there are many hours I could spend at it, but I can't do it. I got an old volume of U. S. Supreme Court Reports the other day which I shall carry with me, and I am determined to read it through and study every case in it. May be by the time I get through with it I will have my thoughts turned more in the channel of my profession than they are now. Spending one's time "in the service of his country" is all very nice to talk about in speeches, but I don't think it will help a body much when they return to civil life and "take up the shovel and the hoe" to earn a living. I can see the difficulties ahead of me when I return to civil life, but they do not appall me; only make me anxious for the time to come when I can "tackle" them.

You remember that sister Tempe once told me at Massillon that I was extravagant. I think she would take that back if she could see me now, wearing stoga boots, coarse woolen shirts, coarse pants, and living on beans, hard tack and fat pork, and enjoying it. The present doesn't bother me. It's the future that looks formidable. But I know it is like a road over a mountain—when viewed from the valley it looks very steep and difficult, but when approached and traveled on its steepness and difficulty disappear as each step of the ascent is made. I presume I shall be somewhere in South Carolina when you get this, but I haven't much idea where, only that it will be as far toward the north line of the state as we can get.

Address me, "Sherman's Army, South Carolina."

Your husband.

Sisters Ferry, Ga., February 4, 1865.

Dear wife:

I received your letter of January 15th yesterday, and I can't tell you how glad I was to get it. We have received orders to march into South Carolina tomorrow morning at 9 o'clock, and I hasten to write you a brief letter (for it is now after 10 o'clock at night) to let you know we are about to move. I can't tell where I may be when this reaches you, but hope to be at Branchville, S. C. The weather has become very fine and during the day one could get along comfortably without a coat. . . .

I have my diary copied up to December 5th. I wish it was done so that I could send it before we march. I suppose you can address me to "Sherman's Army, South Carolina, via New York." The Post Office Department, as well as the rebels, will surely know all the time where Sherman's Army is to be found, and it will get the mail to us some way. On this march we will be homeward bound.

Your husband.

Near Robertsville, S. C., Feb. 6, 1865.

Dear wife:

I learn that positively the last mail will go down the river to Savannah tomorrow morning, and I can't let the opportunity pass without sending you a brief letter. I am satisfied this will be a much harder campaign than that against Savannah, for this state of South Carolina is as full of swamps and bayous as a sieve is of holes, and they will make our marches tedious and difficult. We crossed the river at Sisters Ferry and came to this place yesterday. We have lain still today, filling our wagons with rations and getting everything ready before cutting loose from our "base." We start tomorrow morning at 7 o'clock and I am very glad of it, for I want to keep moving; the faster we march the sooner we'll get home.

The soil is very poor and sandy here. Magnolia and cypress trees grow very large. Our men chop down splendid magnolias to make bridges of and to corduroy roads. As the magnolia timber is not found in the North, I got off my horse yesterday

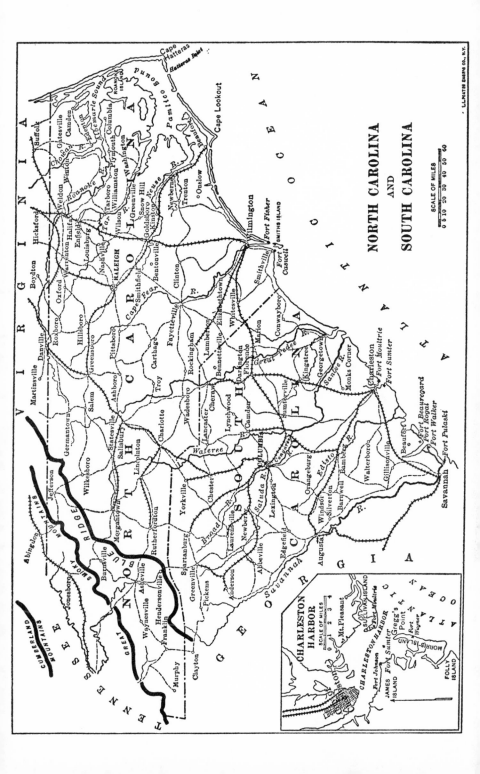

NORTH CAROLINA
AND
SOUTH CAROLINA

SCALE OF MILES
0 10 20 30 40 50 60

· L. L. POATES ENGR'G CO., N.Y.

CHARLESTON HARBOR
SCALE OF MILES
0 1 2 3 4

as we were marching along, and picked a chip off the end of a log about two feet in diameter, which I enclose. I sent you from Savannah an official copy of General [Baird's] recommendation for my promotion to brevet lieutenant colonel. Save it, for if I never get the brevet I want to have this official copy of the recommendation. If I were a "regular" officer I would feel very sure of the brevet, but being only an "irregular," the "regular" gentlemen about the adjutant general's office at Washington will stick the recommendation into a pigeon hole and leave it there "three years, or during the war"; and I shall not lose any sleep on account of it if they do, for I am not begging for brevets, being content with having fairly earned the recommendation.

The last letter I wrote you I supposed would be the last one you would receive from me for some time, and I now suppose this will be the last for, say, three weeks. I have been studying our proposed route on the map this afternoon, as pointed out by the General, and I see we will not have much chance for communication with the North for at least three weeks, and a little bad luck at some point might make it much longer; but we may have no bad luck. It begins to look to me as though this rebellion might close by the North and South uniting in a war against France or against Maximillian in Mexico, which of course will lead to a rupture with France. I regard this as not improbable, and am sorry it is so, for we have had war enough already. But, "sufficient unto the day is the evil thereof." Will write again, first opportunity.

Your husband.

Fayetteville, N. C., March 12, 1865.

Dear wife:

At length I am induced to believe that a line from me may reach you, and though I have but twenty minutes to get my letter ready for the gunboat to Wilmington, I shall employ those minutes to the best advantage. I must be brief and have only a faint hope that this will ever reach you. I have had excellent health. Our entire army is, and has been all the time, in the best possible condition. We have lived just as well as on our march through Georgia, but have waded, swum and bridged more rivers, creeks and swamps every day than can be found in Georgia in a month. The army burned everything it came near in the State of South Carolina, not under orders, but in spite of orders. The men "had it in" for the State and they took it out in their own way. Our track through the State is a desert waste. Since entering North Carolina the wanton destruction has stopped. We entered this State on March 4th and entered this city yesterday about 9 A. M. Our division entered first, with almost no fighting, and we are garrisoning the place, General [Baird] in command of the city. Generals Sherman, Howard, Slocum, Blair and everybody else are here. This is a very old fashioned place, covering about a mile square. There are a good many poor people here— operatives in cotton factories and the arsenal here. There are also a great number of mulattoes here. Nearly all the slaves are half white, and most of them can read and write.

My diary of the Georgia campaign is finished up to the capture of Savannah, but I am afraid to send it by the same boat I send this, for I think it very uncertain about this reaching you, but I shall carry it along and send it to you the first *safe* opportunity I have. We expect to have permanent communication with the coast in ten or twelve days and I can then write some assurance that you will get it. Two gunboats from Wilmington came up the Cape Fear River and reached us here this morning. You may think this a very careless sort of a letter, after having been silent so long, but you will remember I have but few minutes in which to write, and I am but one of a thousand in this army who will have opportunity to send a letter at all this time. In haste.

Your husband.

Near Neuse River, N. C., March 21, 1865.

How do you do? You used to know me but it is so long since you have seen me that I expect you have almost forgotten me, and I, therefore beg to send you this letter of introduction, hoping it may serve to awaken some thoughts of the wanderer, and at the same time assure you that he has not forgotten you. I have not heard from you for two months, but I have written you every time I have had an opportunity of sending a letter away. Whether my letters have reached you I don't know, but I am trying to satisfy myself with the hope that they have. I can't bear to think that you have not heard from me for two months, for I learn that very gloomy reports have reached the North about Sherman's army in North Carolina and South Carolina, and I know you have been imagining all sorts of disasters.

I wrote you a very brief hasty letter from Fayetteville, but when I sent it I didn't much expect it would get through, though I hoped it would, for it is a great satisfaction to me to think that you hear from me though I do not hear from you. I have some hope that this may reach you, for General Sherman, yesterday, communicated with Generals Terry and Schofield, who are marching from Wilmington and Newbern, on the coast, to meet us, and I suppose Schofield is in Goldsboro today, so we may hope for railroad communication with the coast in a few days.

Day before yesterday two Divisions of the 20th Corps, and two Divisions of this, 14th Corps, met the enemy at this point, Bentonville, in heavy force, and were considerably damaged.[1] We were marching on a road about 8 miles south of here, escorting the trains of the Corps, and after midnight night

1. Connolly's last battle. The Union army suffered casualties of 1,646 (killed, wounded, and missing) but forced Johnston, now commanding the Confederates, to withdraw from his entrenchments.

before last received an order to leave one of our brigades with the train, and with the rest of the Division march with all possible speed, and without resting, to the relief of the Divisions mentioned above. We reached here yesterday morning after daylight, but when we arrived everything was quiet. Yesterday about 11 o'clock we were moved to the front and sent forward to reconnoitre the enemy; we found him in force and strongly entrenched, but made no serious attempt to drive him from his works, as that might have brought on a more general engagement, than Sherman was ready for, so at dark we withdrew behind the main line, and are now entirely in reserve. While we were driving in their skirmishers yesterday I received a gentle reminder that "a body ought to be careful" for a rebel bullet struck the limb of a pine tree some five feet above my head, and glancing downward struck the plate of my sword belt and plunged into the leaves at my feet. It didn't hurt any and I was very glad of it.

I should like very much to write out a history of our campaign through South Carolina for you but I am afraid I shall not find an opportunity of doing it, for we never have any assurance that we will remain half a day at any one place, and it is out of the question to write at night after marching all day, but I shall have an immense deal to *tell* you when I get home. My diary of the Georgia campaign is complete to the fall of Savannah, but I shall not venture to send it until we get regular communication established, for I'm afraid it might be lost.

Our army is not burning any property in North Carolina. The country is poor, and through the region we have passed the people were principally engaged in the manufacture of tar and turpentine.

I know all about the tar and turpentine business now, for I have questioned every old man and old woman and negro I

have met by the wayside in regard to the details, and it appears
to me that it will require about two years of steady talking for
me to tell you what I have learned about these people, their pur-
suits and habits.

Before we had marched half way through South Carolina I
was perfectly sickened by the frightful devastation our army was
spreading on every hand. Oh! It was absolutely terrible! Every
house except the church and the negro cabin was burned to
the ground; women, children and old men turned out into the
mud and rain and their houses and furniture first plundered
then burned. I knew it would be so before we entered the state,
but I had no idea how frightful the reality would be. This state
is filled with deserters from the rebel army; they flock to us
every day; they look upon us as their friends. Hundreds of
them have gathered up their families and, with a little bundle
of bedding stowed away in an ox cart or mule cart, they toil
along after our trains, our soldiers sharing their scanty rations
with them, and helping them in every way they can to get to
Goldsboro, where some provisions will be made for feeding
them until they can get off to the North.

The great crisis of the war is rapidly approaching. I presume
we will march from here to Raleigh, which is only about 60
miles distant, and if the enemy lets us obtain possession of
that place as easily as we have the others, Lee will very soon
thereafter be compelled to retire from Richmond. Indeed I
regard the evacuation of Richmond as a certainty now, for
we have army enough here now to force our way to Raleigh,
unless Lee combines with Johnston to prevent it, but to do
that he must evacuate Richmond. But I don't consider Richmond as of much importance to them now; it is rather a burden,
and if it were not for "the looks of the thing" I don't believe
Lee would stay there another day. We know that every thing
is being removed from Richmond, and for several weeks prep-

arations for its evacuation have been going on, and we must look out for a slap in the face as we received at Chickamauga by the sudden reinforcement of the army in our front.

I wonder if the people of the North give this army any credit for the fall of Charleston and Wilmington? We are entitled to the credit of taking both of these places, although we didn't fire a gun at either of them. The first object of this campaign was to take Charleston, the next to take Wilmington, and the next to take Richmond. The latter we have not taken yet but we will take it, unless Grant gets in first which he is likely to do.

Well, what about going home? I have asked myself that question time and again since we first reached Atlanta; I have often thought I could see the time when I would be able to get away, and have been just as often disappointed, so that I am now afraid to come to any conclusion for fear of being again disappointed. As things have turned out it was well that I didn't go home from Savannah, for I couldn't have returned in time to join the Division for this Carolina campaign, and I wouldn't have missed it for anything. Whenever it is at all proper for me to go away on leave, I can go; about that I have no fears, but I don't know when or where we shall lie still long enough for anybody to go away, even for a very short time, with any assurance of finding his command again before the close of the war, and I don't want to be caught dawdling around up North when the last gun is fired. If we should have railroad or water communication all the time I could go, even if the army were moving, for I could easily get to it on my return wherever it might be, but so long as we are without permanent communication it is unsafe for me to go. My three years will expire on the 7th of August, which is but little over four months distant; I cannot possibly be held longer than the 7th of September, but since the beginning of this month I have taken to counting the residue of my term of service by *days*, it seems so much shorter to say "I shall be home in so many *days*" than to say

"I shall be home in—so many *months*"; and I propose now that we try to forget the length of time we have been separated; just rub it out as the schoolboy rubs his "sum" off his slate, and hereafter only look forward and count the *"days"* until I get home.

I am in hopes I can get home within 60 days, but the same hope has been so frequently frustrated that I shall not indulge it too strongly, so I shall now put myself on the safe side and say: "I shall be home in 100 days." Let's count from that now. Tomorrow night when I lie down, whether it be on my cot, or at the root of a tree, or in a fence corner in mud and rain, my sleep will be sweet, for before closing my eyes I shall think: "Only 99 more, then home," and the next night I shall think: "Only 98 more," and so it will go day by day until all those hundred days are gone, and the happy day of our reunion will have come. Then how many things we shall have to talk about, and what happy days will ours then be. But I must not write what is in my heart. . . .

It is understood in the army here that Congress passed some act the effect of which is to increase the pay of officers in the army, but no one here seems to know anything more than that about it, in fact for the last two months we have been so shut out from the rest of the world that we don't know what has been doing except within our own lines. If you or Andrew could get that act without any trouble and mail it to me I should be very glad. We have a report, I don't know how it came, that General Baird's promotion to Brevet Major General was confirmed by the Senate and that General Davis' was not confirmed.[2] I wish I knew the facts about it, but I shall learn about it officially before I can hear from you. I don't know anything about my own brevet, but I presume that amongst the swarm of Generals seeking brevets the more humble rank of Major has

2. The rumor was correct. Baird's Commission bore the date of Sept. 1, 1864; Davis was passed over.

been entirely overlooked. Oh, well! it's all vanity and vexation of spirit. I'm only a "hundred day man" now, and I shan't worry about brevets, but get home as soon as I decently can and go to work to earn brevets in civil life, for although I have been soldiering a good while I don't see that I have any more taste for it now than I had when I began.

Let father and mother know you have heard from me as soon as you receive this for I know they will be very anxious to hear from me. I see Johnathan Wood occasionally. Whenever I happen to be riding near where his ambulance train is I always stop and see him if I have time. The last time I saw him was the day he crossed the Catawba River, in South Carolina; when he drove by I was wading around in mud up to my knees, my clothes all daubed with mud and soaked with rain; I had been up all the night before working in mud and rain to get the trains across the river on the pontoon bridge, and hadn't a mouthful to eat that day; you may imagine I was slightly tired and somewhat hungry when the next night came. We start a man from our headquarters tomorrow morning to take our letters on horseback to Kingston, N. C., and he will have to ride 40 miles, so you see it costs something to send letters from here, the chances are about even too that he will be picked up by rebel cavalry before he gets there, I hope he may not though, for I certainly am very anxious for this letter to get to you. Oh, pshaw! there are a thousand other things I wanted to say to you, but I find I have written a long letter already and have scarcely said anything.

A PASSAGE in Van Horne's *History of the Army of the Cumberland* forms a fitting epilogue to this last letter.

"At Goldsboro, General Sherman proposed a new organization for his combined armies, giving General Schofield the command of the 'center,' and thus designating his forces, retaining for the right wing its old designation, Army of the Tennessee, and styling the two corps of the Army of the Cumberland, the Fourteenth and Twentieth, the 'Army of Georgia.' The left wing had informally borne this name during the march through Georgia and the Carolinas, but these corps were only really detached from the Army of the Cumberland after they had fought their last battle.

"This fact gives the Fourth, Fourteenth, and Twentieth Corps a community of fame and glory. . . . General Sherman had assigned them separate fields of operation, but had not formally separated them until it was too late to give them new historic relations. . . . Indeed, all the achievements of these three corps, in union or separation, are portions of the history of the same army, as by hearty consent each has an interest in the aggregate glory. They have an undivided tenure in the fame of the army, achieved in all the battles from Lookout Mountain to Jonesboro; not less do they hold in common the glory of the fields so widely separated. The shouts of the Fourteenth and Twentieth Corps at Savannah for victory at Nashville, in which the Fourth and their own representatives had a share, and their beloved commander the chief glory, was answered in glad response from every camp in Tennessee and Alabama for the repulse of General Johnston in his attempt to bring defeat and disgrace to the oldest corps of the unequaled Army of the Cumberland." [3]

No fighting of consequence occupied Sherman's army between Bentonville and Johnston's surrender on April 26.

3. Vol. II, 323-24.

INDEX

Abolitionists, Connolly favors, 134, 146

Acheson, Captain J. W., wounded, 258; accompanies Connolly, 269; plays piano, 276, 307–08; Negro servant, 277; joins Connolly's mess, 291; in quicksand, 299

Acworth, Ga., burned, 298

Alexandria, Tenn., described, 87

Allatoona, Ga., battle at, 269

Allen, Dr. H. C., in Battle of Milton, 45n

Antietam, Battle of, 16n

Army of the Cumberland, morale in, 56, 107–08; reorganized, 126; Thomas given command, 128; history summarized, 390–91

Army of Georgia, formed, 391

Army of the Ohio, Buell commands, 17

Army of Tennessee, Bragg commands, 17–18

Atlanta, Ga., campaign opens, 202, 207; first sight of, 234; falls, 256–57; description of, 259–60; burning of, 301–02

Baird, Absalom, approves leave for Connolly, 139, 162; promises action, 142–43; at Ringgold, 160; plays whist, 184–85; reviews target practice, 185; at division review, 188; serenaded, 199; orders advance, 202; describes Big Shanty action, 220n; in action at Jonesboro, 258; recommends Connolly for promotion, 263, 383; on leave, 284–85; returns to duty, 291; bad humor, 299; meets Kilpatrick's scouts, 315–17; sends aid to Kilpatrick, 331–32; abolitionist sympathies, 339; narrow escape, 341–42; friendly to Negroes, 362; promoted, 373; commands at Fayetteville, 384; promotion confirmed, 389

Baird, Mrs. Absalom, visit expected, 265

Baird's division, 127; assaults Missionary Ridge, 155–59; sees hard fighting, 208; in advance from Atlanta, 267

Barry, William F., at Ringgold, 203

Baxter, Morris, killed, 175, 177

Beatty, John, Connolly meets, 19, 124, 125; brigade of, at Tullahoma, 96; banker in civil life, 130n; resigns commission, 169; aspires to Congress, 189, 234

Beatty, Samuel, aspires to Congress, 189

Beecher, Henry Ward, Connolly admires, 134

Bentonville, N. C., Battle of, 385–86

The Library of Congress has cataloged this book as follows:

Connolly, James Austin, 1843–1914.
    Three years in the Army of the Cumberland; the letters and diary of Major James A. Connolly. Edited by Paul M. Angle. Bloomington, Indiana University Press [1959]

    399 p. illus. 21 cm. (Civil War centennial series)

    "Connolly's letters and diary were published originally in the Transactions of the Illinois State Historical Society for the year 1928."

    1. U. S.—Hist.—Civil War—Personal narratives. 2. U. S.—Hist.—Civil War—Regimental histories—Army of the Cumberland. 3. U. S.—Hist.—Civil War—Campaigns and battles. 1. Title

E601.C765   973.781   59–9065 ‡

Library of Congress